Great Britain

Great Britain

Hunter Davis & Frank Herrmann

Hamish Hamilton London

First published in Great Britain 1982
by Hamish Hamilton Ltd
Garden House 57–59 Long Acre London WC2E 9JZ

Copyright © 1982 by Hunter Davies
Photographs copyright © 1982 by Frank Herrmann

Book design by Michael Brown

ISBN 0–241–10755–5

Filmset in Great Britain by Northumberland Press Ltd, Gateshead
Printed in Italy by Arnoldo Mondadori Editore, Verona

Introduction

IT OFTEN looks as though there is not much to celebrate about British life today, when the news is so full of economic gloom, unemployment figures up, just look at the price of petrol, whatever is going to happen to Ireland, never mind the crime figures, all that sex today is disgusting, those hooligans should be deported, and what about the unions, tut, tut, a pretty state we are in.

The positive is so rarely accentuated. Is this because good news doesn't exist, or because it's boring, or because people glory more in bad tidings and grisly details? I think it's because bad news suddenly happens. The good is always with us, only we take it for granted. The bad steals all the headlines.

Stand back, turn around, reflect a moment. Yes, of course, we have so many good things in Great Britain today. Let us please enjoy them. Not as a means of escape, a refuge from the dark present, hiding one's head in the Blackpool sands to avoid the inflation figures, or losing our senses in the White Garden at Sissinghurst to forget the dole queue, but as a way of looking at the whole picture, clearly and openly and in perspective, enjoying the good things, while realising there are other things around which might be better.

So here is some good news, some uplifting places and events and organisations, a selection from the many things that can be enjoyed, which we should be proud of, as we step hesitantly, fearfully, through the Eighties.

Having decided, the problem was where to stop, not where to start. You will undoubtedly have your own favourite places, and be upset we have missed them out, but perhaps you might discover some new pleasures, or some you have hitherto overlooked.

Our catchment area was the whole of Great Britain, everyone and everything in it, past and present, people and places. We didn't want to do another tourist book, another guide to the British countryside. There are more than enough of those. We wanted to cross all the borders and boundaries, picking and choosing from all types of pleasures, all types of places. It might seem strange to go from the Marks and Spencer departmental store in Leeds, describing the hard facts about merchandising, to the Last Night of the Proms, trying to capture what is almost an abstract event, an evening of pure emotion, but the connection seemed absolutely obvious to us. Two Great British institutions.

It was Christopher Sinclair-Stevenson's idea and we started with a list of topics we couldn't miss. We must do a Garden, we all said, and a Cathedral, and a Seaside Town, and a Big Business, a Sporting Occasion, Something Literary, Some Lovely Landscape, An Educational Institution, The River, A Street, A Village, Parliament, The Theatre. The list went on. At the same time, we wanted to move round Great Britain, from the South of England to the North of Scotland, to Wales and to Northern Ireland. We're all in this together. We all have something to celebrate.

Now, why did we choose that cathedral rather than another? Hmm. Can't quite remember now. Oh yes, Durham makes such a good photograph, and anyway we must have something from the North-East. But in celebrating one famous cathedral, or one village, or seaside town, we are, in a way, celebrating all of them.

We had endless arguments over our sporting occasion, and ended up with two, as you will find. Please don't tell us about the ones we should have done. There are just so many famous British sporting events which are viewed with pleasure, perhaps even with envy, by the rest of the world. So, sorry, Wimbledon, Henley, Grand National. Another book, perhaps.

We had planned to do twenty acts of celebration. What arguments that led to. We thought perhaps that one chapter should be about a Great British Person. Someone of our times who in some way sums up some of the greatness of Britain. We thought of Sir Peter Medawar, the Nobel scientist, or Paul McCartney, the pop singer, Henry Moore, Graham Greene, Sebastian Coe. We just could not agree. It seemed unfair to make one person stand alone, amongst the famous edifices and noble landscapes. That is why the book in the end has only nineteen chapters. Each chapter, though apparently on an inanimate object, is full of people, but there is not one chapter solely on one person. (Apart from one, and that is to show his work, not his personality.) Who, or even what or where, would *you* have chosen for a twentieth chapter?

Frank Herrmann and I then went on to spend two years on the book, most of the events being covered in 1980 and 1981, touring the places and events we had chosen, usually together, sometimes making return visits on our own. We tried to capture the feelings and facts on the days we were there, how we felt, what we saw, making it personal and particular, but at the same time, we hope, capturing a flavour that is true to the whole and will last for a few years. It is hard to imagine the Wembley Cup Final being much different next year, or the River Thames at Cookham being changed, but you never know, Eton could close.

One of our objects was to pass on some facts, explain the background, how things work, what the people concerned think they are doing, what it's like behind the scenes. We certainly do not intend an Anatomy of Britain, as we make no claims to be comprehensive, or analytical, but at the same time we hope we have covered a cross-section of British life today, given a feeling of what is happening in some carefully-chosen segments of our society.

We had no brief from any organisation. No publicity body invited us in. Nobody but we ourselves paid our way. We just arrived, and were as amused and critical as often as we were delighted, disagreeing with some views we heard. But our point was to record not to argue.

Most of all, we wanted to pass on our enthusiasm, our delight, hoping that you might share it. So, let us now praise famous things.

Hunter Davies
September, 1981

Contents

1 A GARDEN: SISSINGHURST, KENT 9
One of the prettiest gardens in England, certainly the most literary,
probably the most famous.

2 THE SALE ROOM: SOTHEBY'S 21
The world's biggest and most successful auction house.

3 FOOTBALL: WEMBLEY 34
Scenes from the annual Cup Final and a look at the history and
life of our best-known sports stadium.

4 A VILLAGE: KERSEY 49
Not a well-known village, but a very attractive one, in the depths
of East Anglia, a classic English village in which every townie,
in his heart, would one day like to live.

5 BIG BUSINESS: MARKS AND SPENCER 64
A day in the life of their store in Leeds, where the firm first began,
almost a hundred years ago, plus a visit to their world headquarters
in Baker Street, London.

6 A CATHEDRAL: DURHAM 81
Perhaps the most striking of all our cathedrals, in its situation and
its importance to the north-east of England.

7 A STREET: THE ROYAL MILE, EDINBURGH 93
Surely one of the most interesting streets in the whole of Britain,
perhaps even the world. Where else is there such history, such
excitement, such architecture, in just one mile?

8 ROYALTY: THE QUEEN MOTHER'S SCOTTISH
CASTLES 110
From Glamis to Balmoral and up to the very top of Scotland to
the Castle of Mey: the Queen Mother's life as seen through her
family homes.

9 RAILWAYS: THE RAINHILL TRIALS 123
The celebrations for the 150th anniversary of the Liverpool–
Manchester, the world's first passenger railway.

10 THE SEASIDE: BLACKPOOL 134
The biggest, most successful, most honest seaside resort in the
country.

11 A SCHOOL: ETON COLLEGE 154
Behind the scenes in an educational establishment.

12 PARLIAMENT: NEIL KINNOCK IN WALES 170
The work and life of an M.P. in his constituency, facing the day-to
day problems which the public rarely sees.

13 LANDSCAPE: THE GIANT'S CAUSEWAY 184
Ulster's most dramatic natural wonder.

14 LITERATURE: HARDY'S WESSEX   196
A visit to Wessex, a place which technically does not exist but
which Thomas Hardy has made famous throughout the world.

15 RACING: THE DERBY   212
A day at the races, along with 250,000 others.

16 THE RIVER: THE THAMES AT COOKHAM   229
Messing around in boats on a short, but dramatic, stretch of our
principal river.

17 THE THEATRE: THE ROYAL SHAKESPEARE
COMPANY   245
From a humdrum rehearsal to their bold new plans for the future,
an inside view of the world's biggest theatre company.

18 THE CITY: THE STOCK EXCHANGE   260
Life amongst the brokers, and other excitements.

19 MUSIC: THE PROMENADE CONCERTS   274
In particular, the Last Night of the Proms, the annual distillation
of what it is like to be truly British . . .

1 Sissinghurst

SISSINGHURST Castle has the prettiest garden in Britain. That's my opinion. You immediately say you know a prettier one, then fine. We'll leave in the morning and go and see it.

Sissinghurst Castle is the most *interesting* garden in Britain. You pause and say you know a more interesting garden? What nonsense. This time I simply don't believe it. How can there be anywhere else in Britain with such rich historical, architectural, horticultural and literary associations?

The garden is all on a human scale, which is another and immediate attraction, without any of the formality or grandeur of a French landscaped garden or of the larger English stately homes. For extra measure, the humans associated with the creation of Sissinghurst led their lives in a rather unusual fashion. Some might say a scandalous fashion. Show me a garden *anywhere* with more human interest than Sissinghurst. Right then. Let us proceed.

Down to Sissinghurst we go which is about forty miles south-east of London, deep in the Weald of Kent, bravely ignoring the fact that no words can ever do a garden justice nor skilful photographs convey the slightest scent.

The name 'Castle' is misleading, as it's not a castle, not even a manor house. In fact, as a building, there is not a lot to be seen, apart from two wings and nearby a little tower. The grand manorial days are long since over. There is no Big House.

Most visitors, on first sight, are surprised by its smallness, both by the present buildings and by the six-acre garden. It's what has been done to it all that is so remarkable.

The site was occupied as early as the twelfth century and the house was then large and grand enough to accommodate Edward I and his retinue for four nights in 1305. This house has now completely gone, though most of the moat still exists.

The earliest architectural remains which we see today date from the Tudor period when a new manor was created which was considered suitably magnificent to house Queen Elizabeth I for a three-day visit during her Progress through the Weald in 1573.

By 1730, however, the house had been abandoned, left to be wrecked or ruined, no longer required for habitation, except for a handful of years, between 1756 and 1763, when it was used as a gaol for French prisoners of war. There's an interesting contemporary drawing, on display at Sissinghurst, which shows the prisoners strolling round the courtyard, hanging out their laundry at the foot of the tower, watched by patrolling sentries. (One of the English officers consigned to this depressing job was Edward Gibbon, historian of the decline of the Roman Empire.) It was the French prisoners who called Sissinghurst 'Le Château' and the name 'castle' has clung ever since.

Left: *Sissinghurst Tower, seen from the Cottage Garden.*

During the nineteenth century, Sissinghurst suffered further indignities by being converted into the Parish workhouse which is how it remained for over sixty years.

In the year 1930, Vita Sackville-West and her husband Harold Nicolson were looking for a new home and garden. Their own house, also in Kent, but nearer London, not far from Sevenoaks, was being threatened by the march of commuter developers and the plans by a local farmer to build a chicken farm.

It was completely by chance that they heard about a farm at Sissinghurst being for sale. And it was also by chance that they went on to study the small print which said that the sale, which was of a tenanted farm house and 350 agricultural acres, included 'some old ruins'. They bought the whole property for £12,500 – but it was these 'old ruins' which had captivated them. Vita's first visit had been enough to convince her of the possibilities of the ruin and the few acres around it, even though the site itself was little more than a rubbish dump.

"The major nuisance," so she later wrote, "was the truly appalling mess of rubbish to be cleared away before we could undertake any planting at all. The place had been on the market for several years since the death of the last owner, a farmer, who naturally had not regarded the surroundings of the old castle as a garden, but merely as a convenient dump for his rusty iron, or as allotments for his labourers, or as runs for their chickens. The amount of old bedsteads, old plough-shares, old cabbage stalks, old broken-down earth closets, old matted wire, and mountains of sardine tins, all muddled up in a tangle of bindweed, nettles and ground elder, should have sufficed to daunt anybody.

"Yet the place, when I first saw it on a spring day in 1930, caught instantly at my heart and my imagination. I fell in love; love at first sight. I saw what might be made of it. It was Sleeping Beauty's Garden: but a castle running away into sordidness and squalor; a garden crying out for rescue. It was easy to foresee, even then, what a struggle we should have to redeem it."

V. Sackville-West, as she normally signed herself, rarely using her Christian name, had some money in her own right and came from a grand and aristocratic family. (By a coincidence, it turned out that she was a direct descendant of the Bakers who had built the original Tudor mansion.) She was a poet, novelist, biographer, a friend of many eminent literary people of the day, notably Virginia Woolf and the Bloomsbury set. She was also a gardener and had already created one fine garden at their previous home and wrote extensively on gardening in books and newspapers.

Harold Nicolson, her husband, had no money of his own, but he was equally eminent, as a diplomat, M.P. and a biographer. He wrote the official biography of George V in 1952 and was knighted in 1953. In 1930, when they moved into Sissinghurst, he was in his mid-forties and they had been married for seventeen years. With them came their two young sons, Ben aged fifteen and Nigel aged thirteen.

Harold made plans for the final design of the garden while Vita took charge of the planting, but first they had the enormous task of simply clearing away the rubbish, with the aid of one old gardener and his son, plus occasional help from their own sons. It took them almost two years, just to prepare the site.

None of the old buildings nor the tower had any water, drainage or electricity when they arrived, and they camped at weekends for the first few months in a little room in the tower, slowly making all the buildings habitable. The roof of the stables had to be replaced, and a bedroom and a bathroom were added to one of the cottages in the grounds, but otherwise all the buildings were left basically untouched.

The living arrangements were rather odd. Vita's sitting room, where she did all her literary work and spent most of her time, was in the tower which was considered her own private domain. The boys, as they grew older, lived above the converted stables. Harold's room was in one cottage (South Cottage) while their dining room was in the other cottage, Priest's House. All four of these buildings are separate, so eating and sleeping meant a walk across the garden. However strange, the unit apparently worked and by the outbreak of the Second World War they had achieved their common purpose, the creation of a magical garden.

Vita Sackville-West died in 1962, at Sissinghurst. Her husband died in 1968, also at Sissinghurst. Their younger son Nigel inherited Sissinghurst but, so that death duties could be paid the house and estate passed into the ownership of the National Trust who now run and look after it.

Nigel Nicolson still lives there, in a wing of the stable block. It was his family home and the home where in turn he has brought up his own family. His older brother, the late Benedict Nicolson, the eminent art historian, was always looked upon as the urban son, and so inherited other property from his mother. Nigel was considered the rural son, who would always love and care for Sissinghurst.

He is a tall, kindly, courteous man in his early sixties, a respected literary figure in his own right, the author of many books and the co-founder of a famous publishing house, Weidenfeld and Nicolson. He greeted us at the front arch way and took us for lunch in his own private quarters. He doesn't mind at all that over 100,000 people walk through the gardens and underneath his windows every year.

The National Trust have a staff of six gardeners and care for the gardens as Vita intended, opening the garden and part of the house (the library in the stable block and the Tower) every day except Mondays from April 1 to October 15. There's a tea room in the oast house nearby and a shop for souvenirs and garden produce, and also a bookshop where Nigel's books sell very well.

"I enjoy people coming to Sissinghurst. They no more disturb me than the birds or the bees. I'm very pleased to have them. I can have the gardens to myself in the evenings, and in the mornings until we open at one o'clock. When the season ends, I am quite disappointed.

"The creation of Sissinghurst was like creating a book or painting a picture. As one wants to have a book published or a painting exhibited, so one wants a garden to be put on show."

Upstairs in his part of the house he has thousands of family letters, many of them still unpublished, despite the large number of books which have already been written, or are about to be written, about his parents. Perhaps it was having to walk across the garden all those years, in order to communicate, which made the family such avid letter writers?

"All four of us always wrote to each other. That was how we were brought

Right: *The entrance gateway to Sissinghurst, seen from inside the garden.*
Nigel Nicolson, son of Harold Nicolson and Vita Sackville-West.

up. And we all kept each other's letters. We seldom used the 'phone. The 'phone was for ringing the station to get the train times."

As a young man, Nigel often wondered what would happen to the house and garden when his mother died, but never had the courage to ask her himself. "It was one subject I knew would cause an explosive outburst." So he asked his father to ask his mother if she would ever let the National Trust take it over, but he never found the answer till after her death. In her mass of papers he found a diary in which she answered the question. "Not in my lifetime." However, she made it clear she didn't mind it eventually being owned by the National Trust.

Nigel also found many other revealing documents in her papers, some of a more explosive nature. It took him many years, and great thought, before he decided to publish them. First, though, he said, let me take you round the gardens.

Vita Sackville-West had two basic ideas when she started planting. Firstly, she wanted to make it a romantic garden, in a very English way, with lots of roses, but with hints of a Norman manor house, or even of a deeper, Mediterranean South. Secondly, she wanted the whole garden divided into little sections, separate rooms with separate feelings.

In the early years, she tried to make these different rooms seasonal, having a spring garden, an early summer garden, a late summer garden and then an autumn garden. It was only after the War that she introduced the idea of some of the rooms being separated by colour – orange and yellow for the cottage garden, dark blue and purple for one side of the front courtyard, and then the most original idea of all, a completely white garden.

We had been encouraged by Mr Nicolson, and by his older daughter Juliet, to come down in the first week of July as the White Garden would then be at its finest. Which it was. When Juliet got married they had used the White Garden for the reception and they had chosen July 2, normally the perfect day for the White Garden, but alas, the white rose on the central arch of the garden wasn't quite out that year.

"I came down first thing the morning before," said Nigel, still sad at the memory, "and there were no roses out. On the morning of the wedding, there were three and by the afternoon there were twenty-five. When my second daughter gets married, we'll have to have it a day or two later. Then, we'll have *hundreds* out."

The White Garden is a subtle garden. It doesn't hit you in the eyes or nose like a normal rose garden. You have to discover its cleverness before you realise that yes, every little thing *is* white, or at least a paler shade of grey.

Nigel took us first to sit down in a far corner, on a simple little bench, underneath which a box hedge was growing. "Isn't that a marvellous idea, to have a hedge *underneath* a seat." He pointed out around us all the different textures, sizes, variations and shades of white. His mother, he said, had worked like a painter, not a planter.

It was a joy and a privilege to have him taking us round the garden, with his memories of every tiny corner. Over there, that's where his father once made him walk up and down for hours with a pole and a flag, taking sightings, till yes, that would be the perfect spot for another statue. We came to a gazebo in one corner of the orchard, with marvellous views over Kent, of the corn fields and orchards and hop gardens, with scarcely a man-made object in sight, and he said he had built the gazebo with his brother Ben in memory

Above and below: *The White Garden, Sissinghurst.* Right: *View from the Tower, over the Rose Garden.*

of their father. Throughout the entire garden, and the buildings, are scattered little plaques, objects, statues, given lovingly by one member of the family to another. Sissinghurst is a garden of love, in every sense.

The orchard had a rather wild, unruly look, but at the base of most of the older fruit trees were roses, taking over and blooming on their behalf, now that we were in July and their own blossom months were over. It was Vita's own idea to plant roses up the fruit trees and so give a double flowering each year.

The herb garden and the nuttery are, as one might expect, each devoted to one theme, rather than a colour, but perhaps the most unusual specialist room is a lawn which is completely composed of thyme. I stood for a long time looking down into the mass of purple flowers and could see thousands of bees, working away, yet each keeping its regulation distance, no two bees going for the same flower.

There are no rhododendrons in the entire garden, as Vita was against them, dismissing them as municipal garden plants, nor are there any sweet peas, which is a slight disappointment for her granddaughter Juliet. Vita wasn't interested in growing such things. However, there are scores of plants most people never grow in their normal suburban gardens or see in their municipal parks.

Nigel made us bend down to smell a Cosmos Atrosanguinus, a deep blood-coloured plant, a bit like a poppy. The smell was pure chocolate. It comes from Mexico, one of the two lady gardeners told us, and is not very hardy so few people grow it.

"You have to imagine the beginnings, how everything started small," said Nigel. "There was nothing here at all in this garden. That weeping pear tree beside the statue of a virgin was only a quarter of the size of the statue thirty years ago. Now the tree is much bigger and provides the perfect umbrella for the statue, just as my mother foresaw that one day it would.

"Look at those thistle-like flowers, onopordum they're called. A month ago they were simply not visible. Now they're twelve feet high. Now I'll show you the arum lilies. Look carefully and you'll find one or two that are *absolutely* perfect, with not a blemish.

"I often come down to the White Garden late at night in July, when the full moon is out. It's ethereal. Now and again, a white owl used to fly over, but it has not been seen for several years."

The whole garden did seem perfect, to this amateur gardener, and it is very hard for any untrained eye to be aware of the slightest blemish on anything. Each day you can hear visitors exclaiming in wonderment. It's easy to see why they don't upset Mr Nicolson, despite constantly streaming past his windows. They are *all* garden-worshippers, highly respectful, treading lightly, gazing much of the time in silence, turning only to exclaim to their friends, partly in awe, partly amazement, partly fury. "There's not a slug, not a caterpillar, not even a black spot. It's simply not fair!"

I felt at times just a little depressed, seeing so many marvellous specimens. As befits an upper-class garden, everything is of the finest quality, the best of breeding, the most cultured versions, all beautifully cultivated. By comparison, my own little garden seems full of such sad, impoverished, deprived, second-class citizens.

As for the interiors, the first room which is open to the public is the Library, to the left as you come through the entrance archway, at the end of the wing which was formerly the stable. A lot of work was done to convert it into a library, inserting a large window at one end to give light, building a fireplace and putting in wooden panelling. It is hard to believe these new elements were installed only fifty years ago, as they look so ancient, but in the 1930s there were still many craftsmen willing and able to re-use and re-create old materials. The chimney-piece, for example, is formed from several pieces of an original Elizabethan fireplace which was found in bits, buried in the garden.

It has a wonderful atmosphere today, gracious and literary and nicely faded, and visitors are always very impressed, but Nigel said his parents never really considered it a success.

"My father always thought it was too long for its width. He said it reminded him of a hospital ward in the Crimea. People admire that painting of my mother [painted by de Laszlo at Knole in 1910 when she was eighteen], but she always loathed it. Too pretty, she used to say. It reminded her of her early days when she was a smart débutante. Later she was very anti-smart and preferred to live and dress like a literary recluse."

The Tower should not be missed. It looks so strange and rather lonely from outside, a red brick column, stuck out on its own, left over from some ancient flood. Although Vita in her first impressions listed all the terrible things wrong with the garden, and all the rubbish to be moved, she did say that the beauty of the brickwork was one of the features which captivated her.

'Red brick', on paper, can sound unattractive, almost a term of dismissal, conjuring images of a Victorian school playground, but this Tudor pink red brick is a kaleidoscope of its own, a rainbow of reds. Even on a dull day, its rich texture can make life seem warm and happy.

The Tower now contains a little literary museum, a pilgrimage place for Eng. Lit. students from all over the world. On the second floor are several show-cases containing diaries, letters and manuscripts by Vita and Harold Nicolson. There's the original typescript of his George V biography (probably

The yew hedge Rondel, seen from the Tower.

the best Royal book ever written), full of his bad spellings and typing mistakes, all corrected in hand. I noticed in several letters that they each refer to Sissinghurst as Sissingbags. Nigel said it wasn't a typing error but an old family joke, but he couldn't remember how it began. In an alcove, formed by a turret of the Tower, is the printing press on which Virginia and Leonard Woolf printed the first edition of T. S. Eliot's *The Waste Land* and other early productions of the Hogarth Press.

It seems such a frail and clumsy little machine, no bigger, no more elaborate than a large mangle, yet it had such an enormous impact on the literary world of the Thirties. It still works, said Juliet. Her husband has managed to get it going and has run off invitations cards for parties.

Juliet went to one of the book-filled shelves and pulled down a first edition of what I could see was Virginia Woolf's *To the Lighthouse*. She opened it carefully and pointed to the inscription. "To Vita. The best novel I've ever written." It seemed a rather pompous inscription, for a lady always haunted by doubts about her work, then Juliet turned over the pages of the book itself. They were all blank. Hence the inscription. Another Bloomsbury joke.

On the first floor, below the little museum, is Vita's own sitting room which was her refuge from 1931 to her death in 1962 and it was here that she wrote many of her books. From its windows, she said, she could 'see without being seen'.

The walls are lined with her books, divided into her special interests – gardening, English literature, history, travel – and her possessions and furniture are all round, left exactly as she had them. The walls were first

Above: *wooden garden seat, designed by Sir Edwin Lutyens.*

Left:
South Cottage, where Vita and Harold had their bedrooms.

papered by her in 1930, over the basic red brick. They have been replaced but are now dull and damp-looking. It must have been a very cold room in the winter, though there is an ancient electric fire still under her table which she used. Under one window is a couch, now equally faded, on which she could rest, or where her closest and dearest women friends could rest.

Nigel learned many intimate details of these close women friends, to his own complete surprise, when he read her papers after her death. He eventually revealed what he had found, in his mother's own words, and in his own, in his celebrated book *Portrait of a Marriage*. He anguished long over whether he should tell the world about his mother's relationships with other women, and his father's own inclination to people of his own sex, yet their marriage, for all its strangeness, was a true love match, which endured and grew, despite their different and numerous attachments with other people.

I went up to the top of the Tower before leaving Sissinghurst, climbing the seventy-eight steps of a spiral staircase in the turret, emerging at length on to a little roof. The summer smells drifting up from the garden were like incense, almost halucinatory. I felt I could float down and come to no harm, safe in the richness of nature, though a corner of nature which has been given a little help from its friends.

You get a bird's eye view of all the little gardens and how they connect. At ground level, this is hard to appreciate. You can see exactly what has been done, what has been created, how so much has been grown so lovingly in such a relatively small area. You gaze in wonderment, thinking of what love and what drama, what dreams and hopes and passions, went into Sissinghurst, both outside and inside its walls. Sissinghurst is a monument to all the senses.

Exit left, lady reading in a literary garden. . . .

2 Sotheby's

IT'S EASY to pass Sotheby's without realising. It's just another doorway in Bond Street, no more attractive or alluring or exciting than any other. Bond Street itself is an exciting street, and a walk along it in any month in any year is a litmus test of the capital's chic. Oxford Street round the corner is decidedly provincial, and in places rather tatty. Regent Street is very much a London street, but somehow old-fashioned and county. Bond Street, however, is classic. Even the assistants in the shoe shops and fashion show rooms and galleries of Bond Street seem timelessly superior, expensively understated, quietly exclusive. The customers as they window-shop are cosmopolitan as well as metropolitan, smoking strange-smelling cigarettes, their jackets over their shoulders, a European cut to their clothes. You realise that grey and black can be *such* clever colours.

So you walk past Sotheby's several times, wondering how you could possibly have missed it, perhaps too obsessed by those chauffeur-driven Rolls and Jaguars purring in the gutters, with silent figures in camel coats in the rear seats, holding mysterious parcels, or green baize porters rushing to and from the back doors of dark vans, dragging out mysterious canvases which might be worth millions or nothing, but caring neither way, just another load to be shifted.

If you stand on the opposite side of the street to Sotheby's, having worked out at last which is number 34, you can see it is a reasonably sized building, though still more like a gentleman's modest town house, with the upper two stories painted white, than the headquarters of an international business with an annual turnover of some £200 million. Very discreet, very English. Bond Street buildings aren't big anyway. Pigmies compared with Manhattan.

The main doorway appears to have been blocked up and a newspaper kiosk plonked down in the middle of it, taking up part of the pavement. The kiosk sells the usual London morning papers, and there are the inevitable magazines like *Mayfair* and *Playboy*, prominently displayed to attract the prurient, but on closer inspection it can be seen that a good part of the stall is devoted to the weighty periodicals of the art world, *Apollo*, the *Architectural Review*, and the *Antique Collector*. I noticed the *Burlington Magazine*, which Benedict Nicolson edited for so many years, selling well. There are not many pavement kiosks in London where such worthy publications outsell the girly mags.

Above the kiosk, mounted on the wall, is a black sphinx-like animal with a plaque which says 'Sekhmet, 18th dynasty, circa 1320 B.C.'. You'd never notice it, unless you happened to raise your eyes. Look even higher and you might even catch a glimpse at a front window of the Earl of Westmorland, since circa 1980 the chairman of the firm.

The Bond Street exterior of Sotheby's. The face at the window is that of Lord Westmorland chairman.

The main auction room during a sale of paintings.

The main entrance to Sotheby's is the dark green-painted doorway to the left of the kiosk. A notice board in the same colour tells you which sales are on today. I was looking for a postage stamp sale, one of their run of the mill, bread and butter occasions, not a sale to attract the public or the press.

Sotheby's has now passed into folklore for its sales, on both sides of the Atlantic. The prices realised at their art auctions have risen to such an extent that they bear little relation to most people's normal life. You can add or miss off a few noughts and most people would be completely unaware. It is fantasy money, for most people. Their Robert von Hirsch sale in 1978, for example, realised over £18 million, the largest figure ever achieved for a single art collection. The Mentmore auctions in 1977 came to over £6 million, the highest ever for a house contents. Their most expensive single item, at the time of writing, was Turner's view of Venice, which was sold in their New York auction rooms in May 1980, for 6.4 million dollars, making it the world's most expensive painting. Doubtless, this sum has now been beaten. Why, all those prices are probably now being considered cheap.

What is not realised is that all the obscenely high prices we read about are not typical. The vast bulk of Sotheby's work is much more modest, not to say humdrum. Over sixty percent of the lots sent to Sotheby's for sale each year realise £200 each or less and eighty percent go for under £500.

I therefore didn't feel too nervous about the postage stamp sale. I had chosen it for its lack of glamour but also to make one or two bids myself. The last of the small spenders.

These days, all London auction houses give printed estimates in the catalogue, so you know the worst before you arrive. In the old days, just ten years ago, you had to rely on knowing someone in the firm to give you their pre-sale estimate of what the stuff might fetch, or find a friendly porter to tell you, perhaps slipping him something for his trouble.

Sotheby's were having eight sales in all that day (October 2, 1980). In London, there were two stamp sales, one Ceramics, one English Silver, and one Old Master Prints. In Chester there was a sale of nineteenth-century Carpets and in Exeter a charity auction. In New York there was a sale of Contemporary Paintings. During that month as a whole, they had 139 sales scheduled, including Jewellery in Madison Avenue, New York; French Militaria in Monte Carlo; Turkoman Rugs in Johannesburg; U.S. Furniture in Pennsylvania; English Silver in Los Angeles; Fans, Tea Caddies and Conjuring Manuals in London.

If you look at the sales pages of *The Times* any Tuesday you will see that London's four leading houses, Sotheby's, Christie's, Phillips' and Bonham's, between them hold sixty to seventy auctions a week, or twelve to fifteen every working day. No wonder the rest of the world thinks the British are now auction mad.

The entrance to my stamp sale was round the block in Conduit Street. Despite its modest-looking front door at 34 Bond Street, Sotheby's extends behind the scenes, left and right on either side of the street and deep into the hinterland.

I found myself in a handsome little hall with a gallery and several fine-looking rugs hanging from the walls. A lady at a table at the entrance to the hall made me sign a book and then gave me a white card with a number on it, 642. This was obviously to assist the auctioneer, should I be brave enough to make a bid.

About eighty people were sitting in silence in rows of chairs, most of them middle-aged men in suits but with a sprinkling of women, all of whom seemed to be making notes. The auctioneer stood at the end on a slightly raised wooden rostrum. There was about as much atmosphere as an empty swimming pool. It was my first visit to a London auction room and I was rather disappointed. I'd recently been at a country sale, in the market hall at Wigton in Cumbria, and that had been like a fun fair, with the hall jammed with families, their flasks and sandwiches at the ready, all set for a day's free entertainment.

Sotheby's, by comparison, was like being at a funeral. I couldn't even *see* any stamps. Nothing was held up. No descriptions were given. No details were announced. The average lot took twenty seconds to sell. The auctioneer, a young man in spectacles with a quiet, accentless tone, announced the Lot number, said a price, sometimes a second price, then once, and once only, quietly brought down his hammer. And that was it. He didn't even say Going Going Gone, the way they always do on TV and in film auctions.

I opened my catalogue and slowly picked up which lots were being sold. It was just a General Stamps of the World sale, nothing special, and they were going through an assortment of countries alphabetically. "Lot 213," said the auctioneer. I could see it referred to a 1918 stamp from the Falkland Isles. "£30." The printed estimate in the catalogue said £30–£40, so that sounded right. "£32," he said, having caught the eye of someone in the hall, though despite practically twisting my head off I could see no one in the hall who appeared to be awake, never mind bidding. "At £32." And down came his hammer. With country sales, the auctioneers work themselves into a lather, coming out of the ring as if they've gone ten rounds with Muhammad Ali. This was so civilised I feared I might fall asleep before the lots I was interested in came up.

"Lot 216 must open at £2,200," said the auctioneer, and for once there was just the slightest suspicion of some excitement in the air, though you had to be quick and knowledgeable to catch it. I looked through my catalogue and found that while I'd been blinking we'd moved on from Falkland Isles to France and to a series of letters from Paris sent by Warren Hastings to his son in India. The estimate said only £1,000–1,500. The postal bids had obviously been flooding in and increased its value. After four or five bids, it went for £4,000. The rest of the French lots went for a great deal more than the estimates, some even for ten times as much.

At the end of the French lots, two men and a woman immediately stood up, the woman exclaimed 'Wow', and they all marched briskly out of the room.

I was rather nervous by the time we came to the Great Britain lots, and still slightly confused, worried that I'd stumbled into a secret society, unaware of the hidden rules or the unspoken rituals. It was all going forward at such a speed that I was sure I'd never be able to make my bid known.

The lot I fancied was 252, a Penny Black, estimated at £30, which sounded my level. The bidding started at £50, to my fury, but in the excitement, determined to make my presence felt, I got in a higher bid – £55. The world stood still for a fraction of a second, then charged off again without me, coming to a halt at £70. I sat numb in my seat for a long time, as we raced through other countries and thousands of pounds poured forth all round me, thinking yes, I should have gone to £70. It *must* have been a good Penny Black. I would dearly like to have said I'd bought something in a Sotheby's sale, however modest. In the end, I'd bought nothing.

When the sale finished, I went round to have a word with the auctioneer, Richard Ashton. He looked rather more tired now it was over than he'd been on the rostrum when he'd appeared so calm and controlled, almost bored. Although the sale had been short, lasting only two hours, he said that up to six months' work had gone into it, as well as countless letters, meetings, trips and decisions.

Standing room only, for paintings and public, while an auction is in progress.

Behind him during the sale had stood John Michael, the head of Sotheby's stamp department. He'd taken a morning stamp sale, which had been Tobago stamps. They share the stamp auctions between them.

"Who chased me up that last thousand pounds?" said a dealer, coming up to Mr Michael. The English dealer had successfully bid for one of the French lots, but wanted to know who his rival had been. Mr Michael said it had been one of the French dealers.

They normally know about ninety percent of the people at any of their stamp auctions, either regular dealers or leading collectors. This had been an interesting and rewarding sale, as far as the auctioneers were concerned, because of the French letters. "I knew we were in for some fun," said Mr Michael, "when I saw Frenchmen appear from behind the pillars in the gallery."

These French letters had come to them out of the blue, brought in by a bank, acting for the estate of someone who had just died. (The woman who had exclaimed 'Wow' was not a dealer, as I'd presumed, but one of the beneficiaries.)

The majority of valuable items which change hands at the leading London auction houses are already known to the experts, whether it's stamps or furniture, and there is a history of the times they have been sold in the past. But this French correspondence was completely unknown, never having been seen before by any stamp expert. Both Richard Ashton and John Michael knew from the moment it came in that it would generate great interest amongst the specialists.

They then returned to their office in the depths of the Sotheby's main building in Bond Street, to celebrate the end of another sale, and John Michael opened a bottle of champagne to treat his staff. It's only a two-man department, plus a girl who's training and a secretary, so one bottle was enough to give them a glass each. They used to have dinner out, when a sale was over, but as the two men usually have to catch an early flight to some far corner of the world next day, they now make do with a drink straight afterwards.

Sotheby's might appear to be a huge monolithic organisation, grinding out

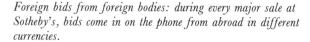

Foreign bids from foreign bodies: during every major sale at Sotheby's, bids come in on the phone from abroad in different currencies.

the millions, but in reality it's made up of many cells, each working individually, almost autonomously. At Bond Street alone there are 19 separate main departments, each with its own staff and own leader. There's Books and Manuscripts, Old Master Drawings, Old Master Paintings, British Paintings, European Art, Prints, Islamic Antiquities, Ceramics and Glass, Chinese Art, Japanese Art, Furniture, Oriental Carpets, Works of Art (e.g. Icons, clocks, musical instruments), Silver, Coins and Medals, Jewellery, Vintage Cars, Wine, and Postage Stamps. They have in all 150 experts, many of them world experts in their fields.

They're like individual entrepreneurs, scouring the whole world for their particular subject, watching trends, observing rivals, reading other people's catalogues, hoping for an inside tip that some collector or some family might one day want to sell, then striking at the right time and persuading them to come to Sotheby's.

The stamps department is about Sotheby's smallest and newest, though the talk in the Bond Street corridors that day was whether Two-Wheelers would eventually supersede it. Strange as it may seem, a forthcoming sale of vintage bicycles and motorcycles was arousing great interest. Could there be a new department in bikes?

John Michael opened the stamp department in October 1978, starting in a cupboard under the stairs. "I was just left to get on with it. I didn't even know how to order a biro." He spent much of his early life in Rhodesia and worked in shipping till 1965, starting off in stamps by selling some of his own, before joining Stanley Gibbons, the stamp dealers.

In his first year at Sotheby's he sold £650,000 of stamps and in the second year £1,400,000. He had hopes of this, his third year, being even higher. "You can't set targets. It just needs one big collection to come in, or not to come in, and everything changes."

The four of them were very excited by having just secured a collection of Hong Kong Stamps, the Ryohei Ishikawa Collection, which they estimated would sell for half a million pounds. They didn't expect ever again in their stamp lives to see such a fine collection of Hong Kong stamps.

On a half million pound sale, Sotheby's ten percent from the vendor and ten percent from the buyer would bring them in £100,000. Mr Michael doesn't consider this extortionate. In the Hong Kong case, he thinks they will have to spend £60,000 alone on the catalogue and travel expenses.

A lot of their day-to-day material arrives at the front door in Bond Street, unasked for, unheralded. If you go in through that green-painted front door and along to the counter, you'll see little huddles of people clutching their treasures, waiting for some Sotheby's expert to give it the once over. All Sotheby's experts are available for anyone who calls (from 9.30 to 4.30 every weekday) and will give an oral opinion of what they think the object is and what it might fetch in a sale. You can bring photographs if the stuff is too big to cart along. The service is free, and you don't have to let them sell it.

When it's stamps, either Mr Ashton or Mr Michael, as the two resident stamp experts, get called down to the counter, which they do around twenty times every day. About a quarter of the items they see end up in their catalogues. They try to fend off telephone calls, asking people to come in, refusing to give blind estimates. If someone says, as they do at least once a day, "I've got a Penny Black here, only it's a red colour," then that's easy to refuse.

They also go out 'on a sweep', which is the Sotheby's in-house phrase to describe their regular provincial campaigns. Sotheby's, like Christie's and others, now advertise heavily in leading local newspapers, announcing that their experts in various fields will assemble on a given day in a local town to look at anything whatsoever anybody wants to bring in. On a sweep day they can look at as many as 200 stamp albums, perhaps accepting ten for sale.

Then of course they have their world-wide tours, either following up tips, or more usually going round Sotheby's far-flung empire. Sotheby Parke Bernet and Company, to give it its official title, has forty-seven auction rooms or offices in twenty different countries. The stamp department looks after the whole world from Bond Street, apart from North America and South Africa, as Sotheby's New York and Johannesburg offices own resident stamp experts. When anyone arrives off the street at a Sotheby's counter with an interesting-looking stamp album, whether it's Zurich or Hong Kong, Melbourne or Buenos Aires, then Mr Ashton or Mr Michael will give it the once over on their next call. If it sounds really exciting, they might fly out at once.

Normally, it takes between three and six months for an item to be sold. You get a receipt when they first agree to take it, then a letter putting in writing their estimate and auction date. If the seller decides to proceed, a reserve price might then be agreed. Nothing else is heard till you get an advance copy of the catalogue, with a list of your lot numbers. Assembling the catalogues can be a nightmare, with the slightest literal likely to cause panic in breasts all round the world.

They both agreed that the biggest problem in their work is people expecting too much. "When the vendor is greedy, it's a right turn off. You can never

A sale of Impressionist paintings.

satisfy them." Another slight moan is that because they work for Sotheby's people think they must be aristocratic, or at least very well connected. It is true that if you look at the list of Sotheby's top brass it is heavy with titles, both here and abroad, and there always seem to be some débutante-looking girls floating around the corridors. Good connections do help in the auction trade, to promote confidence and bring in a certain sort of customer.

"In *this* department we work through hunger. We're certainly not filling in time. We've always been used to going out and getting work, not sitting in the office, waiting for people to come to us."

They'd finished the champagne and their secretary got out her calculator

and announced that the sale had realised £93,000, thanks to those French letters – almost double their pre-sale estimate of £55,000. I thought it was a good moment to bring out some of my spare stamps, swaps which I just happened to have on me. As I'd failed to *buy* anything at Sotheby's, perhaps I could *sell* something at Sotheby's. That would sound equally impressive.

I got out about forty 1841 Penny Reds, many of them with Maltese Crosses on. (I won't confuse you with my philatelic expertise but I thought they were pretty good. Well worth £50. Perhaps even more.) They each looked at them, then put them down, moving round the office in an abstracted fashion, picking up their bags and papers, arranging their desks as if about to leave on urgent business. After a lot of coughing, letting them know I was still here, I eventually asked Mr Michael straight out what he thought. I knew I'd have to wait six months to get in a catalogue, but I was in no hurry.

He was very sorry, but there was no point in taking them. They were worth only a few pounds. I didn't press him to say what he considered 'few' pounds. He had omitted to say in our chat, apparently, that his department virtually *never* takes an individual lot worth under £100. If by chance it fitted in some-how or added interest to a collection they were already selling, then they *might* consider it, but really, anything under £100 just wasn't a commercial proposition.

Ah well, perhaps I'll stick to being a Sotheby's watcher, having failed to be either a buyer or a seller.

I then went to see the present chairman of Sotheby's, the Earl of Westmorland, who took over from his first cousin, Peter Wilson, in 1980. It was Mr Wilson who did most to put Sotheby's on the map, both in Britain and throughout the world, in the last thirty years. Their growth since the war has been phenomenal, but it is often forgotten that Sotheby's has been a comparatively small business, in terms of sales, throughout most of its life.

It was founded in 1733 by a London bookseller and for the next 200 years they were known mainly as 'Auctioneers of Literary Property'. It was not until the 1930s that they overtook Christie's, their longer-established and larger rival, and began to be principally engaged in selling works or art and paintings, with books at last taking a minor role.

For most of the last two centuries, British auction firms have operated in times of stable prices. During several decades auction prices remained exactly the same, though there have been regular fears that prices might even decline, which they did in 1930 and 1940. It is only in the last twenty years that we have become accustomed to inflation being the norm, having to live with the knowledge that the prices of everything will go up, all the time, by leaps and sometimes bounds. This has been one reason for the enormous rise in the prices of works of art. As they will always be limited in supply, people decided to opt for such things as an investment, rather than the money markets.

As recently as 1955, the total annual sales at Sotheby's amounted to only £1.7 million. By 1959 it had increased to just over £5 million. The really huge advances came in the Sixties when, under Peter Wilson, they branched out in the United States and elsewhere and London was finally established, once and for all, as the art centre of the world, a position which until the last War had been held by Paris. Now, with annual sales at over £200 million, Sotheby's is the world's biggest auction house.

Lord Westmorland therefore viewed his promotion to chairman in 1980

Prospective buyer, examining a Chinese vase.

with some trepidation, though he was immensely flattered to get the job, after fourteen years as a director. Before that he had been an insurance broker at Lloyd's, and before that in the wine trade. Peter Wilson had been both an expert and a business man, equally skilled at looking after each side of the firm. In all auction houses there is a division between those with the learning, who can claim to be authorities in their specialised field, and those who are administrators, looking after the business side. Throughout the world, they have 300 experts out of a total staff of nearly 2,000. Lord Westmorland is basically a business man, with no special artistic expertise. On his promotion, he immediately appointed a managing director specifically to look after the experts, leaving him to concentrate on the wider business side.

He is a tall, distinguished gentleman of fifty-seven, a bit like James Callaghan in looks, with a habit of breaking off in conversation to smile to himself. For many years he was a Lord in Waiting to the Queen. Now he is Master of the Horse, one of the three ancient Great Offices in the Royal Household (the other two being the Lord Chamberlain and the Lord Steward), but his position is purely ceremonial. He was in one of the leading coaches for Prince Charles's wedding and always takes part in such things as Trooping the Colour.

He gets a bit upset when people say that Sotheby's is dominated by the upper classes, that success in the firm depends on who you are not what you are, though he admits that traditionally they have always employed a lot of well-connected people. "It helped to have people who knew the old English families, the sort who had possessions which dated back to the Grand Tour. These contacts have been very beneficial. But they also work very hard. Of the three businesses I have worked in – wine, Lloyd's and here – I would say that the people in Sotheby's work hardest of all. They have to do an incredible amount of travelling."

He sees the Eighties as a time of further expansion, especially in the United States. In Britain and Europe, the increasing power of the Heritage lobby has meant that the supply of the very finest objects is already drying up.

Governments and institutions are fighting – and succeeding – to keep their nation's best works of art at home, usually in public hands, which means they will never again come to the sale room.

"In Europe anyway, people generally like to keep what they have inherited. In America, people are more interested in disposing of their possessions. I'm not sure why this should be so. When a father dies in America, a son will very often sell the things the father has collected. In England I suppose such things have been in the family for so many generations, and they are expected to continue there."

He has felt in recent years that Sotheby's has come in for a bit of unfair criticism, mainly from people appalled by the enormous sums changing hands in the auction rooms. "It is not generally realised how much we have done for the country, not just in directly bringing in foreign currency, but in all the indirect ways. I recently had a meeting with the Invisible Exports Committee and they said that we bring in more invisible profits than the Stock Exchange. They include in this the hotel and travel expenses that arise when wealthy people come from all over the world for our big sales.

"I can't think of any other British business of any sort that has been as successful as we have in the post war years. The trouble is, some people don't like to see you making a success of things. Personally, I am very proud to have been connected with the firm in these great years of growth.

"As I go round the world and meet people, on business and in private, their reaction is always the same when they hear I work for Sotheby's. They are *very* jealous ..."

End of sale.

3 Wembley

WEM-BU-LEE, Wem-bu-lee. How strange that such a nondescript suburb of North London should so regularly have its name chanted round the entire nation. How interesting that even when the name is mischanted, split into three syllables as opposed to two, everyone still knows what is being referred to. Wembley has become a state of mind.

You hear that strange, strangulated cry whenever two or three pathetic football fans are huddled together, stuck in the rain on some open terrace in the depths of the Fourth Division when their team is patently being hammered, yet in their hearts they carry the hope that *this* season there just might be the chance that their team will get to Wem-bu-lee, Wem-bu-lee.

Wembley is not the best stadium in the world. Most certainly, as Sir Alf Ramsey used to say, it is not the most modern. There are many stadiums with better facilities. But there is no doubt that it is the best-*known* football stadium in the world. Fans everywhere, from Russia to Brazil, know where Wembley is. Foreign sporting papers can refer simply to their national team's next match being at Wembley, and everyone knows exactly what that means.

Perhaps Wembley's best-known event each year is the Cup Final. When you realise that basically this is a little local match, a contest between teams from two places in England, a country which is now no longer a world leader in many things, least of all football, it is all the more remarkable that each year 500 million people round the world watch it live on T.V.

They had a meeting at Wembley in 1977 to decide whether they could somehow capitalise on all this fame and affection which Wembley has attracted over the years. It was suggested that tours of the stadium might bring in a few pounds. Several people merely smiled. Who on earth would want to trail round an *empty* stadium, being shown a load of old concrete, invited to stare at rows of vacant seats!

It was a wet and miserable Monday in March 1981, yet there was a queue of almost fifty people waiting patiently beside the twin towers for the gates to open for the next tour at two o'clock. They have them on the hour, all the year round, every day except Thursdays, and except the day before, the day of, and the day after, an event. Even in mid-winter, they average 300 people a day. In the summer holidays, when the schools are off, over 1,000 people walk round Wembley. Their annual average is now 100,000. Yet they do little to advertise this tour, though they do put it in their own Wembley programmes. Word of mouth has really been enough.

I stood in the queue with a party of thirty-two boys and staff from the Christian Brothers School in Nenagh, Tipperary. During their week in London, so a teacher told me, they had already done Westminster Abbey, the Imperial War Museum, the Science Museum, Madame Tussaud's, Ice

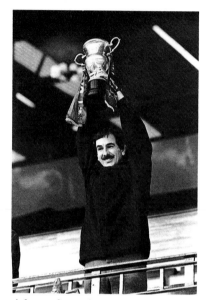

A happy Spurs fan (Hunter Davies) holds aloft the Cup during a Wembley Tour. The Cup is fake but the smile is genuine.

Right: *Crowds coming along Olympic Way for the 1981 Cup Final. Blue was the predominant colour – light blue for Manchester City, darker blue for Tottenham Hotspur.*

Skating and various other excursions. There was also a party of four people from Scotland, a man from London with his son who supports West Ham and was being given a special treat of a day off school as his dad had failed to get him a ticket for the League Cup Final, two ladies from New Zealand, two German men and a couple on their honeymoon from Middlesborough.

I walked in with the honeymoon couple who said it was the second day of their four-day honeymoon in London. The previous day, Sunday, they had looked at the Oxford Street shops, for her sake, but today it was his treat. "If I get to be seventy I don't suppose Middlesborough will ever get to Wembley," said the husband, David, an assistant company secretary. "This is my only chance." His wife Lorraine, a student nurse, said she wasn't a football fan, but she didn't mind coming.

Our guide was Monique, an attractive young lady who spoke with an American accent, though she turned out to be Dutch. There are twelve Wembley guides in all, under the direction of John Feenstra, an Australian whose first job at Wembley was in a maintenance gang, cleaning up the terraces after a big match. He became a guide when the tours started in 1977.

"The most enthusiastic people we get are the Japanese," he said. "They come round in huge parties and spend a fortune on the souvenirs. I remember one very cold winter's day a few years ago when we thought nobody had turned up for the four o'clock tour, the last of the day. Then we noticed this little Japanese boy turning away, thinking we were closed. We decided to give him the tour on his own. 'It's a dream, a dream,' he kept saying all the way round. When we came to the dressing-rooms, we told him to step inside on his own in the dark, and close his eyes. Then we put the light on and told him to open his eyes – and he bloody fainted! Really, he just collapsed. We were worried he was a gonner."

Our guide Monique took us first to the trophy case where she pointed out various historic cups and mementoes, such as a book signed by all the famous people who have been to Wembley over the decades, which appears to mean almost every head of State and every member of the British Royal Family. Then we went into a large room where the post-match T.V. interviews take place. One wall was completely covered in football graffiti. The boys from Tipperary, most of whom turned out to be Liverpool fans, were delighted when one of their masters found the name Shamrock Rovers had been immortalised on the wall.

The lights went out and we were shown a fifteen-minute slide show of highlights from past Wembley performances, complete with sound effects. The chief participants ranged from Cassius Clay to Elton John, two of the many international stars who have appeared at Wembley.

After the film, we set off on a tour of the inside of the stadium, going in an arc round to the North Dressing Room which Monique said was known as the Unlucky Dressing Room. Only three teams who have used it in the last four-teen years have been successful.

There were cheers and gasps from the boys when we entered because the dressing-room had been laid out as if for a match, with fresh strips arranged on each place (though it would have to be for a very unusual match as around fifty different strips were on show, from leading British clubs as well as international teams). They also have several historic strips on show, as worn by people like Stanley Matthews in the 1953 Cup Final and by Nobby Stiles in the 1966 World Cup Semi Final against Portugal.

She told a story in her Dutch-American accent about Stanley Matthews always reading a magazine in the dressing-room before a big match and how one day some other player went up close to see what it was and found it was a copy of the *Beano*. Everyone smiled. It sounds to me more like a story which *appeared* in the *Beano*.

We all obediently filed into the adjoining bathroom and dutifully admired a row of ancient-looking square-shaped sinks and a massive but archaic five-foot-deep plunge bath which the players step into, down a wooden ladder. It takes four hours to fill it up with hot water, said Monique.

The West Ham supporter, like many of the others, had been taking dozens of photographs since we'd started the tour. He lined his young son up beside the bath, then he got him in the dressing-room, caressing all the strips. They have had few things stolen over the years, which is surprising when you think how large the parties are and how many of them are boys from faraway places. Recently a complete Ipswich strip has gone missing. They suspected which boy had taken it, and gave chase, but couldn't catch him.

Having done the dressing-room, ogled the equipment, fantasised over the rituals, breathed in the atmosphere, we then progressed, just as the stars do, to the tunnel which leads out on to the Wembley pitch. This is more like an aircraft hangar than a tunnel, big enough to take a double-decker bus. Monique told us to split into two lines, as if we were two teams, and to wait in the tunnel for her signal to move on.

This is the moment when very often people are near to fainting. Over the loud-speaker system they play the noise of the Wembley roar, so that you proceed down the tunnel, and on to the pitch, with the sound of 100,000 people screaming and shouting in your ears. Alas, that day, the sound system in the tunnel refused to come on. This very often happens after a real match. (The League Cup Final, between West Ham and Liverpool, had been two days previously.)

However, the Irish boys seemed suitably impressed and even overawed as they walked in silence down the tunnel and at last we entered the arena and caught our first sight of that brilliant green turf, the best playing surface in the world, so they like to say at Wembley. We were all strictly warned not to touch it. One man did dare to put a foot on it, unwittingly, just to get a better shot of his son, and screams and oaths could be heard floating across the stadium from the far corner where some groundsmen had obviously spotted this criminal.

We moved slowly round the sandy greyhound track which circles the pitch, taking care not to touch the grass, till we came opposite the Royal Box. Monique made us face the pitch first of all, and pointed out the curve on the surface which is ten inches higher in the middle than at the sides, to help the drainage. So far, a match has never been cancelled at Wembley because of the surface being waterlogged. Then she let us face the Royal Box and imagine all those triumphant scenes from past matches.

A photographer appeared and we were all invited, one by one, to ascend the famous thirty-nine steps, and have *our* photographs taken, holding the Cup in front of the Royal Box. This time, the sound effects did work. As each of us went up, there was the most almighty roaring, filling the stadium, as 100,000 voices sang and cheered at our magnificent achievement. People often cry with emotion at this stage, overcome by the pictures in their head, the recorded roars in their ears. I watched as each one went up and from below they appeared hypnotised, grasping the Cup and waving like mad, dots in an empty landscape, surrounded by a sea of empty seats. When it was my turn, I too felt a gulp, unable to resist waving back to acknowledge the cheers of the invisible fans.

The Cup, by the way, looks like the real F.A. cup but is just an old one they found in a store room. For the first three years they used a cup left over from an old greyhound meeting, which they thought was made of tin, till one day it was valued, found to be solid silver and worth over £3,000.

The tour ended at Wembley's souvenir shop where we were all given a free hot drink or orange juice, and then let loose in the shop to unload our money. They have the usual mugs, medals, plaques, posters, banners and ornaments representing all the best-known British clubs, but by far the most popular item at present is anything to do with Liverpool. They could do more business by forgetting all the other clubs and stocking the shop completely with Liverpool mementoes, but that would of course be rather shortsighted. After all, Wembley is a national stadium. And, who knows, Shamrock Rovers might turn out to be the team of the Nineties.

I asked the honeymoon couple what they had thought of the tour. They both agreed it had been great, really good. In fact it was going to be their cheapest outing in London. Just £1.50 for an afternoon's entertainment was well worth it. (The tour itself lasts one hour, ten minutes.) That night they were going to *Evita* and had spent a fortune on the tickets.

They only had one adverse comment. The dressing-room area had seemed so, sort of, old-fashioned. Those sinks, well, they'd never seen sinks like them before. They were very interested in such things, and were planning to go to the Ideal Home Exhibition next day. They thought that Wembley, of all places, would have up-to-date baths and sinks in their dressing-room. But,

apart from that, they had enjoyed and admired everything and would remember their tour for ever.

Wembley *is* old-fashioned. Many managers over the years have criticised
the facilities and many spectators have longed for better lavatories, more
attractive standing accommodation, less brutal and ugly concrete corridors
in which to saunter. Even in the parts where no expense was spared, in the
Royal Retiring Room or the main dressing-rooms, it all looks now like something out of the 1923 Ideal Home Exhibition. This is part of Wembley's
attraction. Outside, it is an impressive sight, a gigantic bowl with its proud
towers and balustrades. Inside, it is in many ways an ancient monument, a
mausoleum for so many of the nation's memories, a receptacle of our glories,
and quite a few failures.

The first Wembley Cup Final was held in 1923, the year the Stadium was
built. The Stadium was designed to house part of the 1924–25 British Empire
Exhibition, a magnificent scheme, which amazed the world at the time, then
ended in financial disaster, remembered now as much for its folly as for its fun.
The Stadium itself was completed in just 300 working days, an enormous
achievement, and was acclaimed as a miracle of modern engineering, heralding the age of ferro-concrete, just as the Crystal Palace Exhibition, seventy
years earlier, had heralded the age of glass.

The Exhibition site covered some 219 acres in all, with fifteen miles of roads,
and included many halls and galleries. The Palace of Engineering, for example, had a 900-feet-long glazed roof and displayed the new art of milking
cows by electricity and the very latest wonder, the wireless. The whole complex
was a cross between Disneyland, an Olympic Games and a World Expo. It
cost £12 million and it ran for two years, attracting over ten million visitors. At
its peak, 90,000 people poured into Wembley by rail and road every hour.

The Stadium was described as being 'bigger than the Colosseum in Rome',
according to the claims on some souvenir ashtrays, with 'walls higher than the
Walls of Jericho'. Before it was opened, a whole battalion of soldiers stood in
the stadium marking time, just to check that the concrete pillars would stand
up to the vibrations of 100,000 cheering people.

During the Exhibition, the Stadium housed several pageants and an International Rodeo put on by C. B. Cochran, the greatest impresario of his age.
He lost money on it, and later went bankrupt, and the Exhibition's promoters
also realised they had got rather carried away, despite the huge crowds, and
had spent far too much. They had planned for a third year, hoping to recoup
their investment, but went into liquidation. Eventually a private developer
bought the lot, the Stadium and all the Exhibition halls and lakes and side-
shows, for a mere £300,000, paying £30,000 down, promising to pay the rest
when he had demolished the site and sold as much as he could for scrap.

The Palestine Exhibition Building ended up as a laundry in Glasgow. The
West African Building became a jam factory. One of the restaurants was re-
built as the grandstand for Bournemouth and Boscombe F.C.

The Stadium was left, isolated in all its splendour, but even that at one
time seemed doomed. The Football Association were in two minds, after what
had happened at the 1923 Cup Final, not convinced that using Wembley was
worth all the trouble. Despite the massive crowd, their profit for that first
Wembley final had been only £4,714.

Britain gave the game of soccer to the world and it had been the major

Spurs fans and slogans, Cup Final, 1981.

spectator sport in Britain for many years, long before Wembley had ever been thought of. The Football Association had been founded back in 1863 and its first Challenge Cup was instituted in 1871 when it was played for at Kennington Oval. Later, it moved to Fallowfield, Manchester, then to Crystal Palace, then to Old Trafford, Manchester, and then to Chelsea, before coming to Wembley in 1923.

That first Wembley Cup Final, of April 28, 1923, attracted a crowd of 200,000, around 150,000 of whom managed to get in, some of them climbing ladders and digging tunnels. When it was time for the kick-off, the pitch couldn't be seen, nor could two Guards bands who continued playing, despite being lost in the huge crowds that had overflowed on to the pitch. It took over forty minutes to clear enough space on the grass for the match to begin; thanks to the stout work of P.C. Scorey, the only mounted policeman on duty, who slowly circled, in ever-increasing circles, on his white horse Billie, till at last he had gently moved the crowds back off the pitch.

The F.A. decided to persevere with Wembley, despite all the crowd troubles, and by 1932 they had changed the ticket system, taking over the distribution from the Wembley authorities. To make the Stadium viable, as half a dozen football matches a year was soon seen not to be enough to cover the enormous running costs, the Wembley owners introduced greyhound racing in 1927. But for the dogs, the Stadium would probably never have survived. In the 1930s, crowds of 40,000 turned up for the thrice-weekly greyhound meetings. Even now, although little more than 2,000 come for the regular meetings, they still provide Wembley's bread and butter income. Speedway, which was also a great attraction at Wembley in the 1930s, has now all but disappeared.

During the War, the Stadium was used as a camp for thousands of survivors from Dunkirk who spent the first few nights after their rescue sleeping rough in the Stadium's corridors and dressing-rooms.

Just as the British Empire Exhibition of 1924 put Wembley on the world map while the country recovered from the First World War, it was the 1946 Olympics which signified our revival after the Second World War. The Wembley Company made the staging of the XIVth Olympiad in Britain possible by offering the whole site free of charge. They hurriedly had to open and repair their 200-feet-long Empire Pool, which had been added in 1934, then covered over for ice skating instead, because swimming at Wembley, which could accommodate 4,000 people daily, had turned out to be another financial disaster.

As usual with so many great innovations at Wembley, there was a race against the clock to get the new improvements ready in time for the Olympics. When the U.S. team arrived they threatened to pack their bags and return home when they found the track had not yet been laid. On the day itself, the 440 yard hurdles were delayed for half an hour because the lines were still being marked.

Today, Wembley is an enormous complex once again, almost as it was back in 1923. Over the last few years, multi-million-pound additions have been made, notably the £14 million Wembley Conference Centre, opened in 1977, which has an auditorium seating up to 2,700 people. There is also a new 330-bedroom hotel, and the Empire Pool, re-named Wembley Arena, which stages ice shows, gymnastics, boxing, badminton, the Horse of the Year Show.

The Stadium itself has had many improvements, such as a transparent roof put on in 1963 at a cost of £500,000, which completely covers the 100,000 spectators – 55,000 standing, 45,000 seated. In May 1982, the Pope was due there to say mass, another first for the Stadium.

Wembley Stadium is a private concern. Most people assume it must belong to football in some way, just as Lord's belongs to cricket and Twickenham to rugby. All that the Football Association ever does is rent the Stadium, as anyone else might, sharing the gate receipts with Wembley Stadium Ltd,

Above: *Ricardo Villa's remarkable winning goal for Spurs, dribbling through a crowded penalty area.* Right: *Ardilles, Crooks and Archibald rejoice while Villa runs away into the sporting history books.*

75/25, in the F.A.'s favour.

In many ways the Stadium is still a white elephant. They have recently spent £1.5 million on rewiring and on strengthening the barriers, in line with Government rulings, improvements which the general public can never see. It is enormously costly to maintain such a massive edifice, now sixty years old, which covers an area of 73 acres, with half a mile of 76-feet-high walls, two towers 126 feet high, fourteen bars including the Stadium Long Bar (which has a bar counter 129 feet long, the second longest in the world after one in a club in Shanghai), and a press gallery which can seat 240 journalists.

It would, in some ways, be easier to knock the whole thing down and start again, something which even some Wembley officials privately admit would be the best solution to all the maintenance problems. Nobody, at the present time, has the money for such an undertaking. In the meantime, Wembley Stadium Ltd, which is owned by Rediffusion, in turn owned by British Electric Traction, carries on, without any help from the Government or any sporting body, keeping alive part of Britain's national heritage.

On Cup Final day, such thoughts of gloom, such thoughts of the terrifying costs, are forgotten as the Stadium looks its best and the world turns out to admire the pomp and pageantry. On Cup Final day, over 1,500 police are in attendance, 1,000 commissionaires and stewards, 80 car park attendants, 4,000 cars, 500 coaches, 100 first aid men and a catering staff of 400 to serve 25,000 sandwiches, 60,000 beers and 20,000 cups of tea. That's what Martin Corrie says, anyway.

Mr Corrie is Wembley's information officer and one of his jobs is organising all the programmes for Stadium's events. For the 1981 Final, Wembley issued nearly 500,000 copies, which may sound optimistic, when the gate is only 100,000, but Cup Final programmes now start selling ten days before

Manchester City attack the Spurs goal.

the match and go all over the world. This was to be an extra-special Wembley as the F.A. was celebrating its 100th Cup Final. He was very pleased that, despite a bigger-than-ever programme, containing sixty-four pages, he was managing to keep the price down to 80p.

The 1981 Centenary Final was between Tottenham Hotspur and Manchester City, a South-versus-North clash, which always adds extra appeal. From early morning supporters were walking down Olympic Way, named after those 1948 Olympics, lined as usual with stalls selling scarves, banners, badges and food. Chips seemed to be back in fashion with not so many hamburger stalls as in previous years. There were several sandwich-men with religious banners, something you rarely see at ordinary football matches. "Awake to the Righteousness not Sin." "The end of all things is at Hand."

Above the Stadium, there was a constant whirring of helicopters, containing T.V. cameras from the rival networks, and nearby a large air ship, with an advert for Goodyear on its side. Against one wall of the stadium, to the right of the central towers, a monster crane zoomed up into the sky, as if some building worker had found a cheap way of watching the match. In the basket at the end was a T.V. crew from London Weekend.

As always, the crowd was very good-humoured. The rival supporters, when they weren't trying to out-shout the opposition, were putting their arms round each other, saying their team had no chance. You never see *that* at normal football matches.

There were stories in the morning papers of tickets changing hands for £200, which I didn't believe, but I did see one £13 ticket going for £50. All the way from the tube station there were young boys and men asking, pleading, for anyone to sell them a ticket. The crowd these days is young, with teenagers in the majority.

Being there in the flesh means that you miss the action replay of the goals on T.V., though you know they will always be repeated, every week for the next year; but you also miss my favourite spot in the massive T.V. coverage which is now devoted to each year's F.A. Cup – the interviews with the players'

wives. Instead, we had live in the stadium the massed bands of the Royal Marines for two hours before kick off, plus an acrobatic display and then a presentation of the captains from previous finals.

'Abide with me' was sung just before the match, the traditional Cup Final Hymn. For once, many people seemed to join in, except for the extremes in the two rival ends, who probably couldn't hear the band above their own non-stop shouting. It's such a dirge-like, mournful hymn, anyway, not at all suitable for such a joyous occasion.

I watched the Prime Minister Mrs Thatcher and husband Denis, playing with his binoculars. I also noticed in nearby seats Sir Matt Busby, Bill Shankly, Ron Greenwood and Neil Kinnock, M.P. When I say noticed, I was standing on my seat, craning over the heads. Then eventually the Queen Mother arrived, looking radiant, and beautifully neutral, in green.

The details of that match are by now in every record book, and every T.V. film archive. It has to be said that it was not of a very high quality, with Spurs particularly not playing well. It ended in a 1–1 draw, the first drawn Wembley final since 1970. The replay took place at Wembley the following Thursday.

The occasion this time was completely different, with the crowds streaming in much later and more subdued, arriving after a normal working day. Touts were *offering* tickets for sale, at face value. It had much more of the atmosphere of a normal evening match, except that the crowd was 92,000, and they were soon in full voice.

The lead changed hands three times and Spurs finally won 3–2, their hero being the Argentinian, Ricardo Villa, who scored their third and extra-ordinary goal after a solo dribble through a crowded penalty area. In the first match he had suffered the ignominy of being substituted well before the end and had walked slowly round the long Wembley pitch towards the dressing-room. I hoped his bath was ready for him, though I doubted it.

In the end, it was judged by most people to be the best and most exciting final in living memory, a fitting celebration of the hundredth match. Another milestone in Wembley's glorious history.

4 Kersey

KERSEY is a little village in Suffolk. Like the best English villages, the sort beloved by poets, invoked by patriots, praised by politicians, especially in times of national distress or when the poet or patriot is stuck in some foreign field that isn't England, it has a church, a pub, a village hall, just as all perfect-looking English villages should have. Behind the scenes, it probably also has warring families that haven't spoken for centuries, some long-standing row about that horrid bungalow, and perhaps the new vicar is even now proposing a plan which will split the entire village, but we won't go into any of that, even if it does exist. This is a happy book.

We all like to think that we have come from a village, far back in time, when life was fresh and innocent, when we all worked on the land, when pleasures were simple, work was honest and noble and nothing really nasty ever happened. We don't want to hear any boring sociological facts about the dreadful lives the peasants really led in their insanitary homes and their soul-destroying labours in the field, and how they jumped at the chance of getting out. It's the lovely legends about the English countryside we want to believe.

Even now, it keeps us going in our urban chaos. As we go about our tainted, polluted, modern ways, we like to believe that one day, God willing, the football pools allowing, that unwritten bestseller permitting, one day, by Jove, We Will Return.

This is one of the major problems of the modern English village. Those who have returned are all old or, even worse, newcomers. Strangers in our midst. How can they know anything until they have lived here fifty years? Those who have left are the young and active and child-bearing, gone to the bright lights and the flesh pots and the hamburger havens of wicked cities such as, well, Ipswich.

Would Kersey turn out to be that sort of village?

I was walking slowly down the main street, admiring the stillness, the emptiness, one bright but chilly March afternoon. We had chosen Kersey because it looked pretty. Frank Herrmann happened to be driving through, while making for somewhere else, and decided to take a few snaps of the old houses. Lavenham nearby is a much handsomer and bigger and better-known village, a delight to behold, but it is too conscious of its worth, well settled on the tourist map, deservedly a beauty spot. Kersey appeared just to sit there, looking nice, but doing little to attract the tourists. Why, there's neither a public W.C., a car park, nor even a convenient seat to rest one's weary tripod.

Kersey is about ten miles west of Ipswich in that part of deep rural Suffolk

which until comparatively recent times, just thirty years ago, was looked upon as one of the most backward areas of England, full of left-over villages, cottages without water or electricity going for almost nothing, cut off from all modern transport, land down to £20 an acre. Now, the population of Suffolk is suddenly increasing, as it is in many rural counties, while the Inner Cities decay and their populations fall.

Thirty years ago, however, estate agents tried to tempt city folk out with their snips, ripe for conversion, needs some improvement, and the glossy magazines did features on the bargains to be had, forget the Home Counties and the West Country or Wiltshire, come to Suffolk and see the real England, but few people came, at least not in the 1940s and 1950s.

Kersey is a medieval village. That's the first thing that strikes you. It is remarkable that the main street should contain so many buildings that date back to the fourteenth century, timbered houses which lean at perilous angles, bits jutting out, overhanging wings, leaning corners. Many are painted in bright pinks and blues, like the set for a Tudor film, but quite a few remain faded and grey, their beams worn and battered, sagging under the weight of all that history.

It was the medieval woollen trade that made Kersey, and the ancient houses, when first built, were lived in by prosperous weavers and merchants. Kersey Cloth is mentioned in Shakespeare and the village appears in the Domesday book, two claims to fame that separate the *real* English villages from any of those Victorian upstarts.

At first sight, the houses in the main street appear to be in a terrace, or at least built in unison, but on closer inspection they are all different, each with its individual shape, different nooks, different patterns and arrangements. When the wool trade moved north to Yorkshire, and the merchants declined, many of these houses were divided and sub-divided and for several centuries they became simply the homes of local farm labourers, tied cottages, with several families sharing each building. Now, when they are taken over by new-

Street scene, Kersey.

comers, two or three cottages are being knocked back into whole houses, as they were in the beginning.

The second thing that strikes you is the shape of the main street. Kersey is not a village-green village, a cluster round a focal point, but a ribbon which goes up and down. The village nestles in a dip in a steep-sided valley. You go down the hill on one side and into the village, and then up the hill out of it on the other side. There is a stream in the middle which divides the village. One half of this main street is called The Street. The other half is called The Hill. Simple.

Coming down the hill, from either side, you arrive at the little stream. You can cross it by a little bridge at the side, or drive right through it as if it's a ford. On no account, however, must you call it a ford. The locals get very cross. In Kersey, they call it a Water Splash.

The final physical feature to be noted, before we knock on any doors and meet some of the 350 natives, is the church. This stands proudly on one side, overlooking the village. Keeping guard on the other slope are the remains of Kersey Priory, now a private residence. It is strange to have the church outside the heart of the village, cut off on its own hill, but no doubt reassuring, watching over every villager. It is impossible to see the village when you approach from afar, until you are right on top of it, but the church can be seen for miles, a square-tower monument to the medieval wealth that once built Kersey.

Having admired the houses, and the ducks and geese in the Water Splash, I slowly walked up the hill, past the Bell public house, till I came to the village shop, R. C. Stiff and Sons. Above the shop an old wooden sign proclaimed

'Suffolk Cured Bacon, Hams and Chaps'. There was no evidence of such delicacies in the window, just the usual, timeless articles which most village shops have, forgotten lines, covered in dust. People don't window-shop in villages. They know what they've come for. Why bother to have a changing window display?

In the centre of the window were some faded packets of Persil, a special offer in wellies which looked as if they'd been there since the Flood, a jigsaw and a Father Christmas outfit. "With beard, brand new!" I carefully read an advert for bike hire, a notice about Kersey Tuesday Club 'Craft Evening' in the village hall, coffee and biscuits, and a poster for Kersey V.P.A.'s General Meeting, "Everybody welcome to discuss and decide V.P.A. business." What could V.P.A. mean? Vestry Parents Association? Veteran Pigfarmers Amalgamation?

Inside, the shop appeared completely empty but behind a deep-freeze there was a lean, country-looking man in a faded apron quietly arranging some stock. I asked for a postcard, anything of the village, and after a lot of searching, thumbing through a rack, he finally found one. He said he was Mr Stiff, Jack Stiff in fact, and that the shop had been founded by his grandfather Robert Stiff in 1855.

He'd worked in the shop since 1945 when it was being run by his father. As recently as 1955, they had had a staff of twenty-five and a large business in the area, delivering groceries and oil to farmers over a wide radius. They also had a little nursery garden and a garage attached to the shop. Those were the days when it was a real *general* store.

"Now we only have three and a half people. Me, by brother William, my wife Jill and an old man, part-timer, who started when he was fourteen. I'm the last of the line. My two children don't want to go into the shop, and I don't blame them. You do too much for too little return. They're being educated to do something better. My son's at Nottingham University, you know, doing physics.

"We stopped the grocery rounds in 1971. Oh, we just couldn't afford to do it any longer. You either change with the times or go under. We still deliver oil but I don't know for how long. I need to have a Heavy Goods Vehicle licence to drive our lorry, even though we just go round the local farms. In a whole year I don't do more than 3,000 miles. Yet I have to have the same licence as those petrol tankers you see roaring up the M.1. Actually, it's off the road at the moment. The Government says it's to have a tachograph. We'll have to wait. It's such an old lorry it can't be fitted in the normal way. I've just had a health test to drive it. I passed, but in another ten years, well, I doubt if I'll pass it. The laws of the country make everything so hard these days. Is it worth it, I ask myself."

He seemed a happy enough man, despite his moans, and several people came in and out as we chatted, all passing the time of day with him and he attended to them with old-world courtesy. I asked what his best line was these days and he said the cured hams. That was one thing they had kept going. Would I like to see them?

He went slowly to the front door of the shop, peered carefully out, up and down, as if from somewhere huge crowds might suddenly appear, then he locked the door, changed the sign to Closed and took me through the back of the shop to a yard full of old wooden buildings and barns.

He cures 500 hams a year, he said, putting them through a series of complicated processes, starting with dry salt, then brine, then a solution containing dark sugar, dark treacle and some secret ingredients which he could not divulge, a secret handed down through generations of Stiffs. Finally, the hams are smoked over oak sawdust. The smell in each little wooden shed was strong enough to cut up and package on its own, so sweet and rich and aromatic.

Back in the shop, he opened up again, and then stepped out into the street to point to the cottage opposite where he was born. In his day, two families lived in the house. Now it was just one. And the one beside it, which is really only half a house, though it did have a big garden, was now on the market. How much did I think it was worth? Go on, take a guess at the asking price. I didn't dare, in case either way I gave offence, but I was truly amazed when he told me – £72,000.

"When I was a lad, we had a shoemaker, two butchers, a blacksmith, a village policeman, a vicar, now they've all gone. Our vicar lives elsewhere and looks after three parishes. Over the last five years, Kersey's become a dying village. Mind you, I love working in the shop. I wouldn't change that for anything. Nobody else will do it, but I will, just as long as I can."

That was just Jack Stiff being a pessimist, said a genteel old lady coming out of a house further along the street. How could a place with houses, right on the street, selling for over £70,000, be called a dying village? "Jack's father was a big buccaneering type. The shop was bound to decrease in scope when he retired. It's not Jack's fault. I think he really wanted to go off and train to become an accountant. I used to have a very big weekly order with Jack, now he doesn't carry the stock. I honestly think the stock diminished before the customers did. But his ham is lovely. It's the highlight of our Christmas. We always eat it in candlelight."

In the White Horse pub, the one where the locals go, as opposed to the Bell which attracts most visitors, an old man was tut-tutting about the prices being asked for houses. According to him, it was the newcomers, the London folk, coming in with their fancy money, who had put up the prices, making it impossible for the locals to buy. Yes, said another, but who makes the profits when an outsider comes in, think about that then.

Two of Kersey's oldest outsiders are Ralph Hammond Innes and his wife Dorothy who moved into the village in 1947. There is no squire in Kersey, as this part of Suffolk was too poor to attract the big landed estate owners, but at least in Hammond Innes they do have one famous resident. He has a clipped, officer's accent and a military bearing which would fit him to be a squire figure, but he has no desire for such a position. He tries to keep clear of the main social life of the village, much though he loves it. People think that writers enjoy being interrupted, just because they work from home.

Their home is up a turning beside the Splash, and the stream runs on through their garden, but the house itself is hidden from view, behind a massive set of wrought-iron gates. It looks the sort of picture-book house one of England's best-selling authors should live in, a Tudor dream, with every beam intact, the lawns immaculate, the ancient brick paths perfectly laid. It was formerly a barn and has been added to over the years, but a lot of it dates back to the fourteenth century.

They had previously been living in a cottage in Wiltshire, back in 1947,

Kersey's best known residents, Ralph Hammond Innes and his wife Dorothy.

wanted a bigger house, but couldn't afford Wiltshire prices. They were told that Suffolk was cheap and undiscovered. The minute they came to Kersey, they realised the house fitted all their dreams.

"East Anglia was very backward in those days," said Hammond Innes. "Even in the Fifties you used to see ponies and traps in Hadleigh (the nearby little town). It was in the Sixties that the explosion started, with new light industries arriving, overspill from London and then the affluent week-enders.

"There is a little row of council houses, just over the hill, behind the church, and that's today where the *real* locals live. I remember talking to some at the time they moved in, delighted to have a bathroom and inside lavatory, for the first time in their lives, and a bit of comfort.

"Most of the old cottages in the street had been tied cottages for centuries. The agricultural labourers couldn't afford to improve them, and the farmers wouldn't. Farmers tend to be tight at the best of times but they weren't doing well and didn't have much money to improve them. I think if the switch hadn't happened, with the building of the new council houses, many of today's lovely cottages would just have gone. Many in fact *were* condemned. It was the middle classes moving in, with money and time and love to spend, which saved many from literally falling down. I am sure a few farmers did deliberately have them condemned, in order to get rid of the tenants and sell them, and I know some speculators did move in and out just to make a quick profit, but I think on the whole it was the new people who saved the village. Many of them have stayed."

I went on a tour of his house, observing the brick floors which date back to the fifteenth century and came originally from Germany and the Low Countries. "This part of East Anglia had bricks for their houses when the rest of the country had none. Suffolk used to export its wool to Flanders and, as ballast for the return journey they filled them up with bricks. I've seen bricks in Holland in exactly these colours and texture."

I was invited to take pot luck with a lunch which, like the house itself, seemed to be straight from *Country Life* and was delicious. There was a home-

The Water Splash in the middle of the village, with the church behind.

made sorrel soup, grown in their garden, with home-made brown bread, followed by chicory rolled in locally cured ham (thank you, Jack Stiff), covered with a herb and egg sauce. Over lunch, Dorothy talked about the bad old days, when the village was so terribly poor. She has heard from people living in the village of the days when beggars walked from one poorhouse to another. In the 1930s, said Ralph, land fell to £5 an acre.

"I remember 1950 so clearly," continued his wife. "It's one of the few dates I ever get right, that and 1066. That was the year we got electricity and water in our house. Until then, the water had been pumped from our well and we had a generator for the electricity. What energy we needed in those days! We had to hand start an antiquated pumping engine and the electricity plant was always breaking down."

They try to keep out of local action groups, but they played a big part in the restoration of the church bells which was completed in 1970. It started with an appeal for £3,000 to repair the bells, which had last rung in 1887 for Queen Victoria's Jubilee, but then it was discovered that the tower would have to be repaired to take them, and so the target shot up to £26,000, a large sum for a small village to raise. Luckily, Ralph managed to broadcast an appeal on B.B.C. T.V. which brought contributions from all over the country.

"Villages are metamorphosed. That's what happens to them all. It is inevitable. Villages are no longer part of the countryside, lived in solely by agricultural workers, for the simple reason that agricultural workers don't exist any more. They're all mechanics. They don't do hedging or ditching any more. Machines do that. This is an arable area, mainly wheat and barley. It's only with stock that you need any labour, and there's not much of that around. With grain, you can let the contractors come in and do all the hard work.

"You can't possibly say we are dying. Look at our bus service. No village can be dying with so many buses." His secretary, Mrs Anderson, was called for and she confirmed that there was now a bus almost every day of the week: Tuesday, Thursday and Saturday to Ipswich; Wednesday to Bury St Edmunds for market day; Hadleigh for shopping on Fridays; Saturday afternoons for football in Ipswich. That's been very popular this year, with Ipswich playing so well. Such a pity they didn't get to Wembley.

There are today more buses serving Kersey than there were thirty years ago. Eastern Counties retreated some time ago, convinced business was finished, but private enterprise, in the shape of Beeston's Buses and Rule's Buses, stepped in and have made a big success, timing their buses to meet local needs.

Hammond Innes has a studio in London and a place in Wales, but looks upon Kersey as his working home. When he is working he stands at an architect's drawing board to write his books in long hand. He had a slipped disc six years ago and finds standing to write easier than sitting.

Not far from Kersey, he has 230 acres of woodland, which he has had planted. On the latest Ordnance Survey maps, areas once white now appear green, thanks to his planting, which must be an interesting feeling. He knows a lot about forestry and serves on various forestry committees. "I now know enough to realise that East Anglia isn't really the place to plant trees."

He doesn't think he'll ever leave Suffolk and now looks upon himself as almost a native, though he is a Scot, born in Sussex. "It's a marvellous county. Do you know we have 344 churches in Suffolk of architectural importance, more than any other county.

"I could live anywhere in the world and I would be much better off and pay less tax if I did. But what's the point of having money if you don't live where you want to live? I love Britain, dammit. My roots are here. I want to stay.

"I've travelled the world and I know where you can find more sunshine, but I know that sunshine can be hell. Other people have a climate. We have weather. Every day is a surprise. For living in a place all the year round, Britain is unbeatable. British people don't realise this. They think the grass is greener elsewhere. *That's* not even true. We have the greenest grass."

Not far away, in a brand-new house, lives the chairman of the local parish council, Paul Ryde. He too came to live in Kersey in 1947, though he is a

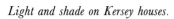

Light and shade on Kersey houses.

Suffolk man, born in Ipswich. He is a senior partner in a six-man veterinary practice in Hadleigh. Most of their business is to do with horses, either blood-stock or leisure ponies, plus a few pigs and cattle. The bloodstock side is growing as people move away from Newmarket and the high prices. He says there's nothing special about being a vet in Suffolk. The animals and their problems are much the same as anywhere else, except they get a lot of tetanus, due to the nature of the soil.

His wife, Nora, is one of the local Stiffs (Jack's sister), and they have two grown-up sons. She was hobbling around on crutches that day, having had a cartilage operation.

He became a parish councillor twenty-seven years ago and sees himself striking the balance in the village. "I've been here long enough to be looked upon as a local, although I can never be one, coming from Ipswich. I did give up the council for three years, but some local villagers thought the outsiders were trying to seize power and change everything, so I came back.

"There is a bit of a Them and Us attitude. The newcomers are now in the majority – and they're very often the ones who are against any changes. What about the village seat, Nora, that was a saga."

The seat saga turned out to have Chekovian subtleties, which could take pages to explain, but briefly, some years ago a couple decided to present the village with a seat. Paul Ryde, as a parish council chairman, thought it a good idea and felt sure it would be welcomed and so worked out where it might go, choosing a site down by the stream, a place where he felt old people, locals and visitors, would like to sit.

"I always like to do things democratic like in this village, so as usual I held a public meeting to get it officially voted. We'd checked first with Suffolk County that such a thing was in our responsibility, as the parish council.

"The village was split. I was amazed. The newcomers were all against and they packed the meeting. You know what village politics are like. The whips go out, folks come in, hands go up. That's democracy. You have to grin and bear. We got heavily beaten.

"All that took one whole year. Meanwhile the seat had been made, of lovely teak, but I had to tell the couple to take it away, as we now didn't want it. I dunno. I suppose in a few years time I might try again ..."

There's an even longer-running saga about the fight to open up the footpaths, a topic which obsesses all villages and one he has personally heard being argued over at every Kersey parish meeting since 1955.

"At my very first meeting we had a retired general in charge. He lost control when two eighty-year-olds started a private argument at the back of the village hall. The place was packed, about a hundred people were there. This old boy was saying there had never been a footpath in a particular place, and the other was calling him a liar. The first old boy said he'd used the path himself as a boy, and could remember taking young so and so there – and he named a girl's name – on several occasions. Well, what an uproar. 'You rotten old bastard!' There had apparently been some scandal about this girl, sixty years ago. Now after all this time the guilty party had suddenly revealed himself. What a meeting that was ...

"I think village footpaths will cause arguments for another twenty-seven years. It's such a complex subject. Hedges have gone, land has changed hands, people argue about what exactly happened in the old days. You can't win.

Kersey villager tends his lettuces in his kitchen garden.

"I did fight Suffolk council's plan to put a W.C. in the village, for the use of visitors. Nobody else was worried at first, till I managed to get hold of the plans and found they'd picked three possible sites. When I showed them to the people who lived beside them, well, they soon complained. We stopped that one."

He and his wife have monitored house changes in the village but think there is no real resentment towards newcomers buying up cottages. Nora brought out a list and counted out thirty-seven cottages that had gone in the last fifteen years, being converted into fifteen houses.

"Some of the newcomers do tend to get on their high horse," he said, "thinking the village is full of idiots who need to be organised. You just can't arrive and try to organise people. You must *infiltrate*.

"A few do-gooders assume they know best, rushing in, telling the locals what to do. You have to *suggest* things, make them think they thought of it, then they'll do it. Country people don't move quickly. You have to sauce them along.

"I think in the end there might be a move back. There's now a lot of elderly people living in the medieval houses, ones that were converted from two or three cottages into one house some years ago. The rates are now so enormous and heating so expensive that I think there will be a change to smaller units. The next wave of development might result in houses being split, just as they used to be."

They too both denied the village was dying. As far as they were concerned, there was one vital and conclusive piece of evidence which easily proved their point. Kersey village still has a village school.

The headmaster, Ronw Bourton, was just finishing his afternoon teaching, taking off his slippers, which he wears in school, about to put on his going-home shoes. He's a tall, quiet man in a two-piece suit with a grey moustache and large M in his buttonhole. "It stands for Mensa. You have to be very intelligent to get into Mensa – and very stupid to stay in it. My membership

Schoolchildren wend their way to Kersey school.

lapsed some years ago but they wrote to me recently and I rejoined. That means I'm *very* stupid ..."

There are thirty-five pupils in Kersey school and two full-time staff. Mr Bourton (his Christian name Ronw is Welsh) takes the Big Class while the other teacher takes the Tiddlers. There's also a part-time teacher, a school secretary, a helper, a cleaner, two cooks, two ladies who take the children every lunch time down the hill to school dinner in the village hall, and a caretaker. That makes the village school the biggest employer in the village, even if their total of eleven does include people who work only an hour a day.

In Mr Bourton's class the age range is from seven to eleven and they have all types of children, from the sons of agricultural labourers to the son of a Ph.D. He was a bit worried that day as he'd worked out that ten children were due to leave the school next term, while only five were due to arrive. When he came in 1967, the roll was forty-five. In the old days, before the First World War, the school had 120 pupils, in the same buildings they still inhabit, right beside the church.

"I have taught in many city schools, but children are so much more delightful in a village like this. It's like a family. They care for each other. You see newcomers arriving in class and being looked after, even the social misfits, ones who might go to the wall in a town school. They have a gentleness that is totally missing in a town. Social heeling happens naturally in this sort of school."

I toured his school, looking in both classrooms, each neat and homely, bright, cheerful, but I was confused by the words on the blackboard in the Big Class. I thought it was some strange Suffolk dialect, and Suffolk dialect as I'd heard in the pub that morning, can be difficult to understand. It turned out to be Esperanto.

"We're learning it together. They're doing as well as I am at the moment."

In one corner of his classroom he has a computer, the first to be used in any Suffolk primary school, so he says. A local gentleman was going to leave

£500 to the church to provide a suitable memorial stone to his wife, then changed his mind and gave it to the school, telling them to buy something useful.

Mr Bourton took me next door to look at the church, pointing out the South Porch, with its delicately-carved pannelled roof, a masterpiece of fifteenth-century craftsmanship, and the arcade of seven stone arches, showing me where the carvings were unfinished. According to Mr Bourton, this was caused by the Black Death of 1348 which carried off so many local workmen, before their job could be finished. Mr Bourton then went to his car and finally put on his going-home shoes and drove home for tea.

I walked for a while round the church graveyard, noticing how all the gravestones were still in place, thanks to Dorothy Hammond Innes and others defeating a plan to have them all lined up round the edges, a dastardly move, allegedly to facilitate the mowing of grass by machines.

Not far from the South Porch I came across the following words on a memorial stone.

> Reader pass on nor waste thy time
> On bad biography or bitter rhyme
> For what I am this humble dust enclose
> And what I was is no affair of yours.

That nicely reveals a certain attitude to the world which many villages, and villagers, often display, turning their backs, refusing all advances. In this case the words are witty and sharp. Perhaps meant to be ironic.

Kersey does offer a warm and welcoming face to the world. It is gently changing with the times, even metamorphosing, without completely ignoring visitors, although so far it doesn't provide W.C.'s or seats for them. Looking down from the churchyard, to the village beneath, straddling the Water Splash, seeing figures silhouetted in the early spring evening, caught in a timeless gossip outside their timbered medieval homes, I began to think that maybe some of the legends about the English village are true.

Final farewell to Kersey.

5 Marks and Spencer

ONE DAY in 1884 a young Jewish refugee called Michael Marks was walking down Kirkgate in the centre of Leeds, looking for a clothing factory. He was a pedlar who for the previous two years, since arriving in England from Poland, had been going round various North Country towns with a pack on his back selling pins, needles, cloths, socks and other small garments. He stopped someone in the street and blurted out the word 'Barrans', which was the name of the factory he was trying to find. The gentleman turned out also to be in the rag trade, a Yorkshireman called Isaac Dewhirst. He had a friend with him who spoke a bit of Yiddish and they got talking to the young pedlar, then aged twenty-one. Mr Dewhirst was so taken by him that he offered to lend him £5 and invited him to come and inspect the stock in his warehouse.

Later that year, Michael Marks decided to open a stall in the open market in Kirkgate. His little stall was unusual in that all his garments were displayed in open baskets, a primitive version of self-service. On the rival stalls, the goods were all mixed up, with no divisions. Michael Marks also made sure that the prices for the goods in each section were clearly marked, a definite move away from the traditional method of haggling. Above the penny section he hung a board with the slogan, 'Don't ask the price, it's a penny'.

This was to prove one of the most successful shop slogans ever used, colloquial and quaint, with Yiddish overtones, yet simple and striking, and it appealed to the industrial working classes, looking for a bargain, attracted by the easy method of inspecting and buying goods. He soon decided to use the same fixed price for everything on his stall, and from then on in his Leeds stall, and in the eight or so stalls he opened in other Yorkshire and Lancashire industrial towns, everything he sold cost one penny.

By 1894, his little chain of Penny Bazaars, as they were called, were doing such thriving business that he realised he needed a partner. He went back to Isaac Dewhirst, from whom he was still buying material, and asked him if he would join, but he refused. Instead, he suggested his cashier, Thomas Spencer. So, in 1894, Mr Spencer joined Mr Marks, putting in £300 for a half-share in the business.

Today, as the 45,000 employees of Marks and Spencer in the United Kingdom get ready to celebrate the firm's centenary in 1984, you won't find any garments priced one penny in any of their 250 department stores. But you will find a firm which still prides itself on its own way of doing things. Marks and Spencer has become part of the language, an institution which cuts across all class barriers, known affectionately as Marks and Sparks by the fourteen million people who go into one of their shops every week.

The Spencers died out long ago but the present chairman, Lord Sieff, is the grandson of the original Michael Marks. One of the firm's main suppliers is still the same Dewhirst company. For almost a hundred years, they have provided clothing for Marks and Spencer, growing and expanding as Marks and Spencer have expanded, one of around 700 suppliers today who provide for the company, manufacturing goods to their orders and specifications. It was Michael Marks who laid down the principle in the early years that he wanted to be a retailer, *not* a manufacturer, and the firm has stuck to this idea ever since.

It is a remarkable firm in so many ways. They rarely advertise, for example, which goes against all modern marketing methods. After all, how could any advertising campaign reach more people than they already reach? So they save their money, knowing that those fourteen million customers who already make a weekly visit can *see* for themselves what's new in their local Marks.

They are terribly British, which in this day and age is a brave principle to stick to, when you think of all the cheaply made clothes from Hong Kong and Taiwan which dominate the counters of so many other shops. Around ninety percent of everything sold by Marks and Spencer is British-made.

No firm in Britain can boast more loyal customers, or more loyal staff. Half of their staff has been with them five or more years. Even people who have never worked for them accept that they are model employers, always concerned for the welfare of their staff.

Over forty percent of the British public buys its underpants and knickers from them and they are by far the country's biggest retailing chain. According to the *Guinness Book of Records*, one of their stores, at Marble Arch in London, takes more money per foot than any other shop in the world.

* * *

Today in Leeds there is an enormous Marks and Spencer store right in the middle of the main shopping area, in Briggate, which has a staff of 350 and covers an area of 51,000 square feet. Round the corner I noticed a little surplus store with a large and defiant notice written on the wall above, 'WE SELL 'OWT'. Could it be a new Michael Marks in the making?

Janet Richardson, aged seventeen, is one of the newest and youngest members of the full-time staff at the Leeds Marks. She has very well-kept red hair, cut short with a fringe. There is a hairdresser supplied by Marks and Spencer, cut and shampoo for only £1, but Janet prefers to get hers done by the outside hairdresser she has always gone to, despite it being much more expensive.

It was one of her early mornings which she doesn't like, as she had to be in at eight o'clock, fifty minutes earlier than usual, and spend an hour stacking the shelves. All the assistants have to do this chore one morning a week. Her father is a charge hand with the council's road mending department and is very proud of the fact that Janet now works for Marks, especially after what she has gone through.

When she first started, just seventeen months previously, her legs ached for the whole of the first week every night when she went home. Then the second week, when she had to do her first spell of stacking, her arms ached. Now she is used to the physical exertion which the job entails. She was working that day in the women's dresses department, the busiest section in the whole of the shop. The spring dresses had come in and they were now selling everything they could get.

Janet Richardson, aged 17, at work at the Leeds branch of Marks and Spencer.

Left: *Janet Richardson, counter assistant, Leeds*. Right: *Lord Sieff, chairman, in the company's head-quarters, Baker Street, London, behind a reproduction of the original Penny Bazaar, set out with some of the goods sold in Leeds, one hundred years ago.*

Ray Dunn, the manager that day. has spent twenty-nine years with Marks, starting at Blackpool on £8 a week as a trainee, before moving in turn to Burnley, Wigan, St Helens, Stockport, Macclesfield (his first post as manager), Birmingham (deputy manager), Bradford and then Leeds in 1977. Those nine changes meant nine changes of homes, and then schools, for his wife and four children. Never for one moment did he think of refusing any move. They were all promotions in the Marks and Spencer hierarchy and he jumped at the chance. He sees Leeds, however, as his last move before retiring.

He often remembers his first view of the large Birmingham store, the first day he arrived to be deputy manager. He'd come from a little store in Maccles-field, "I stood at the front door and I looked across and I couldn't see the back of the store! I thought, God, I'll never manage this."

One problem in his head that day in Leeds was the batting order. Well, an excitement more than a problem. The Leeds store was currently sitting at 13 in the Marks and Spencer top store league. This is worked out on money taken through the till every year in each of the company's 254 stores. Every day, in every store, the till takings (including cheques) go to the bank and the totals are sent to the Marks and Spencer headquarters in Baker Street in London.

In his four years so far at Leeds he had climbed from No 14 to 13, pulling ahead of Bristol, which had been a matter of great satisfaction. Now, with only four months of the financial year to run, he was £40,000 ahead of the number 12 store, Kingston-on-Thames. He talks to their manager on the 'phone once a week, and they compare figures, so he knew exactly their respective positions.

At the same time, he knew that Leeds could never go beyond number 12. Number 11 was Glasgow, Argyle Street, a much bigger store. After that, of course, you're in the super-star league. The number one M. and S. store in Britain is, of course, Marble Arch in London, followed by the other Oxford Street store, known as the Parthenon. Then it's Newcastle, Birmingham, Edinburgh, Croydon, Liverpool, Brent Cross, Manchester, Cardiff, Glasgow Argyle Street and then, fingers crossed, Leeds.

Mr Dunn gets to work at eight each morning, as do all his management staff. The earliest arrivals, at five o'clock, are the warehouse staff, accepting the deliveries of that day's fresh food. If at the end of the day there is anything left that has exceeded the 'sell-by' date, it is sold to staff at half price. The rest is then given free to local charities. In Leeds they divide it between the Crypt (a Church of England charity) and the Little Sisters of Mercy.

As with all M. and S. managers, Mr Dunn's first concern each morning is the post. He has about seven or eight folders, containing around a hundred items, to read each day. They come overnight by road from Baker Street. They gave up the Post Office some years ago, preferring not to rely on their deliveries. It takes him the first hour to go through the folders. That morning he was informed there was going to be a special promotion on luggage, which meant reducing the prices.

All buying is done from Baker Street which knows what each store has sold, and then supplies them accordingly. Baker Street informs them when they have decided on a new line, and tells them exactly what they have been allocated.

M. and S. don't have seasonal Sales, like normal shops, but there are regular reductions on successful lines to make them even more successful. When the order comes from on high in the overnight folder to drop a price, then the local manager sees to it that the goods in question are given extra promotion. The re-arrangement of the counters, to draw attention to the promotion, is left to the individual manager and his staff, though visitors from HQ, who are very frequent, will soon point out if there's a better arrangement.

Recently, for example, Mr Dunn arranged his men's footwear counters in a star shape, as opposed to the normal, parallel lines. He had done this with the ladies' shoes with some success. It was his idea, but the comments from H.Q. were not favourable. It was pointed out that his star shape was reducing the display space by a few feet, so he had to rearrange the counters, back in parallel lines.

Around nine o'clock, he went on his rounds, seeing all the various D.M.'s, departmental managers. He was a bit sorry to have to give the luggage department, which was in a corner of the basement, a better position, with more traffic flow. He had decided he would have to relegate the towels to that corner. "I love the ambience of the towels. They're so colourful, while the luggage looks boring and doesn't catch the eye. But I have to do it for the luggage promotion. So, it's sod the ambience...."

Mr Dunn is short and dapper and cheerful. He describes himself as quite volatile and says he has had lots of rows with colleagues in the past, above and below him. M. and S. might present a bland, rather self-satisfied image to the outside world but inside, so they all maintain, constructive criticism of everything, and everyone, is actively encouraged. Perhaps as M. and S. managers go, Mr Dunn *is* hot-tempered. As the big wide world goes, managers in Marks still seem un-temperamental, conformist, very dutiful, very loyal people.

He then walked across to toiletries and instructed the D.M. in charge of textiles to remove a line of baby clothes. This particular line was being withdrawn. Head Office had decreed it. Customers in several stores had been complaining that the motifs had been coming off. The garment itself had given no trouble, just the motif, so it seemed to me a minor reason for

Marks and Spencer 69

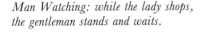

*Man Watching: while the lady shops,
the gentleman stands and waits.*

removing the whole line. "Not at all. We only sell perfect goods in Marks and Spencer. A label which comes loose means an imperfect article." He stood for a while, thinking deep about toiletries, and decided he would boost them by giving them more space. He instructed the relevant D.M., Rick Buckland, who told the warehouse manager who in turn told workmen how to re-arrange the counters.

Mr Buckland, aged twenty-four, is one of four University graduates working in the Leeds store. He is short with a rich moustache and he too looked very dapper in his M. and S. suit. Most management people wear the house product, at work and at home, unlike most of the girl assistants, who in their own free time don't think much of M. and S.'s young casual clothing. When it comes to pure fashion, M. and S. don't pretend to compete. It takes years for an M. and S. trouser leg to narrow, and when it does, the change is hardly perceptible.

Mr Buckland is a B.Sc. in bio-chemistry from the University of Exeter. He is surprised that anyone should be surprised that he is spending his life supervising the sales of ladies' underwear and dresses. He had contemplated M. and S. even before he went to university, at the age of eighteen, when he had an exploratory interview with his local store. They told him that if he had a

chance of a university place, he should take it, then join them afterwards, which he did.

"It was just an academic exercise, getting a degree. I've always fancied the retail trade. I suppose inside me there's something of a barrow boy. I thought M. and S. would be the best training in the world. It would smooth the edges. They have a nicely-structured career path. I got £3,650 when I started and now, two years later I'm a D.M. on £6,250." In those two years, he's worked in five different stores in five different towns.

At ten o'clock, Mr Dunn took his coffee break in his little private dining room, along with five or six of his senior staff, the Inner Cabinet of the Leeds M. and S. The staff quarters, as at all M. and S. stores, are enormous, with thick pile carpets, comfortable sitting areas and immaculate lavatories. I don't think I've been in cleaner lavatories, anywhere in the world. M. and S., as a company, is obsessed by hygiene. The staff themselves all look incredibly hygenic, in their brilliantly clean clothes, fresh faces, perfect make-up, as if they too have all been sent from Baker Street in the over-night bags, ordered by the computer.

Chiropodist at work, looking after a member of the Leeds staff.

That day the chiropodist was in attendance, as he is three days a week. The staff spend their life on their feet, so feet care is essential. A doctor comes once a week. The dentist comes twice a year. The company provides breast and cervical screening for female staff and the wives of male employees.

All staff get served an excellent three-course meal each day, for only 10p, all of it M. and S. produce. This means that in every store, unseen by the public, there is a large catering staff, all equally immaculate, with uniforms and little frilly hats. The staff quarters in each store are equipped with changing rooms, complete with fridge, lockers, free deodorants, creams and lotions, where the staff can change if they are going straight out for the evening. Most have showers, but Leeds hasn't.

Every member of staff gets a Christmas bonus which for counter assistants, who have done a full year, means four weeks' extra pay and everyone after five years is entitled to free shares in the company, depending on the year's profits. In 1981, they got 4.3 percent of their salary each in shares. They are free to sell them on the open market, but most keep them, proud to have shares in themselves. Even when you retire from M. and S., on a non-contributory pension, you get a Christmas present, a hamper or money. Little wonder that M. and S. is a way of life. Their stability figure, for the whole group, is eighty-two percent, which they claim has for a long time been the best in Britain. It means that at the end of any one year eighty-two percent of their employees are still with the firm.

The three senior staff who were sitting with Mr Dunn, having their coffee break, had been with the firm thirty-eight, twenty-six, and twenty-two years respectively, normal figures for senior staff in every M. and S. store.

"What I'm looking for in new staff," said one of the ladies, Gloria Ward, the Staff Manager who began as a sales assistant, "is first of all stability. You have to judge it from their school reports. Then I want good health, because you have to be fit to work in Marks; then an outgoing personality, people who like people and like to help; and then someone who is clean and presentable. They don't *have* to be raving beauties. Tidiness is more important."

Mr Dunn says that his supervisory staff are so loyal to the firm that they will even give advance warning, a year or two ahead, if they are planning to start a family. With such a large female staff (310 out of the total staff of 350 at Leeds are women), leaving to have babies is a constant occurrence. It makes the high stability figures even more remarkable.

After coffee, Mr Dunn then went round various other departments, seeing how the changes were going, noting that the toiletries were now in a better space. "Toiletries had been very undercooked." This is Mr Dunn's own phrase, not Marksism, meaning a counter with insufficient space.

He had a look at the meat counter and inspected the chicken portions. In the last few years M. and S. have revolutionised the chicken market. They were always aware of the potential in fresh chickens, but unwilling to produce the watery, tasteless chickens which many of their rivals were doing. After over three years of experiments, going back to the farmyard, breeding a new strain of chicken, specifying the feed, ignoring conventional battery farms, giving them instead some open space to live in, then developing new chilling techniques to retain the flavour, they finally launched the M. and S. chicken on the world. By 1980, chickens had risen to become their single most successful item, selling at the rate of half a million a week nationwide, beating knickers, jumpers, skirts and trousers in terms of money taken.

In the Leeds store, however, their best-selling department is Ladies' Fashion, which accounts for 31 percent of their income, followed by Menswear 26%, Food 22%, Children's clothes 12%, Lingerie 12%. They like to think of themselves in Leeds as being very clothes-conscious.

Not all new things do well. Records and tapes, tried a year or so ago, were a failure. Mr Dunn had some worries that day about books, another new line. They started well, and were still doing nicely, but he wondered if perhaps there were enough new titles. He observed customers coming back for more books, very satisfied with their purchases, but disappointed to find the old books still on sale.

It was a Tuesday, Market Day in Leeds, so young Janet Richardson, over in dresses was already run off her feet, which is what she likes.

"I hate Mondays. It's so quiet. I often have a few minutes in which there's no customers around, but the rest of the week, well, it's just constant. I've noticed that when it's quiet, I get tireder. I think boredom makes you tired. I never get tired when I'm busy."

Janet knows all about being bored because for the first three months after she left school, with two O levels and six C.S.E.'s, she was unemployed. It is hard to believe that such a presentable, clean, tidy and eager girl should ever have failed to get a job, but such, alas, is the nature of the times in which we live. Unemployment in Leeds, like many places, was running at ten percent.

"I wrote to every shop in the whole of Leeds, and they all said no. I wrote to some several times, and applied for scores of vacancies I'd only heard rumours about. Marks turned me down at least once. Most of my friends from school went into offices, but I always wanted to work in a shop. During those three months on Social Security I was so nervous and worried I developed a rash."

One day, at the Social Security Office, she was sent along under the Manpower Services Scheme to work for M. and S. for six months. This is a Government scheme whereby large firms are asked to take on one or two school leavers each year, who have never worked, and give them work experience. These Work Experience youths are always surplus to requirements, and are not filling vacancies, which is why they are not paid the full rate. They finish after their six months, then some other youths get a chance.

Janet started on only £20 a week, working full-time, but determined to make the most of this sudden opportunity, which seemed to her like a little miracle. M. and S. had always been her first choice, even when she was applying for, and being rejected by, scores of inferior places. "I slogged my heart out. Always early, always working hard, going out of my way to help. I even applied for a cleaning job when I noticed it on the staff board. I didn't *want* it. Sales assistants don't do that sort of job, but I knew it would impress people if I applied. It showed I was so keen to work at M. and S. I would take anything."

After only six weeks, when a real vacancy came up, she was taken on as proper staff, with all the benefits. She's not quite sure what her gross salary is now, but it's very good, she says. "I take home £194 a month. It's better than all my friends. Most of them think they're superior, working in offices, not in a shop, and boast about their cushy lives. They do have it cushy, in some of these offices. I work much harder, but I'm glad of that."

She's already terribly loyal to the company, and gets upset when she sees any of her Supervisors being too kind, so she thinks, to customers taking advantage of their change-anything policy. M. and S. have tightened up a bit in recent years, but the rule is still to change anything faulty or anything that is obviously unworn. The argument, of course, is very often about whether something really has been worn or not. The signs of wear are pretty obvious to the experts, but even so, they often give in, just to keep good public relations.

"I had a woman in the other day with some gloves she wanted changed. I could see they'd been worn, so I said sorry, love. She got very high-handed and said it was disgusting, she'd been shopping at Marks for years, she never thought this would happen, not in Marks of all places. So I had another look at the gloves, I turned them inside out, and I found a label – saying British Home Stores ..."

Mr Dunn had a visitor that day for lunch, Aleck Shepherd, the manager of the Doncaster branch, who was passing through Leeds from an area meeting of M. and S. managers. "We're 49th in the batting order at Doncaster, but if I can take £3,000 more this year, I'll be above Uxbridge."

He is up on Leeds in one respect. In Leeds, they always run out of small sizes first, especially for men. "The average collar size in the West Riding seems to be about $14\frac{1}{2}$ inches", said Mr Dunn. "I think it's because of the high proportion of immigrants in the area, from India and Pakistan, working in the textile industry, who tend to be on the small and thin side. It's the same with women – the 12 and 14 sizes go quickly in Leeds, and we always seem to get stuck with 18s."

Over in Doncaster, so Mr Shepherd is able to boast, they have Big Customers if not Big Spenders. "The main employer in the Doncaster area is the Coal Board. You don't see many small miners, do you. We're always running out of size 16 and 17 collars and 44 to 46-inch chests. We have very thick necks in Doncaster. I'm always telling Baker Street to make up our orders with 'Large Size emphasis'."

They both accept the criticism that Marks is not a place for high fashion changes. That is not their policy. Teenage styles had been tried in the past, such as a line called Miss Michelle, for girls' boutique-type clothes, but it hadn't gone well. Their image, and main custom, is still with the conventional, who want quality at good prices, not the latest fashions.

"There is no room for individuals who want to change the Company's policy," said Mr Dunn. "You have to change to fit the Company. If the individual thinks he can change the Company, he might as well leave. One I'm especially thinking of now has his own multi-million pound clothing business, but he just wouldn't conform when he was here. He always preferred fashion garments anyway."

I complained about the lighting, which I always find too severe in every Marks shop, like an operating theatre, which makes their deliberately bare and uncluttered display counters even more stark and functional.

"You might not have noticed, but the lighting has been softened in recent years. For many years I wore spectacles at work, because of the lights," said Mr Dunn.

"That's funny," said Mr Shepherd. "So did I. I got them specially tinted. Now I've given them up. And remember all those girls who were always getting headaches? It was discovered it was the lighting. You don't get any headaches now."

After lunch, Mr Dunn did his first Collection. This is when the security people go round and empty the tills. Leeds, being such a big and successful branch, needs to empty the tills more than once a day. "We like to maintain a management presence when the Collection is being done."

At 2.30, a women's group from the *Yorkshire Post* arrived to tour the store. Mr Dunn gave them a ten-minute talk about the history of Marks and Spencer.

He's very fond on such occasions of explaining their coat of arms, which includes the white rose of Yorkshire, a tribute to the firm's Leeds beginnings.

When he's out at a social event, in his private capacity, Mr Dunn never reveals he's a Marks and Spencer manager, not if the party is going well. If it's a boring occasion, he might then just let it slip out. "Once it comes out, that's it. *Everyone*, everywhere, has something to say about Marks. People are always giving us ideas. The most frequent suggestion is why don't we have fitting rooms. I can answer that one in my sleep – we've got them in a number of stores in isolated areas, but as every article can be returned, there's normally no need for changing rooms, which anyway require extra space and more staff.

"I can talk for about two hours about Marks without hardly thinking. It's a useful topic for some occasions. But, if the party's good, I want to hear about other people's lives, not talk about my own."

His next engagement that afternoon was to present a cheque for £250 to a representative of the Wharfdale Music Festival. Marks and Spencer are great patrons of the arts. They gave away a million pounds in 1981 to charity. You have to write first to Baker Street, if you think they might help your organisation, but the money is usually given out at a local level. In Leeds, they have given £25,000 towards the Leeds Music Festival. They also help social causes and community ventures.

For the last two hours of that day Mr Dunn worked on the Checking Lists which show what's been sold, what's in stock, what's coming in. It's a painstaking operation, not exactly a favourite occupation with Mr Dunn. Young Janet might not like her early-morning shift stacking shelves, but at least it takes up only one hour a week. Mr Dunn has to spend two hours every Monday and Tuesday, going through these lists which he sends to Baker Street and are the basis of all future supplies.

Janet herself was able to leave at 5.40, ten minutes after the store had closed to the public. She'd had an enjoyable day. She felt pleased the way her dresses

All part of the service – for the staff. Marks and Spencer assistants having their hair done at work.

had looked. She wouldn't wear them herself, as she feels the styles are too old for her, but she likes them all to look nice. She's worked on shoes, children's socks, and books, but likes working on dresses best.

She was particularly pleased that day because her Supervisor had asked if she would contemplate training to be a Deputy Supervisor, quite an honour for a girl only seventeen. She feels she has grown up a lot, and so does her boy friend, in the year and a half she has been at Marks, and acquired much more confidence, but all the same, she feels it's still a bit early for promotion.

"I used to be very shy. It's really brought me out, working here, but I feel a bit young for supervising. I need more experience, more confidence, then I might do it."

She was home by 6.30. After tea and a bit of tele, she was in bed by nine o'clock. Two nights a week she goes to bed very early. They happen to be the days her boy friend works late, but it's also because she feels she *needs* all the sleep she can get. It's a hard life, working at Marks and Spencer.

Mr Dunn finished just after six. He doesn't like to work too late, preferring to start early, but he had some assessments to complete. Every member of staff, at every grade, gets an annual assessment from their immediate superior, two pages of detailed comments on their progress and personality. You can add your own comments, if you disagree, and that too goes on the assessment. Each person gets a copy to keep.

"I've never contemplated leaving Marks for another firm, though there have been people in my career I haven't enjoyed working with. They're a paternalistic firm, for which I thank God. I feel looked after, even cherished, especially in these difficult times for the economy and for the country as a whole. I like to go home at the end of each day feeling all square with life. I've put in a good day for the company. In return they have been good to me.

"One of my proudest memories is of having met both Simon Marks and Israel Sieff. They were both charismatic characters and they loved going around the stores. I'm only sorry the younger staff will never meet them.

"Some people might think it is bad that it should be a family firm, where the sons heve inherited the power. I see it as an asset. I feel safe with them at the helm. Each day I thank fate for having directed my steps to Marks and Spencer."

* * *

It's not just their British H.Q. but their world H.Q. which is situated in London's Baker Street. All that day in Leeds I heard no real complaints against the company, no principles they disagreed with, but I took away a slight feeling that perhaps Baker Street does allow them very little initiative.

Considering the influence it wields over its 40,000 store staff, and the 175,000 people who work for the suppliers, it is quite easy to pass by H.Q. and hardly notice. The building is indeed enormous, taking up a whole block, and inside there are almost 3,000 staff, but outside they present a discreet face to the world, most windows are blank, blinds drawn, almost like a secret Government department.

There appeared to be several sets of front doors but notices at each one directed me elsewhere, till at last I stumbled through one set of doors and came into what looked like a vast hotel foyer, with uniformed security guards,

porters waiting to attend, people queuing up with large packages and important briefcases. The atmosphere was a cross between Broadcasting House and an inter-continental hotel in some Eastern European country. Functional, rather old-fashioned, but very, very clean.

Inside the building they have a reproduction of the original Penny Bazaar stall, set out with some of the goods which would have been sold in a Leeds market, a hundred years ago. The corridors throughout the building seem endless, with identical carpets, colour schemes and doors.

"We have been accused of being clones," said one executive. "M. and S. people don't look alike to me, but other people often say we do. I suppose when you see our employees outside, you can tell them from other office workers in Baker Street. They just look, well, so M. and S."

Officially, the hours in Baker Street are 9 to 5.30, but you never see large crowds coming in or coming out of the building. The majority arrive early and leave late. No one asks them to. They're just so eager to get to work. Yet there is no clocking-in system. Everyone comes and goes by trust. It's almost like those Japanese firms, where they all sing the company song each morning, and everyone lives, not just works, for the company.

We in Britain might take M. and S. for granted but there are always visiting experts arriving at Baker Street, especially from America, who produce weighty reports on the M. and S. retail methods. It confounds any idea that all British workers today might be work-shy and lacking in motivation.

All buying and selling is done from Baker Street, from the thinking-up of new lines to the testing of the first prototypes when they arrive from their suppliers. There is one whole floor which is a huge laboratory, split into little sections. You have to wash your hands, in the usual spotless M. and S. wash basins, before you are allowed to enter any of the food labs.

Through one window I could see three technologists testing glasses of white wine which were laid out on a table. The bottles themselves were hidden under a white cloth, so the testers did not know the name or type of wine. They were trying out Marks and Spencer's own Baden wine against similar German wines produced by their rivals. They hadn't marketed any Baden wine for a year, despite its successful launch some years ago, as it was decided that the quality had gone off.

In another lab, full of instruments and test tubes, like a sterile unit in a modern hospital, a technologist was working on an invention for a new sauce for steak and kidney pie. Nearby, in the textile lab, I watched something called a mace snagger whirling away. This consists of an iron mace-like instrument, with spikes sticking out all round, which was being made to pound various lengths of cloth. Above it, a T.V. screen measured how often it snagged.

At Baker Street, and throughout the stores, the employees are completely un-unionised. No attempt has been made to keep them out. In fact if anyone wants to hold a Union meeting, the management will put a room at their disposal. But under one percent of their total staff of 40,000 is in any union. One reason could be the high proportion of female labour, a lot of it part time, and such people are traditionally hard to unionise, but Marks maintain it is because their workers are already well cared for.

Today, Marks and Spencer also have 190 stores across Canada, though only 58 or so are Marks stores as we know them. The rest trade under different names. The enterprise, begun in 1972, has turned out more expensive than expected, entailing a lot of modernisation, training suppliers, fitting in with Canadian regulations, and so far they have yet to make a profit. However, you will find no one in Baker Street to admit it has been a failure. They are confident they will do well in the end. It's just taken a little longer than expected.

Expansion into Europe, which started just after Canada, has turned out more of a success. They had always been confident of a move to France, if and when they made it, because everyone has always remarked on the enormous number of French people who use their Oxford Street branches. It came as a bit of a surprise, but a salutary warning, when they were about to open their first Paris store in 1975 to find that only two percent of the inhabitants had ever heard of Marks and Spencer. After a few shaky months, and some hard lessons learned, they soon established themselves and now they have two stores in Paris, plus stores in Lyons, Rheims, Strasbourg, Brussels, with more to come.

On the world front generally, business is very healthy and they sell St Michael goods in thirty-eight different countries. In the Far East, for example, you will find mini-Marks in all the main departmental stores, set out just like a British Marks, with the assistants in the same uniform.

Lord Sieff, the present chairman, is very proud of what his family has done in building up the firm, especially the work of his uncle Simon Marks (son of the founder, Michael Marks) and his father, Israel Sieff. It was the two of them who made the firm what it is today, taking it over just after the First World War when it was still a small, local chain of shops.

"Simon and my father were a remarkable team – they were boys at the same school, Manchester Grammar, generally in the same form. They had an almost telepathic relationship with each other.

"One day when he was still at school my father said to Simon, 'Do you know that girl ahead there – she's got nice legs.' 'Yes, I know her quite well, she's my sister.' My father married her and they were married for fifty years. Simon married my father's sister and so brother and sister married brother and sister. We have always been a close-knit family."

Their brand name, St Michael, which appears on every item they sell, refers of course to Michael Marks. "We decided to canonise my grandfather, our founder. After all, St Michael was a guardian angel, so we thought he could be a guardian of quality."

Lord Sieff personally keeps an eye on the Company's quality today, always wearing their suits and trying out their new food products on his guests at his London home. He manages only five hours' sleep a night and is usually one of the earliest to arrive in Baker Street.

He has done a great deal to articulate the principles on which the company operates, and little homilies from the chairman appear in many of their company reports and announcements, uplifting mottoes from a latter-day Samuel Smiles.

"Good human relations have long been one of the foundations on which our business has been built," so it says amongst all the facts and figures in their 1981 Accounts. "They mean concern and care for the individual."

It is probably true, as many people often say, that if only the country as a whole could be run on the same lines as Marks and Spencer, then we would all benefit. It would certainly be very much cleaner.

6 Durham Cathedral

DURHAM Cathedral *looks* like a cathedral. Some cathedrals seem little more than big churches, splendid enough, but stuck amongst the other urban buildings, often dwarfed if not humiliated by everyday activities, they can lose so much of their dignity. On my first visit to Canterbury I failed to find the cathedral. I had seen it from afar but inside the town, driving round the one-way streets, I lost all clues to its situation, and gave up. Canterbury of course is on the flat, which doesn't help. Westminster Abbey has such traffic roaring past that it's difficult to stand back and get it in perspective, without being run over. It's also easy for the stranger to confuse it with the Houses of Parliament. Durham is a knock-out.

Architecturally it is unique, the finest example of early Norman architecture in Europe, and the list of its many wonderful features is always reverently trotted out whenever anyone is writing about Great British Buildings. Historically, it is part of our Island Story. But it is its situation which is so obviously striking and is the first thing which impresses every visitor.

The River Wear makes a sharp meander at Durham, leaving an outcrop of high rock which is in effect a peninsula, surrounded on almost every side by the river, and on this outcrop stand the Cathedral and the Castle and their associated buildings. Whether you are ten miles away on the Pennine slopes, or two miles away passing through the city by train, or standing a few hundred yards away down by the riverside, the Cathedral looms over you, master of all it surveys.

The Sanctuary Knocker at the entrance to Durham Cathedral.

It's a gift for every amateur photographer. You need little energy or imagination to manoeuvre yourself into a position to capture its three magnificent square towers against the sky, all in one shot, yet at the same time get the river gently flowing low down in the immediate foreground, nature's natural border, doing the composition for you. No wonder it has appeared on so many chocolate boxes. It was built for the glory of God, which is often forgotten, as Mr Kodak seems to collect most of the tithes these days.

No exact tourist figures can be given, but Westminster Abbey is generally agreed to be the country's number one church, with three million visitors a year, followed by St Paul's (two million), Canterbury (one million), York Minster (one million), King's College Chapel, Cambridge (one million), and St George's Chapel, Windsor (one million). Durham usually edges into seventh place, with around 700,000 visitors each year.

Seventh is not bad, as there are some forty cathedrals (including certain large churches classed as cathedrals) in England and Wales. In the Church of England hierarchy, the Bishop of Durham is usually considered the number four cleric in the land, after the two Archbishops, Canterbury and York, and then the Bishop of London. (He's also the fourth best paid.)

Bringing in the visitors, or even being high in the ecclesiastical pecking order, is not necessarily the best way to measure a cathedral. It was noticeable that when a survey of all English and Welsh cathedrals was done in 1977 two of the most frequently-given reasons for visiting a cathedral were that it was 'part of the tour I am on' or 'filling in spare time'.

Durham city today is something of a cultural oasis in what has become a rather worn-out mining area, an area which has its charms but is not exactly one which appeals to all foreign tourists. They have traditionally tended to fit in Durham in passing, if at all, en route from York to Edinburgh. The Top Cathedrals, in terms of visitors, all receive a much higher proportion of foreigners than Durham. Durham is unusual in that more than half of its annual visitors are locals.

On my visit, I noticed all day long that the Geordie accent was paramount. This is one of Durham's strengths, and one they are very pleased with. It now seems to be accepted throughout Northumberland and Durham that almost every family makes an annual trip to look at Durham and its cathedral. It is ostensibly just another day out, somewhere nice to go to take the kids, especially if it rains, but at the same time there is a feeling of pride, of coming to look at *their* cathedral. Amongst the cathedral clergy, they like to look upon these trips as modern pilgrimages. This, after all, is how it all began.

St Cuthbert, the most famous saint in the north of England, died in 687 and was buried on Lindisfarne, or Holy Island, off the coast of Northumberland, where the monks cared for his remains for the next 200 years. The Danish raids made them fear for the safety of his shrine and they began a series of wanderings which ended in 995 when they discovered a safe rocky outcrop on the River Wear. Here they built a little white church to shelter the saint's body and in due course, with the coming of the Normans, it was decided to build a much more magnificent building, one worthy enough to house the shrine of St Cuthbert. The Cathedral was begun in 1093 and finished in 1133, a short time in which to complete such a vast edifice.

The Cathedral's outside measurements are 500 feet long and 200 wide, which is almost the area of two Wembley football pitches, yet the whole structure was planned from the beginning to be the first cathedral in Northern Europe to be covered by a stone ribbed, vaulted roof. It was a technological breakthrough which, almost 900 years later, can fill any architect, or bricklayer, with awe.

Not content with the St Cuthbert remains, one of the Durham monks called Aelfred had sneaked off to Jarrow in 1022 and stolen the remains of the Venerable Bede, the North's other great saintly figure and one of England's most important scholars and historians. The Normans did make slight amends by bringing what was left of the Jarrow community of monks to Durham.

Religious relics, of any sort, were a big draw in the Middle Ages, and any cathedral worthy of the name had to have its share. Kings and prelates from all over Europe made pilgrimages to Durham to worship at St Cuthbert's shrine, though the list of objects in the fourteenth century which were said to be part of that shrine sounds a little suspect. The more extraordinary exhibits included a piece of the manger of Our Lord, part of the rod of Moses, a piece of the throne of the twelve Apostles and assorted garments and anatomical portions which had once, allegedly, belonged to other equally famous saints. For good measure, no doubt 'part of the medieval tour I am

Durham Cathedral at twilight, seen from the River Wear.

on', visitors could also see the claw and several eggs from a griffin, the fabulous creature which was supposed to be part eagle and part lion. The English Tourist Board could certainly do with some of those objects today.

The Reformation removed a lot of such relics, but also, alas, a great many real treasures and architectural masterpieces. Many great churches and abbeys never recovered, but it did not stop the power or importance of Durham Cathedral. Its fortress-like position, with the Castle alongside, the home of the Durham Bishops, made it impregnable in the days before cannon and it was the only English city near the Borders which the Scots never took.

The *physical* power of Durham Cathedral, and its strategic importance for the whole of the North-East, helped to make the Prince Bishop of Durham, as he became known, the most powerful figure in the whole of the North, a law unto himself, with enormous wealth and influence, the power to mint his own currency, have his own court and surround himself with loyal Barons with their own loyal soldiers. It was only as recently as 1836 that the Bishop of Durham ceased to have the title of Prince.

Today, the Bishop lives out at Auckland Castle, at Bishop Auckland, his predecessor having kindly given up Durham Castle in 1832 on the foundation of Durham University, England's third oldest, after Oxford and Cambridge, which therefore celebrates its 150th anniversary in 1982.

As in all cathedrals today, the body responsible for running the Cathedral is the Dean and Chapter. The local Bishop is in many ways a visitor, though naturally a very important one, to whom they owe final allegiance as they are part of the diocese. But it is the Dean you have to ask if you want permission to use a cathedral. Prince Charles had to ask the Dean of St Paul's for permission to get married in his church, just as any group of Durham miners, wanting to hold a service in their local cathedral, have to ask the Dean of Durham.

Peter Baelz, who became Dean in 1980, lives in the College, Durham's name for its cathedral close, a beautiful elongated square of historic houses and gardens tucked away behind the Cathedral, which you enter through a gateway, half-hidden on the North Bailey. I was a student at Durham for four years but I had never in all those years been inside the College, imagining it was private, which it is not.

Dean Baelz is an eminent theologian. For the previous twenty years he had been in academic life, at Cambridge and then Oxford where he was Canon of Christ Church and Professor of Moral and Pastoral Theology. He looked rather severe and remote on first sight but proved affable and kindly and with a rather surprising hobby which I didn't discover till I was leaving.

He started as a curate in Birmingham but has never had any cathedral or administrative experience, so he was surprised to find how much organisational work goes into a cathedral. Altogether, he has about seventy people, from clerics to gardeners, involved with him in the day-to-day running of the Cathedral. "Whenever a crisis happens I think what it must be like to be running a really big organisation, like British Leyland. You need a bureaucracy, to get things done, but you have to take care there is still communication with everyone."

The Chapter consists of six residentiary canons, more than at any other cathedral. The norm is to have between two and four. (Canterbury and London have four, York has three.) Two of Durham's six resident canons, who all live in the College, are always Professors of Theology at the University, which accounts for the large number. Two of the Canons are also Archdeacons who assist the Bishop in the administration of the diocese. There are also twenty-four Honorary Canons, appointed by the Bishop for their services out in the diocese, who have a stall in the Choir and a few other privileges, but they are not involved in the running of the Cathedral.

Next, amongst the Cathedral's resident staff, comes a Precentor and a Vicar Choral who sing the services and share the conduct of the worship. A Chorister School which has 130 boys, many of them boarders, produces the choristers who sing about 400 services every year. Durham School, a boys' public school, is also associated with the Cathedral, and the Dean is chairman of the Governors.

Then there's a Chapter Clerk, a layman, with an office staff of nine, who is responsible for the business affairs; a Head Verger and four assistant vergers; a Clerk of Works and six stone-masons, four joiners, twelve yard staff, four gardeners.

That day, the Dean was concerned with interviewing a new tenor for the choir, who would also be teaching in the school, and then getting ready to welcome a pilgrimage of 800 people for a service in the Cathedral. There are special services all round the year, for the Miners' Gala, for the sitting of the Courts, for the University, for the Methodists, for Midwives, for almost any organisation which feels like celebrating its existence in Durham Cathedral. (Write to the Dean and he will pass it on to the Precentor to work out a suitable time. The Chapter has then to decide. You probably won't be refused, if yours is a decent outfit, with local connections, and there will be no charge.)

Durham is fortunate, touch wood and touch stone, that at the moment there is nothing basically wrong with the building, nor is it falling into the river, which is what was discovered to be happening to the nearby castle some time ago. But most of the building is sandstone, which needs careful handling, and so they have a twenty-five year maintenance plan. Dr Baelz doesn't expect that during his Deanship he will ever see the Cathedral without some bits of scaffolding.

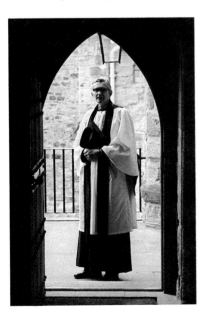

The Dean of Durham, Dr Peter Baelz.

"I do have a sense of the *Present* in this cathedral which I don't find in some cathedrals. I visited the Acropolis recently and I thought of all the gods, dead and vanished, which at the time they thought never would vanish. I can't believe that this would ever happen *here*.

"It is true people come in not knowing where they are, and ask if this place is still used, and my hackles rise when I see people sucking ice cream or lighting cigarettes, but, all the same, I think most people are aware that there is something spiritual going on.

"It is very easy to become isolated. The history of the Church of England, and of Durham Cathedral, is of power and privilege. Our physical position can work against us. There is a feeling that we are still high and remote, above normal life. Everyone has to come *up* to Durham Cathedral. It's not a through way. The physical situation can develop an attitude of mind.

"I want to be more part of the community, to help schools and the unemployed, to be more human, and at the same time more Godly. I want humanity to discover the depths of being human."

Outside, in the greenery of the College, he pointed to where he keeps his

recent acquisition, a 70cc blue Honda which he often uses for trips up Weardale. He has taken up motor cycling late in life, progressing in the last few years from a moped to a proper motor bike. "I'm doing the things I never did when I was young."

I walked round to Palace Green, the large and magnificent lawn which separates the Cathedral from the Castle, the home of University College, passing many bright and noisy students. It was the first day of a new term. In my day, some twenty years ago, a great deal of them came from the local area, from County Durham, Northumberland and Cumberland, but now the students seem to be much more Southern, with public school accents, fair-haired and privileged-looking, the pick of Anglo-Saxon youth. While the University has gone national, even posh, the Cathedral has stayed local.

I decided to start my tour of the Cathedral proper at the front door and the famous Sanctuary Knocker. If the Cathedral historians are proudest of the Cuthbert and Bede connections, this door-knocker is what probably appeals most to the ordinary families on their day out. It is the single most recognized symbol of Durham Cathedral, judging by the amount of souvenir versions which sell in all the local shops. Exiled Geordies, in all parts of the world, often have a reproduction Sanctuary Knocker on their front door, to remind them of home.

The Knocker was made around 1140 of bronze in the shape of a lion's face, with the mane fanning out behind like the rays of the sun, the sort of gargoyle effect which appears on many ancient pieces of English stone sculpture. In the Middle Ages, anyone on the run was given sanctuary in Durham Cathedral, if he could once reach the Knocker. I stood at the front door and inspected it, noting that the bronze looked suitably green with age, just as I'd always remembered it. It was only later, when I was inside, that I discovered that the one on the front door is a replica, the original having recently been taken inside for safety.

The main doorway leads into the nave where at once you see the massive stone pillars which stand throughout the Cathedral, supporting the vaulted roof. They are in themselves masterpieces of sculpture, and engineering, each decorated with differently-carved patterns and designs. (In the great churches of France, such pillars would normally be painted.) At the tops of the pillars, shafts shoot up to support the roof, making further patterns and archways, which seem to give endless views, some arched, some framed, as you look round the Cathedral in all directions.

In the South Transept there is a large and beautifully-painted clock face, dating back to the time of Prior Castell in 1495. It was about the only object which escaped destruction in 1650 when 4,000 Scots prisoners, caught at the Battle of Dunbar, were locked up in the Cathedral. They were left with no food or heat and burned anything made of wood they could get hold of. The clock is said to have been spared because of a carving on it of a Scottish thistle. I tried to get a close look, but it was being filmed by a B.B.C. T.V. crew. It never chimes, as opposed to the clock in the tower which chimes endlessly, and beautifully, but has no face.

In the Choir, I climbed up to the highly ornate Bishop's Throne, built in the fourteenth century by Bishop Hatfield, after whom one of the University's colleges is named. One purpose of a cathedral, after all, was to seat the Bishop – the word 'cathedral' comes from cathedra, the Greek word for chair. Being

The Sanctuary Knocker, made around 1140, depicting a lion's head with tendril-like mane radiating from behind the face. The best known symbol of Durham Cathedral, reproduced on thousands of suburban doorways round the world.

a *Prince* Bishop, very conscious of his exalted position, he was very keen to have what he was able to boast was the highest episcopal throne in Christendom.

Not far away is the tomb of St Cuthbert. He lies underneath a simple stone slab on the floor guarded by four tall candlesticks. The Venerable Bede's tomb is in the Galilee Chapel, at the opposite end of the Cathedral. He has a more imposing resting place, beneath a raised marble tombstone, surrounded by discreet red ropes, just in case any monk from a rival establishment should think of spiriting him away again.

I then went for a short walk round the Cloisters, which turned out longer than I intended as I got my bearings wrong and couldn't remember where I had come in. In the days of the Abbey, the daily life of the monks revolved round these cloisters and they were obviously a good place for gossiping, with several discreet hiding places. In one corner, I followed a sign upstairs to the Monks' Dormitory, a vast fourteenth-century room with original timbers. There was a collection of sculptured stones on display, belonging to the Cathedral, but rather unattractively displayed, so I didn't stay long.

The Dormitory had been rather empty, and I'd wondered where all the large parties of visitors had gone. I discovered them when I returned downstairs, crowded into the book shop and restaurant in the Undercroft. This had a very jolly family atmosphere. I had thought of having lunch here, as the Cathedral's restaurant is even in the Good Food Guide, another unique distinction, but it was too crowded and I didn't want to queue. I bought some guidebooks and postcards from a helpful though rather harassed young salesman.

Next to the restaurant is the Treasury, a relatively new creation in the Cathedral, as are the restaurant and bookshop. In the Treasury they have the original Sanctuary Knocker as well as silver and precious ornaments, books, altar plate, candlesticks, seals, bibles and many priceless manuscripts from the time of Bede and earlier. I stood with a mother and her little girl

Graduation day at Durham University on Palace Green, beside the Cathedral.

who were together drawing the pectoral cross which had belonged to St Cuthbert and was found in his coffin. After the Knocker, the St Cuthbert Cross is the Cathedral's next most recognized symbol. The mother was pointing out where it had been repaired. It was old, apparently, even before St Cuthbert had used it in the seventh century.

I tracked down the Head Verger who was sitting in the South Transept, taking money from visitors going up the Tower. His name is Owen Rees and he has been a verger for fifteen years, previously at Ely and Wells, before coming to Durham six years ago. As the Dean indicated, there really are cathedral people.

The vergers do most of the routine jobs, from dusting tables and pews, putting out seats, arranging vestments, guarding the building and guiding the tourists round. "Basically, we're public relations men. Our job is to care for people." He'd been on duty at 6.45 that morning, his early shift, ready for opening time at 7.15. The day ends at six when the Cathedral closes, or eight in the summer. He was wearing a black cassock and had a cherubic, polished head and gleaming face, smiling sideways to himself whenever he took money from the visitors, thanking each one personally.

He and the four other vergers take round parties by arrangement, and will also answer questions from individuals, such as 'Do you still have services?' and 'Are there any monks left?', which are the two commonest questions. The previous year, they had taken round 600 parties of school children and had helped to organise fifty-five special services, over and above the Cathedral's 1,100 normal day-to-day services.

It is easily forgotten that it is a daily place of worship, not a museum, though the ordinary attendance figures appear to be low, smaller than in some local suburban churches. The first service each day is at 7.30 with Communion, when there are usually between five and fifteen in the congregation. Matins is said at nine, when usually only the Canons are present, while at Evensong at five o'clock there are around twenty.

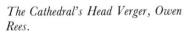

The Cathedral's Head Verger, Owen Rees.

On Sundays, Matins is sung at 10.15 and there is a Sung Eucharist at 11.30. This is the biggest service of the normal week with around 150 attending. During Festivals, like Easter or Christmas, then of course the numbers are much larger. The biggest congregations are for the Special Services such as the annual service for the Miners' Gala when up to 2,000 people attend and the carol services at Christmas when the cathedral is packed to the door.

One of the Verger's duties is to attend to any rowdies, and he usually has to chuck out someone at least once a week. "I don't like having to boot anyone out of a cathedral, but you have to, for smoking, or misbehaving. It's usually just a few local lads, from the pit villages, unemployed, with nothing to do when the ice rink's closed, who come in to chase the girls and they can get a bit boisterous. In the winter you get the school truants. They come in to keep warm."

I ended my tour back in the College and went to visit Canon Ronald Coppin, one of the six Residentiary Canons, whose special job is the Cathedral Library. They have 40,000 books, 23,000 of which are pre-1800, and 300 medieval manuscripts, the most important of which is an eighth-century Gospel Book. Canon Coppin himself is not a trained librarian, he just happens to be the canon who was given the library job. He spends more of his time looking after in-service training for the 350 clergy in the diocese. Unlike the Dean, he is an experienced clerical administrator, having been at Durham for seven years and previously at Church House, Westminster.

He thinks one of the special things about Durham Cathedral is its contact with the University, which keeps them in touch with young people, and with current academic thinking. "With two Professors as Canons, you can't get away with sloppy arguments at Chapter meetings."

He feels that places like York and Westminster Abbey can easily become dominated by tourism, which therefore takes more of the Cathedral's work.

Right: *Looking along the Nave.*
Below: *A quiet corner of the Cloisters.*

"We are of course getting more all the time. The coach parties which used to stop for coffee on the way to Edinburgh now stay overnight in the city."

As those figures for their normal services show, nobody really goes for daily worship in a cathedral any more, not when you compare it with the millions who go just to gape. So why not sit back and count the tourists? What use anyway is a Cathedral in the 1980s? Isn't it just a big museum?

"Some previous Deans of Durham have thought that there was no need at all to do anything. The building was powerful enough to bring people in. That is seventy-five percent of the truth. Doing too much of the wrong thing would ruin it. Our object should be to heighten what is already there.

"In recent years we have come round more to accommodating visitors, hence the restaurant, bookshop, new lavatories. We want to let people see we're pleased to see them, to give a positive welcome, which is part, after all, of the monastic tradition. We have to do all that without, shall we say, becoming too chatty. So, that's our first object and it's very simple – to welcome people.

"Secondly, we want them to understand. People can be repelled if you become too like a schoolteacher, so that has to be done carefully. We want to explain what has gone before and, most of all, what we are doing today. How you reveal this is very difficult, although what we want them to understand is very simple. Our purpose is to worship God."

In the near future they hope to be revealing their purpose further by organising a special exhibition area for children, where things can be seen and touched. They've also discussed the possibility of recorded organ music, as several visitors have been disappointed that in a cathedral they couldn't hear an organ playing, except at services. However, the Chapter decided that taped music would be too false, though the discussions still go on.

"One of the 'funniosities' of this place is that there are no enclosed areas, unlike Westminster Abbey or Windsor. It's hard for a visitor to find a place to be absolutely quiet and peaceful. We haven't solved that one either."

I then went down to the river, to gaze up at the Cathedral from Prebends Bridge, and read Sir Walter Scott's words, carved in stone on the bridge:

> Grey towers of Durham, yet well I love
> thy mixed and massive piles, half church
> of God, half castle against the Scot.

I too love Durham Cathedral. Not just for its massive presence, its exterior magnificence, which was what always attracted me to it, but now also for what they are trying to do inside.

7 The Royal Mile, Edinburgh

I WASTED the first half-hour in Edinburgh trying to get money to park my car, stopping passers-by, begging for change, soliciting help, searching the streets for a shop. What an admission of inefficiency. I had so much to do and so much to see and the precious moments were rushing away. The Royal Mile was somewhere up above me, the most historic thoroughfare in Scotland's most historic city, so how ridiculous to be worrying about petty things like ten pence pieces for a parking machine.

The Royal Mile stretches exactly one mile, from the Castle at one end to the Palace of Holyroodhouse at the other, the ancient route which Scotland's Kings and Queens have taken when going from one to the other. At one time, most of Scotland's noblemen had a residence on the Royal Mile, handy for the Palace when they were due to pay court, convenient for the Castle, should their help be needed.

Technically, there's no such street as 'The Royal Mile' and you won't find it on Edinburgh's street map, though the Council has lovingly put up a series of golden 'The Royal Mile' name plaques along the route, alongside the real street names. It is, however, one continuous thoroughfare, linking the two ancient buildings, which just happens to split itself into three sections. The section near the Castle is called the Lawnmarket; the end section is the Canongate; while in the middle is the High Street. Each has its own distinct flavour. (Just to be pedantic, and the Scots can be very pedantic, given half a chance, the Royal Mile contains *five* streets, if you also include two little link bits at either end, Castlehill and the Abbey Strand.)

Guides at Edinburgh Castle, complete with tartan trews.

The Royal Mile is in the Old Town of Edinburgh. In effect it *is* the Old Town, if you include in the Royal Mile all the odd little bits and pieces which criss-cross or radiate from it. The route has often been compared to the skeleton of a herring, with the Castle as the head and the Palace the tail, and innumerable little alleyways running off like bones from the central spine. These alleyways are a vital feature of the Royal Mile, and easily missed as they appear slight and insignificant, apparently leading nowhere, till you wander down and find whole settlements, tall tenements clustered round hidden courtyards, unseen from the public street. Most of them are called 'Closes', which usually means they are cul de sacs, entries only to the tenements behind. A 'Wynd' means it is open right through, from end to end. There are over a hundred such closes and wynds in the Old Town.

The Old Town at one time, back in medieval days, was Edinburgh. There wasn't anything else. It was cut off by a loch (now filled in to become Princes Street Gardens), and so space had to be maximised. As in New York, they had to build up as they couldn't go sideways, though this was before New York was even called New York. Some of the houses, still standing, were

built in the seventeenth century, and reached a height of eleven storeys. They were amongst the world's first skyscrapers. There are many buildings along the Royal Mile which have had six centuries of continuous habitation – while the two big monumental buildings, at either end, have histories which go back over eight centuries. The Old Town is indeed an old town.

In the eighteenth century there was a dramatic population and building explosion in Edinburgh, and everything changed. Parliament formally approved a plan to expand the city and a competition was held and won by a twenty-three-year-old architect, James Craig. He drew up a master plan for a new Georgian town which resulted in one of the finest architectural designs that Europe has ever seen. This New Town, as it was called, to distinguish it from what then became the Old Town, is still one of Edinburgh's greatest glories and not to be missed. Perhaps the finest of the Georgian squares and crescents is Charlotte Square which was designed in 1791 by Robert Adam, who was born in Fife, although by then he had become Britain's most eminent architect.

Anyway, back to the Old Town. Over the next two centuries it suffered an almost total eclipse, socially and architecturally. The nobs all moved into the New Town, naturally enough, desirous of space and gracefulness instead of cramming into those frightful high-rise tenements. Many of the buildings became slums, insanitary and dangerous, inhabited by the poor, the deprived and the criminal. The smells were notorious. Slops and refuse were simply chucked out of the tenement windows into the courtyards, or on to the people below, with or without the warning shout of 'Gardy-loo' – or 'Gardez l'eau'. Edinburgh is still often known as Auld Reikie, because of those nineteenth-century smokes.

It is only in relatively recent times, within the last thirty years, that the Old Town has been rescued from two centuries of neglect, though even now many visitors to Edinburgh, including those from elsewhere in Scotland, who should know better about their own history, think that the only street which matters in Edinburgh is Princes Street. This famous thoroughfare, which is open on one side, with marvellous views up to the Castle and the Old Town, and has on its other flank the Georgian squares of the New Town, is a street which can be missed, at least by sensitive souls. The views looking out and up from it are breathtaking, but there's little pleasure in walking along it. Few streets in Britain can be as horrible as Oxford Street in London, but on a busy day it has to be said that Princes Street, despite being prettier, is now in the same league. It's just another shopping precinct, full of chain stores. All the same, Edinburgh is fortunate in having three such distinctive central areas – the Old, the New and Princes Street – all within walking distance.

Edinburgh is one of Europe's capitals, not just the capital city of Scotland, and has always had its own life, not dependent on London or the South. In every other provincial city in Britain, it has been considered natural for the bright young man to head for London, if he wanted to succeed and make his name. Edinburgh has always been an end in itself.

The University has been a seat of European learning for four centuries (it celebrates its 400th birthday in 1983), and the city has been a centre for printing and literature for even longer. Scotland's first printing press was established in Edinburgh in 1507 and many of Britain's great publishing and

Overleaf: The Royal Mile, looking up from Princes Street.

printing houses began in Edinburgh, though some have been transplanted elsewhere, such as the Encyclopaedia Britannica, which was begun in Edinburgh in 1768.

The golden age of the Old Town was probably the eighteenth century when Smollett lived in the Canongate, on the Royal Mile, and Oliver Goldsmith (although Irish) studied medicine, and Scotland's most famous poet, Robert Burns, arrived to become an idol of Edinburgh society, followed in turn by Sir Walter Scott, the most popular British writer of his day. Then there were Sir Henry Raeburn, the painter, Robert Adam and his brother James, the architects, Adam Smith, the economist, and David Hume, the philosopher. It was in Edinburgh that Sir James Simpson in 1847 first used chloroform in surgery. Alexander Graham Bell, inventor of the telephone, was born in Edinburgh in 1847 and attended the University.

It is strange that Edinburgh should have given birth or sustenance to so many notable men, yet it has never been a very large town, always dwarfed in size by Glasgow. Its population today is still under half a million, and it only just manages to get into the top ten British towns in terms of population, coming eighth after London, Birmingham, Glasgow, Liverpool, Manchester, Sheffield and Leeds. Its fame has always outshone its numbers and it provides an extra fascination, in exploring the Old Town, to come across tracks at almost every corner of the famous who have gone before.

If you start at the Castle, as I was about to, then you are immediately picking over the trail of one of Scotland's all-time dramatic and romantic characters, Mary Queen of Scots. It was in the Castle that the ill-fated Queen gave birth in 1566 to a son who became King James VI of Scotland and I of England.

Outside the Castle, on the forecourt, is the Castle Esplanade. Over 250,000 spectators cram into this long, barrack-like square each year and watch the Military Tattoo which takes place during the Edinburgh Festival. There were a couple of soldiers on view, patrolling back and forward stiffly, watched by a gaggle of giggling teenage girls.

I then went through the Gatehouse and into the Castle proper, passing the statues of Robert the Bruce and William Wallace, and round and up to the Argyle Battery. I was gazing over the battlements – which was like looking down on the city from an aeroplane – wondering if I should really explore any further, as the buildings above seemed so grey and forbidding, when a gentleman in tartan trousers leaned over my shoulder and said, "That's the Firth of Forth."

I couldn't actually see any signs of water, but I nodded wisely all the same.

"No, you canna see it today. Heat haze. But that's where it is. On a clear day, you can see eighty miles."

He said he was one of the twenty wardens who patrol the Castle, watching for rowdies, stopping people throwing themselves off, answering questions. Oh, the usual sorts of questions, where's the gents, why do you wear those funny tartan trousers, how old is the Castle. An American visitor, leaning over and looking down on Waverley Station, had recently asked him why they had built the Castle so near to the railway.

According to the Official Guide to the Castle, the lump of volcanic rock on which the Castle stands has had some sort of encampment on it since the sixth century. The earliest records of the present Castle date back to the

The Castle from Princes Street.

eleventh century, but no one is really sure when it was first built. Until the seventeenth century it housed most of Scotland's kings and queens, give or take a few decades when it fell into English hands. The last action it saw was in 1745 when Bonny Prince Charlie made a half-hearted attempt to storm the battlements. By the eighteenth century, the Royal households preferred the more comfortable accommodation provided a mile away, in the Palace of Holyroodhouse, and the Castle eventually became a token fortress, a symbol of Scotland's pride and history rather than a Royal residence.

The most ancient part of the Castle is at the very top, St Margaret's Chapel, which was built around 1076 and is the oldest building in Edinburgh. Margaret was an English Princess who married Malcolm Canmore, King of Scots, in 1069. The Chapel was rediscovered in 1846 and restored to its twelfth-century condition and is a very simple, but impressive little building, just sixteen feet wide by thirty-two feet long, carefully whitewashed inside with a central chancel arch built by King David in memory of his mother. When I saw it, it was filled with beautiful fresh flowers. Each week since 1942, when Princess Margaret placed the first bowl in the Chapel, girls called Margaret from different parts of Scotland have arranged the flowers.

I looked around outside for Mons Meg, the Castle's famous fifteenth-century canon which fired a salute when Mary Queen of Scots became engaged to the Dauphin of France, and was used on many other Royal occasions. According to the Official Guide, it should have been near St Margaret's Chapel, but I could see no sign of it. I went inside a building and met another

Warden, stationed in a doorway, reading a book called *The Grand Seduction*. They have a little library of paperbacks, he explained, so when you are on duty in a quiet spot you can relax with a book, though he much preferred to be patrolling.

Mons Meg, oh yes, he said, she had been taken indoors. It was thought the inclement Edinburgh weather, after 500 years, wasn't doing her any good. She had been put in the Castle's prison where she would remain. The prison was closed that day, so I couldn't see her. I didn't really fancy going into the bowels of the Castle anyway, on such a sunny day, and wanted to get walking at last down the Royal Mile.

I then explored the rest of the Lawnmarket, poking down the little closes, marvelling at the hidden tenements, many of which had obviously been recently renovated. There were plaques at most of the narrow entrances, giving useful information about the famous people who had lived up each close. I was looking particularly for Wardop's Court, the home of a lady called Lorna Blackie whose name I'd been given as the Vice-Chairman of the Old Town Association.

I found the courtyard, and the tenement block, but it appeared to be derelict, or in the throes of renovation, judging by some scaffolding. I briefly looked inside a bare stone staircase which reminded me of a Gorbals slum, so I came out again, deciding I must have the wrong address. There was a 'phone box outside the entrance to the close, on the Royal Mile itself, so I rang her and yes, it was her right address.

I went back to the tenement and slowly climbed the stone stairs, passing on the way several smart-looking doorways, hidden on the landings, which I hadn't noticed before. One of the doors said 'James Douglas-Hamilton, Advocate'. This is the Edinburgh home of Lord James Douglas-Hamilton, Conservative M.P. for Edinburgh West and brother of the present Duke of Hamilton. Nice to know some of Scotland's aristocracy still have a home on the Royal Mile.

Miss Blackie had another visitor, a neighbour called Duncan Robertson who was collecting subscriptions for the local branch of the Scottish National Party. He lives on a staircase across the Royal Mile and is doing research at the University, having spent twelve years teaching in Athens. Edinburgh has often been called the Athens of the North, because of its fine buildings and strong philosophical heritage, so I asked him for comparisons. He said there were many similarities – each surrounded by hills, each with a dominant building, Edinburgh with its Castle and Athens with the Acropolis. Only the weather was completely different.

They both said that living on the Royal Mile, at least in their part of it, the Lawnmarket, was like living in a village. Whenever you went out you met someone you knew. When Lorna came in 1960 there were many more children and families, but now the professional classes had moved in and at the same time Edinburgh University had converted several of the old family tenements into student residences. The change she really minded was the increase in the shops selling tartan junk. "There used to be a butcher, three grocers, a newsagent and a chemist on the Lawnmarket when I arrived, now they've all gone." It was a cry I'd heard many times before.

As the Old Town was allowed to decay for most of the last 200 years, its population falling from 40,000 in 1850, to 20,000 in 1931, down to 4,000

in 1971, it means that at least it has been spared the horrors of modern development, such as ring roads, new office blocks, shopping precincts. However, when people suddenly became aware of their heritage, in the early 1950s, and the preservationists started campaigning, they found that the old buildings were in a terrible condition. Edinburgh has 6,700 listed buildings, most of them in the Old Town. The cost of renovating them has in some cases been as high as £45,000 per flat.

"Old Edinburgh is really too big and expensive a problem for the locals," said Lorna. "We need millions of pounds. There should be an international appeal, like the one to save Venice. The Old Town is unique in Europe, yet until three years ago it wasn't even listed as a Conservation Area."

Thanks to the Old Town Association, the locals are at least doing their bit to safeguard the future, battling to save the Old Town, striving to keep a balance, between the needs of the tourists and the needs of the locals, pressing for more service shops and fewer wine bars.

For the last fourteen years, Lorna has been a business woman, co-founding a chain of clothes shops called Campus which began in the Grassmarket, in the Old Town. They expanded to Glasgow, Oxford and Nottingham, till she decided to sell out her share. She was now thinking of going back to journalism in Edinburgh, which she had done in the past. "It's a strange feeling at the moment, leaving the business. It feels like being divorced."

I still couldn't get over the surprise of her flat. It had seemed so cold and cheerless, climbing up the stone staircase, yet inside it was warm and luxurious, beautiful rooms hung with fine paintings, ancient books, precious objects, with magnificent views from the rear windows, overlooking the gardens of Princes Street, a panorama of Edinburgh's grand public galleries and classical buildings. Her front view was dramatically different, mean and sordid by comparison, looking straight into the other stone tenements, though she herself finds this view just as interesting as the more obvious glamorous one.

The two faces of Scotland? Narrow and mean and dour on the one hand. Romantic and picturesque on the other. She agreed that Scotland, and the Scottish character, can betray both these elements. "You can see it in two of our greatest heroes – Mary Queen of Scots, a glamorous, romantic figure, as opposed to the dour John Knox. They both have their following."

John Knox's house is further along the Royal Mile, on the same side, but now we are in the High Street, the more bustling middle section, with many *real*-looking shops around, selling things like fruit and newspapers, as opposed to the more touristy shops and galleries of the Lawnmarket end.

Knox's house *looks* suitably old, with its overhanging wooden rooms, odd gable ends and outside staircases, whereas it's hard to realise at first how old most of the hidden-away tenements are, as they are flat-fronted and unadorned. Knox's house dates from around 1490 and he lived here with his family from about 1561 to 1572 (the precise dates are not known), when he was Minister of St Giles, on the opposite side of the road. Knox is the man mostly responsible for the Reformation in Scotland, the leader of the revolution which broke away from the Catholic Church and established Scotland as a Protestant country.

He was a contemporary of the other two great European Protestant reformers, Luther and Calvin, and was influenced by Calvin when for a time he was exiled in Geneva. He was a man of action, not just words, and was

a fine writer and historian, but he tends to be remembered today for his uncompromising and narrow attitudes.

There's a shop on the ground floor of the house, as there was in Knox's day, now selling the usual tartan stuff, and you have to climb the outside staircase to get into the house itself which is open as a museum. The young girl on the doorway took my money, but was unable to answer my questions on the differences, if any, between Knox, Luther and Calvin. She was helping out for just a few weeks, she said, but people were always asking her that, so she was going to consult her father, a Minister, next weekend.

I looked round the rooms, rather bare and sombre, but containing some interesting books and furniture, and came across an American couple laughing at a Knox manuscript.

"'All papists are infidels,'" so the man was reading aloud to his wife. "What a big mouth that John Knox must have been. Look at this bit, honey, he's getting really worried about Mary Queen of Scots being a papist. He must have been a real thorn in her flesh."

"He sounds like a tyrant to me, dear."

They said they came from Detroit, Michigan, and they had actually come to the shop below to get a sweater, but couldn't find one big enough and had wandered by mistake upstairs into John Knox's house.

There are dozens of little museums and galleries up and down the Royal Mile, on either side, many of which are easy to miss, and equally easy to wander into by mistake. A few doors along, now in the Canongate, I went into the Tolbooth, attracted by its massive clock and French château-style roof.

At one time, Canongate was a separate borough and the Tolbooth, built in 1591, its civic centre, courtroom, jail and tax office. (Tolls were collected in little booths.) Two uniformed attendants were shuffling papers at a counter in a large empty room, hung with rather nice-looking watercolours, and I asked if perhaps they were closed. "I wish we were," came the dour reply. Then he smiled and said, go on, look round, it's all free.

Next door, I stumbled into a building which hadn't appeared in any of the guide books I was clutching. The atmosphere was so different from the Tolbooth, warm and jolly, full of happy families, all very busy and occupied. It turned out to be a brass-rubbing centre.

I tried in vain to get into Canongate Church which was soundly locked, a handsome building, built in 1688, slightly set back from the road so you don't see it until you are right upon it. Instead I walked slowly round the gravestones, looking for the burial place of Adam Smith, one of the many Edinburgh notables buried here, but failed to find him.

I had a look in the window of a shop called the Himalayan Shop, wondering what on earth such a place was doing in the Royal Mile. It seemed to be selling ethnic jackets and boots. I happened to glance across the other side of the road, which I had been trying to stop myself from doing, saving it up for the return walk, and through a gap in the buildings I saw a view which did look like the Himalayas, a mountainous mass of rocks and crags, hanging menacingly over the Old Town. It was Salisbury Crags, so I worked out from the map, which runs into the green slopes of Arthur's Seat. It was rather eerie, suddenly to see a mountain, right inside a city.

The last few hundred yards down the Canongate are fairly uninspiring, with bits of modern council developments. The houses have a scrag-end feeling, as if they know all the real life is elsewhere. I began to imagine that perhaps I'd got lost. The Palace of Holyroodhouse couldn't possibly be stuck here, amongst all this down-town facelessness, then I turned through some iron gates and immediately I was right amongst the green and open mountain countryside I'd seen earlier, with the Palace before me, like a trick from a children's fairy story.

The Palace originated as a guest house for the twelfth-century Abbey of Holyrood, now an adjoining and romantic-looking ruin, and the oldest parts were completed in 1529 by James V. Its most celebrated resident was Mary Queen of Scots who lived here for six dramatic years. For a start, she had John Knox to contend with, railing against her popery, then the unhappy marriage to Lord Darnley, but the main drama centred round David Riccio, her Italian secretary.

One Saturday evening, March 9, 1566, Lord Darnley and some supporters burst into the Queen's private quarters in the Palace and attacked Riccio, accusing him of being the Queen's lover. He held on to the Queen's skirts, begging for help, though the Queen could do little as she was six months pregnant and a pistol was being pointed at her stomach. Riccio was dragged out, still screaming, and stabbed more than fifty times.

Just a year after Riccio's murder, Darnley himself was removed, his house blown up and he himself found strangled in his night-shirt. Mary then married the probable murderer, the Earl of Bothwell. The story is pure Hollywood, not Holyrood, and little wonder it has been used so many times in so many forms, from opera to films. It was almost as if Mary had been deliberately picking different sorts of men each time, helping future casting departments: first, the tragic young boy, the French Dauphin; next, the aristocratic but dissolute Lord Darnley; then the artistic and effeminate-looking Italian Riccio; then finally the Heathcliffian Bothwell. That's how I see them, anyway. Then in the last reel she ends up a prisoner, and has her head chopped off.

I was therefore greatly looking forward to my guided tour of the set, I

Right: *Lady Stair's House in one of the ancient courtyards which radiate from the Royal Mile.*

Left: *Curving shop fronts of the Grassmarket.* Below: *Roofs and churches in the Royal Mile, looking towards the Firth of Forth from the Castle.*

mean the Palace, which turned out a bit of a disappointment as the guide was a mumbler and the Palace inside had an uninhabited, anonymous feeling. The State rooms are magnificent enough, but somehow ordinarily magnificent, like State apartments anywhere, from Hampton Court to Windsor Castle. The guide did apologise for some tatty carpeting, which he said would *not* of course be on show when the Queen was in residence.

As we followed him silently through the State rooms, he instructed us to keep behind the rope, with him on the inside, making the same joke as we entered each room. "You take the High Road and I'll take the Low Road." At one stage he talked about the Queen being 'coronated', a new verb which I rather liked.

The private quarters used by Mary Queen of Scots were older and more interesting and they did have a strange atmosphere. Queen Victoria, when she stayed in the Palace, always found they made her sad as she thought of 'poor Queen Mary, supping here when poor Riccio was murdered'. In a corner there was a rather battered telephone, left lying around for no apparent reason. A wee girl beside me asked her mother if it was used by Mary Queen of Scots. "No, hen, Mary didna' hae nae 'phone."

It was when I was going back up the Royal Mile that I realised it is on a hill, with the slope going down from the Castle to the Palace, following the ridge. On the way, I went into several museums on the other side this time, such as Huntly House, which had some interesting local Edinburgh relics, but the one I enjoyed most was the Museum of Childhood in the High Street, a treasure house of toys and games, clothes and objects used by or associated with children over the last century.

I noticed that one of the tartan gift shops, Scotscraft of Galashiels, had in its window a sign saying 'Retiral Sale', providing me with another new word. I went in and asked the lady at the counter why she hadn't used the word Retirement, or had Retiral got a special local meaning? "Who are you?" she said, suspiciously. I said I was just a tourist, walking around. I wasn't snooping for the V.A.T. man or even Webster's Dictionary. "Where are you from?" She stared at me again, still as suspicious, so I made an excuse and withdrew.

Further along, I went into another gift shop called the Tappit Hen and found the lady this time very friendly and loquacious. She said she was called Mairi Stewart and she'd run the shop for twelve years.

"When I began there were only two firms in Scotland producing Scottish gifts – Caithness glass and Govancraft pottery. Now there are hundreds. The quality is super, really tremendous, especially the jewellery. Look at this silver work, and this enamel by Norman Grant, and what about this pewter. It's super stuff and very reasonable."

The Americans are apparently very keen on the pewter, the English on bits of small silver, and the Japanese on anything with a Union Jack on, but perhaps the best-selling line at present, so she said, were the hand-knitted jumpers done in modern designs which sold from around £27. They were *really* super.

"The craze for thimbles is still continuing. I can't get enough of them, in wood, silver, anything, either antique or modern. *Everybody* is now collecting thimbles."

Her one guiding principle, when ordering new goods, is very simple – they must be portable. People can't park in the Royal Mile, so they have a long way

St. Giles' Cathedral.

to walk. Foreigners anyway now come by plane and they can't carry much.

I then reached St Giles' Cathedral, the major building at the heart of the Royal Mile, which I had carefully tried to avoid staring at when walking down the other side, which is hard to do, considering its size and its distinctive spire, shaped like a crown. I had a look up for its famous golden weathercock but it had recently been brought inside, after renovation. Just a year previously, a policeman had noticed that the weathercock, which has been on the roof of the Cathedral for four centuries, was swinging rather dangerously. The High Street was closed while it was inspected, then brought down and repaired.

There should not of course be a cathedral in Scotland today, as the Church of Scotland has no bishops and no hierarchy. St Giles' proper name is the High Kirk of Edinburgh, but it is still commonly known as a cathedral, which is what Charles I elevated it to, when he introduced bishops, but they departed in 1688 when pure Presbyterianism was re-established.

There has been a church on the site since 854. The oldest parts date back to 1120 and for over 800 years it has been the spiritual centre of Edinburgh, despite suffering fire and pillage at the hands of English invaders and being the scene of many bitter religious and political disputes amongst the Scots themselves.

It has been added to and altered over the years, the most recent addition being the Chapel of the Order of the Thistle which was designed by Sir Robert Lorimer and inaugurated in 1911. The Knighthood of the Thistle is Scotland's chief order of chivalry. The chapel is in the south-east corner of St Giles' and is a beautiful and surprisingly ornate memorial. Scottish churches, even St Giles', tend towards the dour rather than the decorative, functional rather than fantastic. This little chapel is said to be the most lavish church building to be erected in Scotland since the Middle Ages.

Outside St Giles', I sat on a wooden bench in the evening sun, admiring all the public buildings which were about to close for the evening, as it was now just after five o'clock. Near the front door of the Cathedral is a heart-shaped design, set in the cobble-stones, which marks the site of an old building, the Old Tolbooth, which was once a prison. It was demolished in 1817 but lives on in literature as Sir Walter Scott used it as the setting for the opening of his novel *The Heart of Midlothian*.

Everything soon appeared empty and deserted. The law-abiding shop-keepers and officials had all gone home to their families, as no doubt John Knox would have approved. It was time for respectable tourists to find their transport and get on their way. If I hadn't known that all along the Royal Mile, down the closes, and inside the old tenements, real life was going on, I might have come away thinking that the Old Town was a museum. Thanks to the efforts of preservationists in the last thirty years, saving so many of the old buildings, it is now a living entity. It is a street which needs a month to explore properly, not a day, a street which once again has become the most interesting street in Britain.

The Heart of Midlothian.

8 The Queen Mother's Scottish Castles

AFTER leaving the streets of Edinburgh I set off north for the wilds of rural Scotland to look for the Scottish homes of the Queen Mother, Britain's most popular person.

Is that an exaggeration, a tease, a ridiculous sweeping statement, a piece of Royal genuflection? Well, in my lifetime, I cannot think of anyone that the British public has loved *more* than the Queen Mother. Winston Churchill, now he was pretty popular, but at times in some quarters he was pretty unpopular. The present Queen is of course exceedingly well-liked, but she is still in mid-reign, so we all fervently hope, while her mother is as old as the century. We have known her for a very long time. There is a warmth of national affection for her which will be hard ever again to equal.

Lady Longford, in her 1981 biography of the Queen Mother, went so far as to say that she is 'without doubt the most popular Queen Consort in our history'. *In our history*. That does seem a slight exaggeration. Our Kings have been marrying Queens for many centuries now, so a lot of names come into the reckoning. As one goes through that long, German-dominated list – remember Queen Mary, Queen Alexandra, Queen Caroline, Queen Charlotte, and all the way back to the Normans – an obvious fact does stand out: the Queen Mother was the first truly *British* Queen Consort for centuries.

The Scots have always been particularly proud of Elizabeth Angela Marguerite Bowes-Lyon, as she was born on August 4, 1900. Her Scottish blood is unquestionably of the highest. It therefore came as a bit of a disappointment to me in 1980, reading all the purple prose which greeted her eightieth birthday, to discover that she was born in England, either at the family's English home in Hertfordshire, or in London itself (there is some confusion about her precise birthplace, but this is not the time to go into all that). I believe she herself has tried to keep her English birth quiet all these years. We all know, really, that her *true* home is Glamis Castle, the ancient seat of her family, the Earls of Strathmore.

I expected Glamis to be in wild Highland countryside. No reason. Being Scottish-born, I should have known better. It's probably Shakespeare's fault, setting *Macbeth* there, making everyone think of wild witches, frightening forests, dark deeds. It is situated not far from Forfar, about twelve miles north of Dundee, in lush, farming country, flat and featureless, almost Home Counties. I could have been anywhere in Britain, despite passing such romantic-sounding names on the signposts as Blairgowrie and Kirriemuir, names reminiscent of Highland gatherings or rugby club sing-songs.

As our stately homes go, Blenheim is far more impressive. Chatsworth is grander. But Glamis Castle has *warmth*. Is that where the Queen Mum gets it from? It's built of local pink-red stone and is in what is called the Scottish

Glamis Castle, family home of the Queen Mother.

Baronial style, having overtones of a French château, with little round turrets at almost every corner. It seemed from the outside a manageable size, not obscenely huge like Blenheim, that is if you are fortunate enough to have a staff of forty which is what it takes today to look after Glamis Castle and its 16,000-acre estate.

It also looked in tip-top condition, the paint mint-fresh on every surface, not a cobweb in sight, no signs of wear and tear. In an average year, over 80,000 come to see the Castle, the gardens, nature trail, tearoom, giftshop and other delights. It must cost them a fortune in upkeep. The Bowes-Lyon family, fortunately, is rather affluent.

The 17th Earl of Strathmore and Kinghorne, who lives there today with his family, is a descendant of Sir John Lyon who lived in Glamis in 1372. He married Princess Joanna, daughter of the Scottish King, Robert II, and since then the Castle has been visited and inhabited by many members of the Scottish and British Royal Families.

Mary Queen of Scots stayed at Glamis and her visit is well documented. The English Ambassador reported to Queen Elizabeth that 'despite Fowle and Colde weather, I never saw her merrier, never dismayed'. Cromwell quartered his troops at Glamis. In 1715, during the first Rising, the 4th Earl of Strathmore entertained James, the Old Pretender. Beds were made up for eighty-eight gentlemen during his visit.

The Queen Mother's father, the 14th Earl of Strathmore, inherited £250,000 in 1904 – about the equivalent of ten million pounds today – as well as the title. He married Cecilia Cavendish-Bentinck, great-granddaughter of the Duke of Portland who was twice Prime Minister. So, whatever way you look at the Queen Mother's lineage, there was ample aristocratic blood, and even some royal, flowing through her veins when, as Lady Elizabeth Bowes-Lyon, she came to marry George V's second son on April 26, 1923. There was a suggestion at the time that she was a 'commoner', from some impoverished Scottish family, which was certainly not true, in any sense.

We set off on a tour of the Castle, under the care of a young guide who was most attentive. I had my wife and two of my children with me on this occasion. One of the first things we were shown was an old seventeenth-century chest in the Crypt, brass-bound and studded, which contained the dressing-up clothes the little Princesses had used. They were all real, genuine Tudor tunics, not the sort hired from a costumier. We were allowed to touch them, and I just managed to stop my seven-year-old daughter Flora from putting them on.

Princess Margaret was born at Glamis Castle on August 21, 1930, and both she and her big sister, Princess Elizabeth, played games in the castle during their holidays with their Scottish grandparents, using that dressing-up box.

From the Crypt, we climbed the 143 stairs to the Tower. Each step is carved from a separate stone and is big enough to take five Scotsmen, walking abreast. "Do you hear the heart beat?" the guide asked Flora. "It's the ghost of Glamis . . ."

Sure enough, down the winding stairs came the noise of a deep ghostly heart, beating away. Flora was suitably scared, as no doubt all children over the ages have been, when first mounting these massive circular stone stairs. The Queen Mother, who often took people on tours of the Castle when she was a girl, used to play the same trick on her little friends, as did the present Queen.

Entrance to Glamis Castle.

At the top, we came to a huge clock ticking away. The guide said it was his job to wind it twice a week, giving thirty-five winds each time. The weights weigh ten stone.

We climbed even higher, above the clock, and came out on to the roof itself, which is not open to the public. Even here, every inch of the black railings, with their thistle and rose motifs, was in pristine condition. Major additions were made to the Castle in 1606, when the French-château overtones were added to the original L-shaped medieval Scottish keep. The guide pointed out, over the roofs, the window of the nursery where Princess Margaret was born, now part of the present Earl's private quarters, which means it can't be seen. We moved below to Royal Rooms which can be seen, such as King Malcolm's room, where he is supposed to have died, and the Queen Mother's suite, where she often used to stay.

On her marriage, she and the Duke of York were given this apartment in the Castle by her mother, Lady Strathmore. The rooms retain the same decor and furnishings as they had in the 1930s. The Queen Mother's sitting room is particularly homely, comfy and chintzy, compared with the many grand and spectacular drawing rooms elsewhere in the Castle. Our guide said if he could take any room home to his house, he'd take this.

In the Queen Mother's bedroom, they now have a four-poster bed which her mother, Lady Strathmore, used. On the tapestry, round the top, she embroidered the initials of all her children. The Queen Mother was the last of nine children – she had five elder brothers and three sisters, one of whom died in childhood.

The King's Room, next door, also has a four-poster, this time belonging to Patrick, a seventeenth-century Earl of Strathmore. In neither of these rooms are you allowed to inspect the W.C., but beside the King's bed Flora spotted a china potty. The guide said everyone always spots that. It's the single most popular exhibit with visiting Americans.

Duncan's Hall is the oldest and most creepy part of the Castle. It's easy to imagine Macbeth choosing to murder Duncan here, which is what everybody always says. A pity it's not true. The Queen, when she took Prince Charles round for the first time, describing her Bowes-Lyon family connections to him, naturally told him that this was where Duncan was murdered by Macbeth. Prince Charles, being an educated young man, is said to have told his mother she was talking nonsense.

Macbeth did kill Duncan, though not in his bed as Shakespeare says, and not in Glamis Castle. It happened in the north of Scotland, near Elgin, in 1040, around 200 years *before* the present castle was built. Macbeth was in fact a good and successful King, and he reigned happily for seventeen years after getting rid of Duncan, till he in turn was killed by Duncan's son Malcolm.

However, Macbeth was indeed Thane (or Lord) of Glamis and he did live at Glamis, so the guide told us, near the site of the present castle. And there are enough true stories about blood pouring all over Glamis's stone floors, during various other Scottish battles, to give Shakespeare, and our Royal family, some justification for any poetic license.

*   *   *

When the Duke of York unexpectedly succeeded his brother as King in December 1936, Balmoral became his and his wife's main Scottish home. He loved Balmoral just as much as his father had done and from then until his tragic death in 1952 he and his family spent eight weeks there every autumn, just as the present Queen still does.

"The Aberdeenshire people," so he wrote to his mother, Queen Mary, on his first visit to Balmoral as King in 1937, "turned out well for our drive from Aberdeen, and we saw many friends at their own gates. When we got to the gate here, about 100 of the employees pulled the Balmoral Victoria with us four in it ... all the way to the Castle, in silence, except for pipers who marched ahead playing ... It was their own idea."

Balmoral Castle is about the same size as Glamis, at least they look equally big from the outside. It is built of local grey granite which on a rainy day can make it seem rather forbidding, but the situation is remarkable, far more dramatic than Glamis's, with soaring, snow-capped mountains on the skyline, then wild heather foothills, tall pines lower down and, beside the Castle itself, the beautiful valley of the River Dee.

The public is allowed in the grounds from May to July, before the Royal Family arrive for their long autumn holiday. You can't see inside the Castle, though when I was there plans were being finalised for the Ballroom to be opened as a museum of Victoriana.

The estate is much bigger than Glamis, with some 42,000 acres, but they manage today with the same number of employees, around forty, a lot fewer than the hundred or so who were there to greet the Queen Mother on her first arrival as Queen in 1937.

Balmoral is a modern castle, compared with Glamis, but it has been part

Balmoral Castle, in a setting which Hollywood could never better.

of British folklore for the last 130 years, ever since Prince Albert bought the estate and put it, and the Highlands, on the tourist map.

Albert and the young Victoria first spent a holiday on Deeside in 1848, leasing a holiday home at Balmoral before buying 11,000 acres for £31,000 in 1852. "I seldom walk less than four hours a day," wrote the Queen, "and when I come in I feel as if I want to go out again."

Charles Greville, on a visit, found their holiday home pretty, but very small. "They live there without any state whatever ... not merely like private gentle-folks, but like very small gentlefolks, small house, small rooms, small establish-ments ... They live with the greatest simplicity and ease. She is running in and out of the house all day long and often goes about alone, walks in the cottages, sits down and chats with the old women."

This was in the original little castle on the estate. As Queen Victoria's family quickly grew, and they spent longer and longer there every autumn, there was soon little room to put up all her Ministers who were forced, often against their will, to make the 500-mile trek up to Deeside to report to her. In 1853, Victoria and Albert began to build a brand-new castle, just a hundred yards away from the old one, which they continued to use till the new one was finished in 1857. (You can see the foundation stone near the entrance porch.)

Just three days after they had moved in, they received the news that Sebastopol had at last fallen, which meant wild celebrations, healths being drunk in whisky, and pipes and gunfire all night. A few days later, there were more celebrations when Prince Frederick of Prussia, who was staying with them, asked for the hand of the Princess Royal, their eldest daughter.

The architect of the new castle was William Smith, City Architect of Aberdeen, under the guidance, of course, of dear Albert. As the Queen so often noted in her diary, the Prince seemed to be occupied with the architect all morning. Albert then went on to re-design the whole estate, creating new plantations, new farms and model dairies. They rushed up with great excite-ment every autumn, just to see if all last year's plans had been completed.

Albert died of typhoid fever in 1861, after only four years together in their dream castle. The following season, the Queen finished the building work in hand which Albert had planned, but for the next thirty-nine years of her reign she made few alterations, although some cottages were occasionally built for her staff, such as one called 'Baile na Coille' for her faithful, and famous, Highland servant, John Brown. Today it is lived in by the resident factor.

As the years went by, Victoria spent longer and longer each autumn at Balmoral, and was always loath to leave. "The departure from Scotland, that loved and blessed land," so she wrote in 1869, "was very painful and the *sehnsucht* [longing] for it and the proportionate disgust on returning to this gloomiest of places [Windsor, where Albert died] very great. It is not all the pure air, the quiet and the beautiful scenery which renders it so delightful – it is the atmosphere of loving affection and hearty attachments of the people around Balmoral which *warms* the heart and does one good."

Later Monarchs loved it almost as passionately, and their personal monuments and mementoes are everywhere in the gardens, from the entrance gates erected by George V, a stone compass put up by George VI, a garden devised by Queen Mary, to a drinking fountain in memory of Noble, one of Victoria's dogs. "For more than 15 years the favourite Collie and dear and faithful companion of Queen Victoria." He died in 1887, aged sixteen and a half.

Today, minor alterations and additions are still being made by the present Royal Family, and one of the first things I saw in the gardens was a new Japanese-style water garden. There were sunken baskets at the bottom, so I was told, but they hadn't yet flowered. The lake had been personally excavated by the Duke of Edinburgh, borrowing a bulldozer from the army. "You should see the mess they had to clear up afterwards," someone told me later in Ballater. "It became the Duke's latest toy." The end result, after all the fun, looked splendid all the same.

When the Queen visits Balmoral every autumn, the Factor and the main Keepers, about ten in all, are there to meet her on her arrival at the main gates, just as they met her father and mother. She shakes hands with them, and has a personal word, and during her stay meets most of the people who work on the estate, as well as looking up those who have retired.

Everybody tells you that the Queen is never in. Like Victoria, she is out of doors all day long, regardless of the weather, though the weather on Deeside is often excellent. This might come as a surprise to those English people who expect the Highlands to be rainy. On my brief visit, in April, I came back with a sun tan. On her first stay at Balmoral in 1848, Queen Victoria had been highly delighted with the weather.

"The soil is the dryest and best known almost anywhere," so she wrote to her uncle, the King of the Belgians, on September 13, 1848, "and all the hills are as sound and hard as the road. The climate is also dry and in general not very cold. There is a deer forest and on the opposite hill (which does not belong to us), grouse. Albert has, however, no luck this year. The children are very well and enjoying themselves much. The boys always wear their Highland dress."

This dry climate causes problems today for Balmoral's six gardeners. Like most gardeners, they like rain once a week, but they don't always get it. As in Victorian times, their whole annual effort is geared to having their best and most magnificent shows in the autumn, ready for the Royal family's arrival. I talked to one gardener who was moaning about the dry Easter we'd

just had, hoping for a few showers. In 1976, an annus mirabilis as far as British weather goes, so hot and dry had been the summer that almost everything had flowered and gone *before* the Queen arrived.

I inspected the greenhouses, which even in April looked full of colour and greenery, but I was told that was nothing. You should see it in the autumn. I noticed that they were using little polystyrene containers for their potting plants. These are rescued from the waste bins in the tea garden, then washed out and used by the gardening staff. Very economical.

There's a nine-hole golf course on the estate, which estate workers can use when the Queen is not there, and a cricket pitch. Right in front of the castle's main windows was a barbed wire enclosure, cutting off a bit of the field, which looked to me decidedly unattractive. Who would want to look out on that? I was told this was where they put the Balmoral estate's fold of Highland cattle, bought by the Queen in 1955. While at Balmoral she likes to wake up every morning and look out of her window and see animals.

The land across the River Dee still doesn't belong to them, but to the Laird of Invercauld. By comparison, the Queen is a minor landowner. The Invercauld estate is about 180,000 acres, over four times the size of Balmoral. However, the Queen can walk up to twenty miles on her private land, unseen by the crowds, unobserved by the press, and like her predecessors she greatly values this privacy. (Only Edward VII was not absolutely enraptured by Balmoral, having other and more social pursuits in the south, but even he usually managed four weeks at Balmoral.)

The Queen, as Monarch, now owns Balmoral Castle, so the Queen Mother uses a smaller house on the Balmoral estate, Birkhall, which is not open to the public. It's only a five-minute drive away, beside a rather precarious-looking chain bridge over the river. The Queen Mother is also never in when she is at Balmoral, out in all weathers, having picnics, walking, fishing.

The Queen Mother takes great interest in the Birkhall gardens. She doesn't actually do any digging, but she supervises and suggests. Like Queen Victoria in the old days, she rushes up each September (and often May as well), to see if her new ideas have taken root. One gardener told me that she had suggested the previous year some African shrubs might be tried, as a friend had given her a book about gardens in Kenya, but no local gardeners thought *they* had the slightest chance, despite Deeside's famous climate.

*   *   *

The Queen Mother's own personal residence in Scotland today is the Castle of Mey. Not many people venture as far as Mey, even devoted writers of those endless books about the Royal Family. I wasn't sure myself where it was, till I looked it up on the map. Deeside, and its temperate climate, is by comparison in the Deep South. It took me another six hours of hard driving to get up from Deeside to Mey which is right on the northern tip of the Scottish mainland, just beside John o'Groats. People often think Scotland finishes at Inverness, but Inverness was only the first stop on our long journey north.

The final fifty miles of the road up the east coast, from Dornoch up to Wick, were quite spectacular, almost Cornish, with deep inlets and neat painted cottages, not at all the wild and desolated coast line which I had imagined.

As we got nearer to John o'Groats, however, the fields gave way to wilder moorland and there was a feeling of being on a massive plateau, stuck somewhere on the edge of the world. When we finally got on to the north coast, the furthermost part of Britain, it looked so ominous ahead, as if it *was* the end of the world. We booked into a hotel near the Castle of Mey at Dunnet, then had an evening walk of two hours on the Dunnet sands, in beautiful isolation, bathed by a glorious sunset.

Next morning, we went round to take a look at the Castle of Mey, by which time a wind had got up. It was then easy to imagine what it must be like in winter. The entrance drive is lined with sycamore trees, all of which have been driven to distraction by the wind, bent and gnarled, toppling over, clinging to one another for protection and self-preservation, creating a secret entrance tunnel to the Castle.

This part of Caithness is notorious for its wind. If anything grows above wall height, the wind has it. In the local fields there are slabs of Caithness stones arranged in rows, demarkation lines instead of hedges. Getting anything to grow, even hedges, is exceedingly hard. You plant cabbages, apparently, and the wind sends them straight into the air. What made the Queen Mother buy a castle in such a windswept, desperate area?

She was staying in Caithness with a friend, Lady Vyner, in 1953, not long after the King had died, and she was told how sad it was that the Castle of Mey was empty and might be pulled down. The Queen Mother had never visited the Castle before, or had any connection with it, but she took one look and decided to buy it.

You can't see it from the road, which is a boring road anyway, with some council houses along it, except for one brief glimpse, and even that tells you nothing about it. You have to go down the drive (which the public is not allowed to do) and through the defeated trees to realise that, perched beside the sea is a beautiful sandstone castle, smaller than Glamis and Balmoral, a gem on a windswept coast.

It dates back to the eighteenth century, when it was owned by the Earl of Caithness. The Queen Mother has spent a fortune renovating it, and it shows. Even so, the wind still howls and there is little protection. The rear garden of the castle leads straight down to a rocky shore. The view across, on a good day, is of the Island of Hoy in the Orkneys, some nine miles away.

The Castle of Mey is not on the tourist routes, like Balmoral and Glamis, and they get few visitors coming to look at it, which means the locals are friendly, whenever any strangers do turn up, directing them to the Castle gates. A party of French youths had recently been found on the Queen Mother's front lawn, dancing about and filming each other. They were chased by a member of the staff, and told it was private property. Later it was discovered they'd left behind a souvenir of their visit. Beside the front gate they'd put up a notice 'Bed and Breakfast, £1.50'.

Another time, a strange American gentleman managed to get into the Castle itself, and engaged one of the staff in deep conversation. She'd been most alarmed, not just by his conversation but by a large black bag which he had been carrying. Some time later, he was picked up by the local police. They carefully opened the black bag – only to discover a paint brush, which he was going to use to paint the Castle, and a packet of cabbage seeds for the garden. He maintained he'd met the Queen Mother in Canada and she had told him he needed work done on her Castle.

The River Dee.

When the Queen Mother is in residence of course, there is strict security throughout the grounds and the surrounding areas, though she hates being followed and protected.

The entrance hall is large and in two sections, with a pair of curved steps going up and round to the higher level. The front door is enormous and very heavy, so much so that it is impossible to open when the winds are at their highest. Inside the Castle there are many personal objects, given to her by friends and relations, such as Lord Charteris (the Queen's former private secretary) and Prince Philip, a couple of whose paintings are on the wall. In the porch are various bits of art which the Queen Mother has bought at Caithness sales, including tapestry and two cushions made by an eighty-five-year-old local lady. On a table she has a collection of shells which she has gathered from the local beaches. John o'Groats beach, particularly, is noted for its shells and fossils, and I took my family there afterwards to collect some.

The Castle of Mey is the Queen Mother's own private home, the first she has personally ever possessed, unlike Glamis which was her family home and unlike Balmoral, a Royal home. She worked with great energy and enthusiasm on the re-building of this ruined little Castle in the early years of her bereavement, using it as a means of recovery, easing her return to full activity, at the same time providing herself for the rest of her life with a place for privacy and peace. She well deserves it.

9 The Rainhill Railway Trials

BRITAIN gave railways to the world, though the world these days is probably not quite aware of the fact. America and Russia both think their railways are older, and like every developed country they have their own railway history, with companies and engines and coast-to-coast exploits which their schoolchildren learn about, but Britain got in first. Hurrah.

In 1980, during the Liverpool–Manchester celebrations, a reproduction of 'Rocket' was built which went on various tours round Britain and Europe. While it was in Cannes, showing its paces, one of the organisers heard people in the street say to one another, 'C'est Américain'. He quickly stuck a Union Jack on the front. Just to let them know the truth.

Britain is still doing many wonderful things with new and experimental railway technology, such as the Advanced Passenger Train, but it seems to be the age of steam which has captured public imagination, as it has in most other countries. Once steam disappeared from British Railways in the 1960s, being replaced by diesel or electric, it immediately became an art form. Everything to do with the old steam railways, their companies or their rolling stock, their timetables, posters, name plates, even the old platform tickets, became collectors' items.

By getting in first with railways, naturally Britain has had something of a monopoly on the world's railway anniversaries. In 1975, for example, we celebrated with great excitement the 150th anniversary of the world's first public railway, the Stockton and Darlington; but even more exciting were the Rainhill celebrations in 1980 for another 150th anniversary, the Liverpool–Manchester, the world's first passenger railway. Behind both these historic railways was George Stephenson, the Father of Railways.

Cornishmen will scream and shout and say that Richard Trevithick began it all and they have a point. Trevithick did, in 1801, build a locomotive, probably the world's first machine that ran under its own steam, and in 1808 he had one performing in a little circle in London, near the site of Euston Station, but he got bored, failed to solve the many problems, such as a proper track, and went off to work on dopier ideas, like an under-water steam dredger. Trevithick was a genius, one of Britain's greatest inventors, but he could never stick to one thing.

Yorkshire folk will also protest and point to John Blenkinsop of Middleton near Leeds who in 1813 managed to run a locomotive in his colliery. It was a success for a while, but it was clumsy and very slow. The wheels had cogs which fitted into a rack on the track, to stop it falling over. It was thought in those early days that it was physically impossible to run a locomotive on smooth rails.

There were other developers, in different parts of the country, but all these

early railway experiments were either looked upon as novelties, just a passing fancy, or of purely colliery use, with no public potential. It was George Stephenson who *made* the railways.

Stephenson made railways in the sense that he made them work, struggled and persevered when others had given up, solving all the many problems, from the tracks to the boilers, from wheels to viaducts. When you consider that he started work at eight, without any schooling, and that he picked up his expertise by trial and error, was in turn despised by the professional engineers, humiliated by politicians, then that has to be called true genius.

Stephenson was born at Wylam-on-Tyne, not far from Newcastle, in 1781. Rail-ways had been a feature of the north-eastern collieries for decades – paths laid with rails along which horses pulled the coal trucks from the collieries to the loading bays on the Tyne or the Wear.

Stephenson's first job was keeping cows off Wylam's colliery horse-drawn track, then he progressed to helping on the stationary steam engines, of the sort invented by James Watt, which pumped water out of the pits. Eventually, he became the colliery's resident engineer. He was aware of experiments which had been tried to get a steam engine moving on its own, instead of having it stationary, because several of the most important early developments had taken place on Tyneside. William Hedley of Wylam, for example, who gave his name later to his 'Puffing Billy', produced his first loco in 1813.

After 1814, by which time Stephenson had moved to Killingworth Colliery, most people had begun to give up experiments on locomotives. Stephenson was virtually on his own for the next ten years, convinced that he would prove

everyone wrong and make railways work. He built sixteen locomotives and laid down several colliery lines during these ten years, improving and developing all the time, till in 1825 he astounded the experts by successfully building the world's first *public* railway, using locomotives, the Stockton and Darlington.

The world as a whole was not particularly astounded, as the S. and D. was very much a local event, built for the coal trade, but in 1830, when his Liverpool and Manchester line opened to national acclaim and excitement, passenger railways finally arrived and Britain, and the world, went railway daft.

The Victorians made Stephenson into a hero, thanks to his biographer Samuel Smiles, embodying in him all the known virtues, though he was a perverse and rough Geordie, always convinced he was right about everything.

In modern times, his fame has lessened somewhat, though every schoolboy knows about 'Rocket' (which was in fact built by his son Robert). Engineers as a rule aren't looked upon as glamorous figures today. Publishers and literary editors are more interested in Bloomsbury than in Brunel. Our heroes now come in rather different, rather flimsier forms.

Stephenson died in 1848, by which time he had seen his work change the face of the civilised world. Literally. Not many people can truthfully say that. Europe, Asia, the Americas, North Africa, Australia, were criss-crossed by railway lines. The world became linked mechanically. Until Stephenson, life had moved at the speed of the fastest horses. After him, time and distance, transport and speed, were never the same again.

Even during the construction of the Liverpool–Manchester, it had still not finally been decided whether to employ locomotives on the completed railway, or whether having fixed engines at the side of the track, to pull the coaches along, might be just as good. It was decided therefore to hold Railway Trials at Rainhill. Several primitive locomotives took part, but the trials were won in great style by 'Rocket', the Stephenson engine, which reached a speed of 30 m.p.h. and astounded the enormous crowd.

The recent celebrations at Rainhill were in praise of George, as much as of his engines, using the same stretch of line where George had triumphed in 1829. We went for the first day of the three-day 'Rocket 150' Cavalcade which British Rail had organised, at a cost of nearly one million pounds. We booked into the Adelphi Hotel in Liverpool, which is a railway relic in itself, next to Lime Street, with public rooms about the size of railway stations, then went to have a quick look at the engines at Bold Colliery, near St Helens, getting ready for the next day's big Cavalcade.

It was obviously going to be a big day for Brasso. Gallon tins of it were being rubbed lovingly into all the polishable parts of the old steam locomotives. Almost all the old engines, some thirty of which were going to be steaming away next day, are in private hands – owned by railway preservation societies, private people or museums. They're therefore tended and cosseted by amateurs, who always work themselves into a lather, when they're doing something they love. After every bout of polishing and fussing, they stood back to photograph the results, then they did a bit more polishing. Then they had themselves photographed, doing the polishing. All railway enthusiasts are camera mad.

Apart from 'Rocket', two other repro-locomotives from the 1829 trials had been built, 'Novelty' and 'Sans Pareil'. In the original trials, 'Novelty' had

Lion, the oldest working loco in the parade, built 1838.

Sans Pareil,
a reproduction of the 1829 entry.

a lot of mechanical problems and never completed the tests. The repro-'Novelty' was apparently suffering the same problems. History repeating itself. But 'Rocket' was in great form, steaming away for all the cameramen, doing its tricks. The Coal Board had arranged for a pretty girl, Miss Coal Board, to be photographed shovelling on coal, hoping that it would provide some good caption material for the newspapers, but to true steam fans the smell of steam is quite enough of a sensual pleasure.

We got to Rainhill very early next morning, but were forced to park almost a mile away. British Rail had built a long series of grandstands, held up by scaffolding, on either side of the one-mile stretch of line at Rainhill. This was obviously where most of their money had gone, arranging this special seating for 50,000 people for each of the three days. There seemed far more than 50,000 as we explored up and down the dusty paths, marvelling at how an empty stretch of countryside had been transformed overnight into a veritable town.

Over 400 stalls had been set up in an arena beside the track, turning it into a fairground and a fun palace, most of them selling some sort of railway souvenirs. Scores of railway societies had taken stalls, hoping to spread their message, and shift some books and literature. I bought a book about the Somerset and Dorset railway, as the pictures looked pretty, but decided against *The Power of the Duchess*, though the title sounded exciting. The Lewis Carroll Society had a stall selling plates and dishes with L. and M. motifs on, but I couldn't quite see the connection between *Alice in Wonderland* and Railways. I contemplated joining the Isle of Man Steam Railway Supporters, wondering

if they could possibly be as big as the Manchester United Supporters Club. I went into one tent which announced in large letters outside, 'God's Wonderful Railways'. As all enthusiasts know, this is how Great Western Railway fans often transcribe their initials. Inside, I was given a leaflet instucting me to Confess my Sins to Him, issued by the Evangelical Tract Society. Railways had just been their cover.

British Caledonian Airways had a stall, presumably trying to make railway enthusiasts take up flying, so did the Northern Stock Exchange, Sedgefield District Council, Everest Double Glazing, all a bit remote from railways, but they gave an interesting variety to the hundreds of railway stalls which naturally dominated Rainhill that day.

I got back into my grandstand seat by 1.30, for the official opening of the Cavalcade by the chairman of B.R., Sir Peter Parker, and the Minister of Transport, but nothing happened. Eventually, we heard the devastating news that 'Rocket' had been derailed three times and wouldn't now lead the Cavalcade, though it was hoped it would bring up the rear. After all that showing off! Now, 150 years later, 'Novelty' had got its own back. In coming off the line, 'Rocket' had also blocked 'Sans Pareil', so its place in the Cavalcade now looked in danger.

After further delays, making the start an hour late, the great Cavalcade at last got going with 'Lion' having the honour of leading the procession, its wood-pannelled boiler gleaming, its green tender glistening. It was a very apt leader. 'Lion' is thought to be the oldest original working steam loco in the country. She was built in 1838 for the Liverpool and Manchester and gave the line more than twenty years of stout service. She appeared in 1930 for the hundredth anniversary celebrations of the L. and M. and was used in the film *The Titfield Thunderbolt*, taking the star role, so she was used to having thousands of eyes feasting on her vital parts. Normally, she resides in the Merseyside County Museum. She got an affectionate cheer from the crowd, and whistled in return, though as a rule railway enthusiasts don't let their emotions show.

Next came a Midland Railway 1887 express passenger locomotive, a

Spinner design, one of the prettiest locomotives ever built. All early loco-motives look pretty, like hand-coloured toys, though it is perhaps the benefit of age and rose-coloured spectacles, plus the loving care and attention lavished on their paintwork, which makes them appear such works of art.

'Hardwicke', another very popular loco, also got its own special cheer. It is painted black, yet it was like looking at a colour picture, such was the richness and depth of reflections in its gleaming bodywork. 'Hardwicke' was used by the London and North-Western Railway on its late nineteenth-century races to the north. On a non-stop journey between Crewe and Carlisle, in the 1890s, it averaged 67 m.p.h.

The Cavalcade moved on before us, in roughly chronological order. As we got into the twentieth century, the engines grew bigger and stronger, their vital organs more covered up, their bodies more streamlined.

The 'Flying Scotsman', designed in the 1920s by Sir Nigel Gresley, one of railway's all-time great engineers, still looked massively powerful, after all these years. It was the first loco to run non-stop from King's Cross to Edin-burgh and the first to reach 100 m.p.h.

As 'Sir Nigel Gresley' himself approached, the loco not the man, the gentle-man next to me appeared to be almost shaking with excitement. This was Gresley's futuristic masterpiece, a streamlined A4 Pacific, a breed which today has its own fan club, the A4 Society. They were the stars of the 1930s and one of them, 'Mallard', beat the world record with a speed of 126 m.p.h. in 1938. 'Sir Nigel' was painted a brilliant blue, the classic L.N.E.R. colour, and as he approached he gave a deep, reverberating whistle. "That sound goes right to the back of my neck," said the man beside me.

Many of the engines were pulling carriages behind them, equally beautifully preserved, complete with drivers and passengers in period costume. Southern Railway's 'Golden Arrow' train contained three Pullman coaches, from the 1920s to the 1960s, in deep chocolate brown, emeralds and greens, posh enough to be Royal trains. By comparison, luxury has gone out of dining cars today.

After the steam locos, the diesels and electrics looked decidedly uncouth

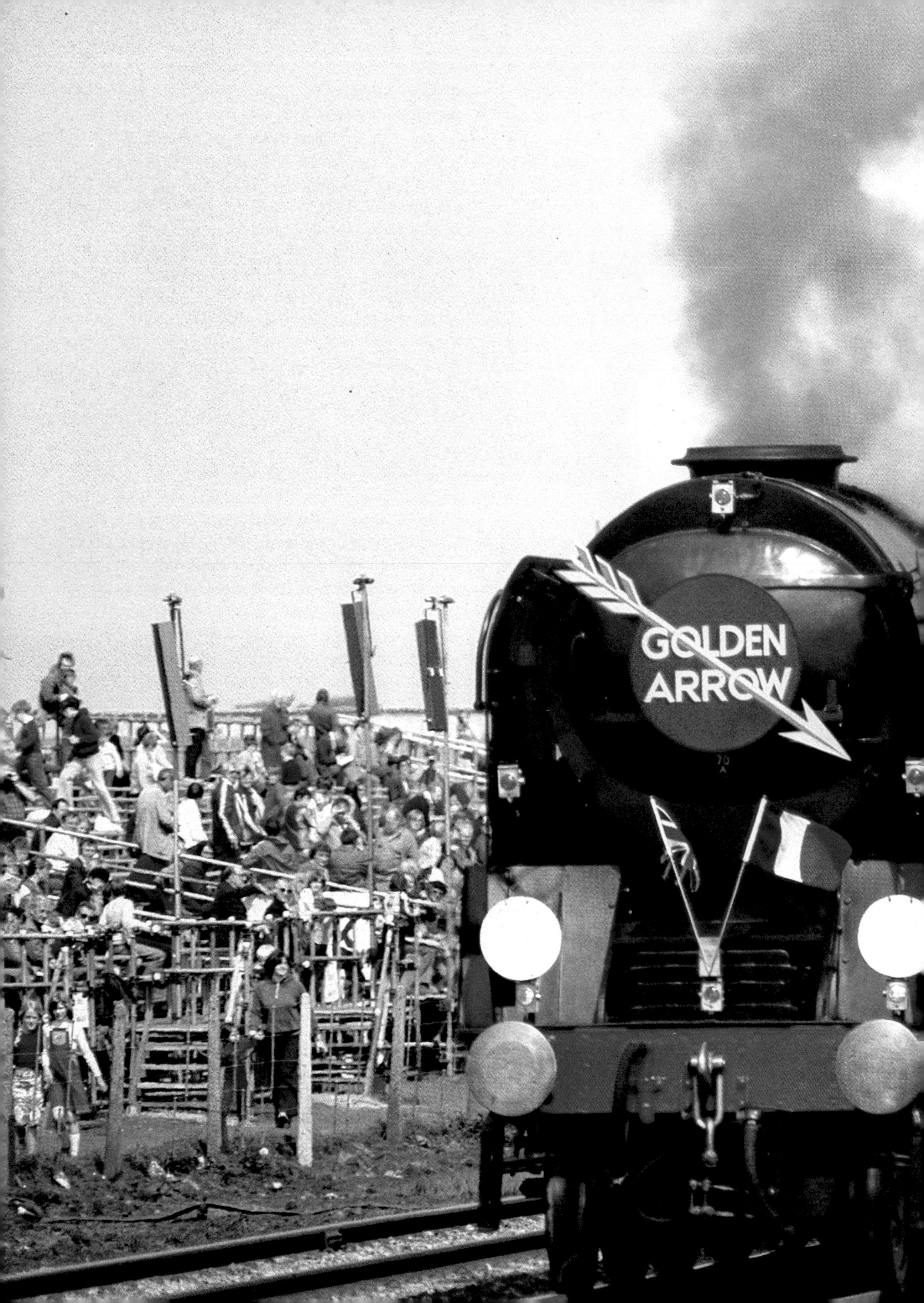
GOLDEN
ARROW

and utilitarian, like factory robots, though the Deltic diesel-electrics did give
a satisfyingly deep throbbing roar. My friend beside me, obviously not a
prejudiced enthusiast, willing to admire all periods of engines – which is not
always the case with railways fans – said the sound of the Deltics also made
him shiver. What can his home life be like?

British Rail, as they had organised the day, also included a selection of
their modern freightliner wagons in the Cavalcade, some of which looked
rather worn and dusty, but perhaps they'd just come from work, dirty after
a hard day. Many were for transporting fertilisers, according to signs on the
side, and some carried trade names, like Godfrey Davis. "What's all this
garbage?" said my friend.

He told me, confidentially, that he'd heard that at the engine sheds last
night some enthusiast had built a big wooden key and stuck it in the side
of one of B.R.'s Western Region Diesels, making it look like a toy. Then
taken photographs of it. What a wheeze!

The Advanced Passenger Train finally appeared, the scheduled top-of-the-
bill performer. It too gave a deep two-tone whistle and it did look very
impressive and streamlined, with dark glass on the windows, making it seem
mysterious and exclusive. Both the A.P.T. and the High Speed Train, which
preceded it, are magnificent beasts, yet I think I preferred the sleek lines of
Sir Nigel Gresley, who got in first with the notion of streamlining, fifty
years earlier. Today's speeds, of course, are a great deal better, as is the comfort, thanks to all the modern devices.

The High Speed Train, which is what we see in the B.R. adverts, and on
the Inter-City 125 services, has a diesel engine, front and rear. B.R. has
claimed its H.S.T. broke the world record for a scheduled, time-tabled
passenger train journey, with an average speed of 111.7 m.p.h. on the
Paddington–Chippenham run in 1979. At its fastest, the H.S.T. can do 143
m.p.h.

The A.P.T., on the other hand, is electric, with the power car in the middle
and a tilt mechanism which can take it round corners in safety and comfort

at great speed. It is said to be a world leader in engineering, and it is hoped it will bring future prestige, and sales, to British Rail. When it gets into full operation, it is expected to break all speed records on the scheduled services. It has already recorded speeds of 160 m.p.h.

We all waited in vain for the reproduction 'Rocket' to appear, despite its accidents, but alas that day it never made it, nor did 'Sans Pareil', but 'Novelty' did emerge, pulled by a diesel. However, on the subsequent two days of the Cavalcade, 50,000-strong crowds each day were able to see all three repro-locomotives turn out and show some of their paces.

On paper, all that happened during that 150 Cavalcade was that a load of railway stock, most of it very old, went up a stretch of line, and then back down again. No races. No speeds. No touching the exhibits. Just a slow, leisurely crawl, mannequins on a mechanical catwalk.

In reality, it was a piece of history, 150 years of man's amazing achievements in the world of transportation. You didn't have to be a railway fan and know about things like wheel ratios to appreciate the beauty of it all. It was a wondrous sight. I felt honoured to have been there.

British Rail get upset if one goes on too much about the steam stuff, about the romance of 'Rocket' and the glories of Gresley, and they have a point. Their modern trains are in their own way equally exciting, and they should be acknowledged. B.R. need the encouragement, just as much as George Stephenson did, as they have to fight national battles, in hard economic times, to get the money from the Government for their future developments. At the time of writing, they appear to be winning the argument to get more cash for electrification. It's not much use having startled the world with their Advanced Passenger Train if they can't afford to run it properly. That day at Rainhill, when I saw my first A.P.T. in the flesh, it was being *pushed* by a diesel freight loco. Such ignominy. They could do little else as that stretch of the track at Rainhill had not been electrified.

Old and New
Lion and the A.P.T.

So let us praise all great British engines. Past and present.

10 Blackpool

WHILE in Lancashire, why not visit Blackpool? You say, no thanks. You would rather stick to places like Sissinghurst.

It is easy to feel superior, ready to mock the working people of Britain at play, to tut-tut at all the vulgarity, to turn up a refined nose at the cheap amusements, to smile condescendingly at the fat ladies on the lurid postcards and the equally fat families in real life, baring their flesh and their feelings as they stuff themselves with nasty food. You shouldn't go, if that's how you feel, if that's how you're convinced it is, without ever having been. But, you would be foolish *never* to go.

Blackpool is a phenomenon. It is not just the greatest and most successful seaside town in Britain, but the biggest in the whole of Europe. Past and present, it is part of British social history. Nobody interested in human life should miss it.

During the last year, many tourist resorts in Britain have felt inflation eroding their customers and their profits. From London to the Lake District, hotels have reported up to a thirty percent drop in customers. Of all the holiday towns in Britain, only Blackpool has maintained its trade.

Blackpool realised many years ago the three elements which have always made it a winner. Indoor Amusements, that's the first reason. You can hide yourself away in one of Blackpool's enormous entertainment complexes for the whole week of your stay, with scores of pleasures to choose from, and need never come out into daylight. The weather, therefore, can be made irrelevant in Blackpool.

Above: *Figure of fun*. Right: *Rock around the clock*.

Secondly, Blackpool is cheap. Given the high price of everything in this day and age, the cost of Blackpool is amazingly low. There can be few better bargains in mass catering and mass entertainment anywhere in the world. The average price in the average guest house in 1981 was still only around £6. This included an evening meal, plus bed and breakfast. Even Benidorm can't compete with that. And, as for London, the price would be nearer £70.

Blackpool did feel a slight pinch in the Sixties when the cheap package tours to Spain first came in, giving the punters Blackpool *with* sun, but the enormous increase in fuel costs has put up the price of planes and Spanish workers are now on realistic salaries. A foreign holiday is not the bargain it once was for working families, not in the penny-pinching Eighties, and not with high unemployment. The thing about Blackpool is that you can trim your holiday very easily to suit your pocket.

Hard selling, that's the third reason. Blackpool is in show business, so every year there's a new exciting gimmick, some even more wonderful attractions, yet another astounding permutation of the old but well-tried themes. Blackpool works very hard to sell itself, from the Corporation down to local land-

ladies, advertising heavily, pumping out endless brochures, cut price holidays, special attractions, special trips. Perhaps the best idea they ever had, when they were wondering how to prolong the season, looking for a way to bring in the holidaymakers in the darker, wetter, days of September and October, was the Illuminations. You *must* have heard of Blackpool Illuminations.

On the face of it, the attraction seems bizarre. All they do is every autumn hang a load of lights along the promenade. It's the scale of it which impresses everyone – 375,000 different lamps, seventy-five miles of cable, all strung out in a series of gaudy tableaux. The production in 1981 cost £770,000, with a large proportion of this cost coming from the rates. It certainly pulls them in, and has done so since they were first switched on in 1912 during a visit by Princess Louise. "The Illuminations represent the most dynamic tourism project ever undertaken anywhere in the World," so the Council's brochure modestly claims. The facts certainly speak for themselves. During those late two months, September and October, when most of Britain's seaside resorts are closing for the winter, eight million come to Blackpool and spend an extra £50 million. In the season as a whole, £100 million gets spent in Blackpool.

It all began back in 1735 when the first recorded paying guests arrived – staying in an isolated cottage near a deserted beach where the North Pier now stands. Twenty years later there were still only four ale houses, and by 1780 just four hotels. In 1788 William Hutton, a Midlands shopkeeper and traveller, visited Blackpool but found only a few houses strung out along the

long beach. "Although about fifty houses grace the sea bank, it does not merit the name of a village because they are scattered to the extent of a mile. About six of these are appropriated for the reception of company. In some of the others are lodged the inferior classes whose sole motive for visiting this airy region is health." The name Blackpool came from a stream which flowed into the sea through some peat bogs and was always discoloured, forming a black pool.

The coming of the railways completely transformed Blackpool, as they transformed every other town and resort in Britain. From the moment the railway reached walking distance of the front, when Talbot Road station was opened in 1846, millions of people in Lancashire and Yorkshire were suddenly within striking distance for cheap day trips. (Even more important today in this carbound age, Blackpool has the M55 running right to the town – the only seaside resort in the whole of Britain with its own Motorway.)

The entertainment boom got into its stride on a mass scale from the 1860s onwards with promoters introducing new delights every season. Two of Blackpool's magnificent piers date from this period – the North Pier, which opened in 1863, followed by the Central Pier in 1868. Then came the South Pier in 1894. The original Opera House opened in 1889 and the Tower in 1894. By the 1890s, when Blackpool's resident population had risen to 35,000, they were accommodating 250,000 holidaymakers a year. Today, the town's population is around 150,000, and there are 200,000 bookable beds.

Every year, at least one of the major Political Parties holds its annual conference in Blackpool, but there are other, less newsworthy conferences going on there all the year round. The posh hotel is the Imperial which has 152 bedrooms. Delegates usually congregate in places like the Winter Gardens or the Opera House, each of which can seat around 3,000 people.

Although two theatres have closed in recent years, there are still eight theatres in Blackpool with live shows, the largest number outside London's West End, plus eleven cinemas, six ballrooms, nineteen parks, cabaret clubs, discos, bingo halls, a waxworks, a zoo, and of course their seven miles of promenade. Mass entertainment centres are still being built, the newest being Coral Island, with every sort of amusement under one roof, but the latest

Right: *Helter Skelter at the Pleasure Beach.* Left: *Stopping for pleasure outside a Blackpool shop.*

Blackpool streets – cowboys and cowgirls.

building craze is for bigger and better shopping centres. The new £10 m. Hounds Hill shopping centre opened in 1980 which includes a Marks and Spencer super store. People on holiday in Blackpool seem determined to get rid of their money any way they can.

I spent a day at Blackpool, a very hot Thursday at the end of July, the height of the summer season, with two of my children, and the first place where they wanted to get rid of their money was the Pleasure Beach.

The Pleasure Beach is not on the beach, but on the inland side of the promenade, near the South Pier, and is a forty-acre fun fair. The big new attraction that day was the Revolution which is supposed to have cost £1 million to instal and is claimed to be the very latest in roller coasters, a gleaming, all-steel train which gives 'brand new, bone chilling, heart startling, palm sweating thrill rides'. You get locked in with padded bars and then it loops the loop, going through 360-degree circles. Then it reverses, and goes backwards through the same loop.

The look of it was quite enough to make my bones sweat and palms chill, and luckily Flora and Jake were equally frightened. I took Flora instead on the ghost train, price 35 pence. "Do not stand up! This Ride is run by a Skeleton Staff!" It seemed to go on for hours and was scaring enough for me.

We simply gaped at the rest of the rides, and so saved a lot of money. There seemed to be every variation of going along on a track, far more than George Stephenson had ever thought of, with overhead or hanging trains, boat trains, tunnel trains, water-shoot rides, space vehicles, electric cars, ski-lift trains, racing cars, and steam trains. It was impossible to find one good vantage point, however high we climbed, from which we could see all the rides and shows, so we went into an underground restaurant, with boat rides going past us while we ate hamburgers.

I was struck by how clean it all was, despite the thousands of people milling round, most of them guzzling. I felt myself go into a sort of trance, hypnotised by all the flashing stalls and roundabouts, watching people already in a trance, listening to the manic laughter, the canned screams, the amplified music, the souped-up roar of the side-shows.

We left the Pleasure Beach and walked along the Promenade, looking for the Golden Mile, another of Blackpool's famous attractions, but not knowing what to look for. Flora was desperate to get there, convinced it must be an amusement arcade, one mile long, where she could spend *all* her money. We asked several people for the Golden Mile, but they didn't seem to know where it was, just vaguely pointed further along the Promenade. The sun was getting hotter and we were all exhausted, despite endless Cokes and ice creams.

The Golden Mile was never a mile long, just a stretch of the front near the Central Pier of about 400 yards leading from the old Central Station. It became famous in the 1920s and '30s for its concentration of fortune-tellers, rock-sellers, singing booths, side-shows and other attractions. One of the Golden Mile's most notorious exhibitions was the Rev. Harold Francis Davidson, the Rector of Stiffkey, who was de-frocked in 1932 for consorting with prostitutes and was then signed up by a Blackpool showman, Luke Gannon. Over 100,000 paid 2d a time to see him crouch in a barrel, alongside the 'lobster clawed man and the fattest woman on earth'. In 1937, he moved on to Skegness where he appeared in another side-show, this time with a lion. Alas he accidentally trod on the lion's tail one day and received a mauling from which he died. Moral, he should have stayed in Blackpool.

The Golden Mile stretch now looks much like the rest of the seven-mile promenade, with its amusement arcades, shops, stalls, but it also has various giant entertainment blocks, the biggest and newest of which is the Coral Island complex, on the site of the old station, which contains snack bars, restaurants, discos, dancing and seating for 1,500.

The Tower is also part of the Golden Mile, but Flora was a bit put off by the price when we came to the entrance. All she wanted to do was go up in the lift to the top of the Tower, but they charge you £1 just to get into

the Tower building, which we didn't want to do, and then another 60p to go up the Tower itself. It was the only time all day Blackpool hadn't seemed cheap. Well, it's the kiddies' holidays, isn't it, so I forked out and up we zoomed.

It's a copy of the Eiffel Tower and has probably been Blackpool's best-known symbol since it was opened on Whit Monday, 1894. It is 518 feet high and contains five million bricks. There was an interesting display at the bottom of the Tower, with lovely period photographs of former days, but I couldn't find anywhere to buy copies. A place like Brighton, with its middle-class clientele, would be pushing such tasteful nostalgia, but in Blackpool everything always has to be new and modern. Every season something different. I would also have liked to have bought a picture history of Blackpool, showing the different fashions in mass enjoyment over the last hundred years, but I couldn't see any for sale.

The view from the top of the Tower was terrific. Jake said he could see the Isle of Man and I strained hard and I could just see land, far out to sea, but it might have been North Wales, or possibly Blackpool's North Shore.

I was glad in the end that we had paid to see everything in the Tower building. The ballroom alone was worth the admission. Alas, Reg Dixon doesn't play the organ any more, but a smart lady in evening dress, who announced that she was called Cathie Haigh, was on stage entertaining the afternoon customers, most of whom were middle-aged ladies, dancing very elaborately with each other, plus some little girls dancing with their dads. Flora refused to dance with me. Instead, she watched mesmerised from the high gilt-encrusted balcony. Jake thought it was boring and went off to find the amusement arcade. The ballroom can accommodate 2,500 dancers while 4,000 can watch from the two tiers of balconies. It's a beautiful period piece, straight from the 1930s.

We found Jake downstairs watching and listening to a life-size talking, moving model of Ken Dodd. "Doddy's Here!" announced the notice. "He talks! He sings! Ken Dodd is at the Tower!" Then in lower letters beneath it added, "But not in person." It was a most elaborate model which appeared to work with the help of some back-projected film camera.

Then at last we were out again in the fresh air to explore the nearest pier, the North Pier, Blackpool's oldest. We'd passed the other two piers, walking earlier along the promenade, but Jake and Flora wouldn't go on them as they had been determined to find the Golden Mile and spend their money. I'd also wanted to examine several ironwork shelters along the promenade, decorated like pagodas, but the children wouldn't explore them either.

The North Pier was designed for 'quality visitors', so they said back in 1863. It's now a listed building. When you think that the piers in most English seaside resorts are either closed, crumbling, or falling into the sea, it is reassuring to know that all three of Blackpool's Victorian piers are in excellent condition, still with live shows, amusements stalls, bars, shops and people promenading, sunbathing or just sitting and watching one another on the splendid wrought-iron benches.

Earlier in the morning we had had a quick look at the beach, which had been a great disappointment after having read in the guide books about the fabulous seven miles of wonderful golden sands. It was high tide and there was just some very muddy, brown water, full of debris, lapping against an even

higher pile of debris on a tiny strip of unattractive beach. Even so, a few white-skinned couples had been holding hands, pathetically running in and out amongst the beer cans and rubbish.

Now, later in the day, as we sat on the Pier on the ornate chairs, I looked down and could see that the tide had gone out. The beach was now beautifully clean and broad and, if not golden, at least a lighter shade of brown, with enough room for everyone to spread out and enjoy themselves, with donkeys and side-shows beginning to be set up.

I went into a bar at the end of the Pier and came face to face with a gang of young men in leather cowboy hats emblazoned with the initials J.R., all of them naked to the waist, each with about six pints of beer lined up in front of them. "If you're proud to be a Geordie, clap your hands." They sang, or shouted, this several times, rather aggressively, looking for someone to contradict them, but there were no takers. They weren't drunk, just rather merry, causing no harm, at least not so far, but I decided to take my drink outside in the sun, just in case.

There did seem a phenomenal amount of bare flesh that day in Blackpool, most of it very white and extremely flabby. Everyone must strip off the minute they leave their digs in the morning, ready for action, a hard day's enjoying themselves ahead, so they don't want to be encumbered with too many clothes. Most of the iron seats on the Pier were occupied by elderly couples, many hand in hand, content just to watch the passing show, to give their feet a rest and let their memories wander.

We took one of the electric trams back along the Promenade to the Pleasure Beach, where we'd begun. Blackpool had the first electric trams in Britain, and is now the last place in Britain to run them commercially. I could have gone up and down in them several times, as they brought back memories of my own childhood, but Flora and Jake wanted to be off, this time to buy popcorn and find some more amusement arcades.

In London, and in most big cities, amusement arcades tend to be squalid

Blackpool: Pleasure bent.

and sordid, full of depressing and depressed people. In Blackpool, they're cheerful and bright, with well-dressed holiday-makers, families and grandmas. I still hate them, and fought against them all day, but you could never call them sordid. It was the noise most of all that got me, my only real complaint against Blackpool, but then I have a phobia about noise. The majority of the population appear to *demand* noise when they're enjoying themselves.

Strangely enough, the people working in Blackpool, the stall-holders and the attendants, seemed so subdued, many of them uniformed, clean and polite, almost American in their quiet efficiency. There was no feeling of rapacious-

Landlady of the Year, Hazel Parr, ready to welcome happy holiday makers to Haldene.

ness, no sense of being conned, nobody shouting to entice you into some show, as in most fairgrounds throughout the world. They seemed to know themselves that they were giving value for money, so there was no need for spurious money-grabbing tricks. They just quietly get on with making people happy.

Around a quarter of Blackpool's adult population, some 12,500, are engaged in the tourist trade in some form, most of them in the hotel and guest house industry. There are 3,970 hotels and guest houses in the town, so it has to be called an industry. It proved fortunate during the war when Blackpool put up 37,500 evacuees, without anyone hardly noticing.

There's been an increase in recent years in self-service accommodation, perhaps because holidaymakers want to save money, or perhaps to avoid the traditional battle-axe landlady who won't allow visitors in the bedrooms, locks the front door at ten and refuses to give you a key. This image is all wrong of course, says the Blackpool Hotel and Guest House Association.

Even the smallest guest house today seems to have a bar, and there are usually photographs in their adverts to prove it, festooned with mementoes and knick-knacks. "Lovely cocktail bar where you may invite your friends. Sun lounge with Hammond Organ. Own keys to bedrooms and front door ON ARRIVAL. Free access to hotel at all times. Colour TV, Baby listening, free showers, early morning tea. Come as a guest – leave as a friend."

The names of these guest houses have hardly changed since the turn of the century. There are some new ones, like Casa Blanca, and jokey ones like Cosy Nook, but the most frequent single category of guest house nomenclature is that with Royal overtones. I counted dozens of them – Balmoral, Sandhurst, Sandringham, Windsor, Belvedere.

We went for coffee with Hazel Parr, a highly recommended landlady, an award winner in fact, having just been made Blackpool's Landlady of the Year.

Hazel Parr never cooks chips, which straightaway ruins the image of the traditional landlady. It's like having a Journalist of the Year who never puts his foot in the door or a Civil Servant of the Year who refuses tea. What is happening to all our stereotypes? Mrs Parr does, however, serve up taped music with every meal as she likes her guests to sing along with their food.

They didn't line up all the landladies on the promenade, arms folded, or even have them parading in saucy aprons. It's all very dignified in Blackpool these days, not to say intellectual. Mrs Parr received her Landlady of the Year trophy for having the highest marks in the Small Hotel and Guest House Keepers Course at Blackpool College of Technology. She shouldn't really allow herself to be called a landlady, but she doesn't mind. She's officially a Small Guest House Keeper.

She passed her exams first class. Oh, you know, portion control, bulk buying, the obvious sort of things landladies, sorry Small Guest House Keepers, have to know these days. In her final exam she had to cost and plan a buffet for 150 people, and then cook it for twenty-five. She included lots of fancy things like Tuna Fish Mould, Crunchy Garlic Chicken, Quiche Lorraine, which she normally would never serve in her own guest house. Her guests prefer blander fare, stuff they can recognise at a glance. "I stick to meat and two veg. They've got to be knowing what it is. I could never do curry or garlic. When you put down their plate, it's got to be obvious."

The absence of chips at Haldene, which is what her guest house in Gynn Avenue, Blackpool, is called, comes partly from her dislike of making chips

B. and B. in Blackpool: Or Small Hotel and Guest Houses, according to Blackpool's Small Hotel and Guest House Association. There are 3,970 such places in Blackpool offering a total of 200,000 beds.

in bulk. "I can't get them the way I like. They can get them everywhere else in Blackpool, so I feel I don't have to bother."

She's an attractive, cheerful, very talkative lady of forty, married with a seven-year-old son, and came into landladying almost by chance five years ago. For the previous twelve years she'd been a chauffeur at British Leyland.

Her husband Ron was in the Austin Morris division where redundancies were frequent and he fully expected to be paid off. As they felt the end was coming, they looked round for another livelihood and so sold their own house in the Midlands and bought a little guest house of ten bedrooms in Blackpool.

The moment they decided to change their life, a strange thing happened. Not only was her husband retained, he started to shoot up the B.L. hierarchy. He's now Regional Manager of Landrover and Rangerover for the North of England, one of the divisions of B.L. which *does* do very well. They're obviously winners. Not only does Hazel have her Landlady of the Year trophy displayed near the T.V. but her Trophy for being Lady Expert Driver in the North of England. She's also got ballroom dancing prizes.

She does all the cooking and cleaning single-handed for her twenty or so guests and then does all the washing-up afterwards by hand. She thinks she can do it better than any machine and refuses to be persuaded otherwise. The only thing she minds about doing the washing-up is that she misses all the after-meal chats with her guests. One secret of her success is obviously her passionate interest in every customer.

"I make them sit down and have a cup of tea the minute they arrive. You can see newcomers thinking, 'Will it be on the bill?' People can stay in bed all day as far as I'm concerned. I'll just clean round them." She doesn't chuck them out early on the last day either. She hates to see families trudging round Blackpool, carrying their cases, just because a landlady has forced them out at ten in the morning. "I try to run it like a home, the sort of place I'd like to come to. I've slept in every bed for at least one night, just to see if there's anything annoying, like pipes running."

Her prices are remarkably low, even for Blackpool. Bed, breakfast and evening meal that summer was only £6 a night – though it was due to go up by another £1 during the autumn for the Illuminations. This was not to cash in on the increased demand but because her heating bills are higher.

Thanks to the Illuminations, all Blackpool landladies have of course a very long season, compared with other resorts. In Mrs Parr's case, she has four mini-seasons, each one dominated and given a special flavour by the different sorts of customers. Between Easter and Whit, when the season begins, she gets the swimmers. She's just one minute away from Blackpool's Derby Baths which is usually the venue for the British National swimming championships. The new season therefore starts off rather noisily, as the swimmers are young and boisterous. It means she has to be up very early, for their first training sessions. She does all she can to help them, organising three sittings for break-  fast, which landladies normally never do. (In most places you're there when it's served, or you've had it.) She also has to be flexible as swimmers often leave suddenly, as they get beaten in their heats and go home a day or two earlier than they expected. Her notice-board was full of old postcards from all round the world, including the last Olympics in Moscow, from swimmers who still keep in touch.

The next wave of visitors is somewhat quieter. In June she gets the pensioners,

older people on a fixed income who come for the cost-cutting holidays, heavily advertised in all Blackpool's brochures. Her part of Blackpool, the North Shore, is traditionally more select, so the locals like to think. The noisy end, where the teenagers go, is towards the Central and South Piers, near the Pleasure Beach.

Come the school holidays, in July and August, the noise returns with the family parties. The final two months of the season, September and October, are dominated by weekend coach parties, works outings who come for the Illuminations, arriving on Friday and leaving Sunday.

For some reason which she doesn't quite understand, around fifty percent of her guests each year now come from Staffordshire. Once such a trend begins, it grows, as Staffordshire friends recommend other Staffordshire friends. Next come the Scots, who make up twenty percent of her guests, then around ten percent each from the South of England, the rest of the North of England, and Northern Ireland.

There was a honeymoon couple from Northern Ireland who had just arrived that day, to find the rest of the guests had put false teeth and balloons in their bed. "That's the sort of people we have. Everybody takes it in good part."

They all feel so at home, she says, that they're always pressing to help her with the washing-up. Most of them do make their own beds, despite her telling them not to. They say they feel strange, if they don't make their own beds.

She always rotates the same seven meals throughout the whole season, so if you stay two weeks, you get everything twice. On Saturday it's steak and kidney pie, roast on Sunday, lamb chops on Monday, roast pork on Tuesday, salad on Wednesday, chicken on Thursday and fish on Friday.

She always feels exhausted at the end of every season and is quite relieved the day she closes for the winter. "Then I miss them terribly, once we are closed, but they always send me Christmas cards giving me all their news, booking for next year and telling me which room they'd like this time."

One final little secret, she says, is her weekly raffle, though she was a bit worried about revealing details as other Blackpool landladies might decide to do the same. She puts a raffle ticket, for free, under every plate on Saturday night, and the winner gets a bottle of wine. "Sweet wine of course. You've got to have something that everyone will like."

There's no doubt that people like Blackpool. Those who still might be feeling superior, determined never to go, should really think again, but book up quickly. The *facts* prove how popular Blackpool is, and everyone in Blackpool, from Council officials to award-winning landladies, can quickly trot out a relevant statistic.

Perhaps the most impressive fact about Blackpool is that every year fifty percent of the people who have a holiday there have had *ten* previous holidays in Blackpool. Say no more.

On the road: another holiday over for two of Blackpool's six million annual visitors.

11 Eton

As THERE are those who are prejudiced against the pleasures of Blackpool, without ever having been there, so there are people prejudiced against the privileges of Eton, without knowing very much about it.

We all know *something* about Eton. It is very hard to avoid. The outside world is endlessly fascinated by it, and by the people who have gone there, and the slightest tit-bit makes news. It would be silly to call it the best school in the world, as the only true test of a school is whether you consider it best for your child. But it would be hard to argue against those who say it is the best-*known* school in the world. Visiting Eton, therefore, is not like visiting another school. Visiting Eton is like visiting an institution.

My first visit to Eton was as a guest. I got a letter from the school's Literary Society one day, asking me to give a talk, and of course I graciously accepted, always willing to help a school, of any sort.

I arrived early and wandered up and down Eton High Street, sniggering at the antique shops, wondering if they'd been erected by a film studio, cut out replicas of olde worlde England. I peered through the windows of several bespoke tailors, their fronts apparently unaltered since the nineteenth century, full of dusty shelves and Dickensian assistants waiting for the young gentlemen.

The school buildings dominate one end of the High Street and are magnificent, more like Oxbridge than Oxford, dreaming spires and mysterious quadrangles, cloistered courtyards, historic towers and a chapel the size of a cathedral.

I couldn't see the famous playing fields, but they were probably behind, down by the river, stretching on for ever. It all seemed so unfair. I've never been worried about not having gone to a public school, nor would I want my children to go to one, but Eton's *physical* beauty came as a shock. Why can't everyone be educated inside an architectural gem?

Twenty of Britain's Prime Ministers went to Eton, from Walpole, Wellington, Pitt, Gladstone, Disraeli, Canning and Grey to Macmillan and Douglas-Home. They must have walked up and down this High Street, when they weren't in the tailors, being measured, and the surroundings must have left a deep impression on them. After Eton, only the Palace of Westminster can be a suitable enough setting for one's place of work.

The School House I was looking for, Evans's, looked like a Cotswold hotel. I asked for the housemaster in charge, Mr Payne, as instructed, and was led into his drawing room where I was met by the sound of high, braying, expensive adult voices. Several other guests, and masters, were obviously having drinks and I felt rather out of it, though I was courteously introduced. Most of them soon departed and a little group of us were left to have dinner together, before the Lit. Soc. meeting proper began.

There were just six of us – three adults and three boys. I was one of the

Right: *The statue of Henry VI, who founded Eton College in 1440 with behind, Lupton's Tower, built in 1520.*

adults, or passing myself off as one, plus the housemaster himself and a visiting Fellow (or Governor) of Eton who was an eminent Q.C. The three boys were officers of the School's Literary Society. They were in their school uniform, white ties and tails, which for some reason I thought had gone out. I'd smiled when I first caught sight of them, little old men with their deep voices and funny clothes, especially one who had on a very fancy waistcoat, which he stuck his thumbs into with great ceremony. This was to let the world see he was a member of Pop, the exclusive Eton society.

I'd expected some awful school stodge, when I'd been told we'd eat before-hand, but it was like a private dinner party in a grand country house, with excellent food and wine flowing liberally, and lots of sparkling conversation. As you would expect, the boys were fluent and polite, not in awe or over-respectful to the master or the two visitors, nor were they suspicious.

We eventually moved into a pannelled hall where about sixty boys had been patiently waiting while we had been stuffing ourselves, all of them in white ties and tails, like a uniformed Inquisition. I was to talk about Wordsworth. Well, it was a Literary Society. I chuntered on for about an hour, telling them about the marvellous biography I'd recently had published, and then called for questions. The questions fell into two areas. What was it like in the dressing-room at Spurs when you were writing *The Glory Game*, or can you tell us what it was really like to meet the Beatles? I could have saved my breath on old Wordsworth. Their real interests were the same as the boys' in any British school.

Then it was back into the drawing room, with the master pouring out foaming glasses of beer for the boys, and we sat by the log fire, all terribly civilised. I have to admit, despite a feeling of being a class traitor, that I greatly enjoyed it, but then what else would one have expected? You can't have such lavish entertainment from a state school. And they are, in theory, the pick of the nation's young manhood, so one would hope for a high measure of intelligence and courtesy.

I asked the Q.C. what he thought as we left. As a Fellow, an ex-pupil and an ex-parent, he had seen the school at close hand over the last thirty years. He considered there had been big changes since the Sixties. It was still a very liberal school, where boys were encouraged to be mature and independent, but they now seemed to him to be much less in awe of the school hierarchy. In his day, the head was a truly awesome figure. That had all gone. It didn't seem a big change to me, just a minor sign of the times.

It was a random visit. I only saw what I saw, or what I was allowed to see. Was it all a façade? Had I just been presented with the public face?

*   *   *

A few months later I went back on a more professional visit, to spend a day with Frank Herrmann, looking at any parts of the school we cared to inspect, given complete freedom to talk to any of the boys and masters. A new head master had just taken over, so it was good of him to agree to our presence, when he had so much else to think about.

Bobby Butler-Sloss, Secretary of the Literary Society, the boy who had invited me the first time, gave up the day to show us round, despite being in the last stages of working for his Oxbridge entrance. Over 130 were sitting

Two boys in School Yard, closely followed by the Head Master of Eton, Eric Anderson.

the exams that week and it was expected that well over half would get in. The previous year, they had achieved forty open scholarships to Oxford and Cambridge, a record even for Eton, making it the most 'successful' school in the country, beating for once their old rivals, Manchester Grammar School. Eton now averages thirty-five scholarships a year, a result of the deliberate attempt in the last decade by the previous head master, Michael McCrum, to raise the school's academic standards.

This was something of a surprise. I half-believed the caricature image of an Etonian as some chinless lordling, strutting around aristocratically in his funny clothes. I knew there were some clever people there, but not *that* many. The days of getting in simply by being a chinless wonder, however well-connected, are now over.

There are two basic ways of getting into Eton – one is to get your name on a House List and the other is to get on the General List. Names on a House List are put there from birth. In theory, they'll accept any name on this list, but in practice it's only those with Etonian connections who immediately on the birth of a son put down his name with a housemaster, or prospective housemaster. Future housemasters, usually existing Eton teachers, are often told years ahead that they will be taking over a house, and are allowed to start assembling their own list.

Once a boy reaches thirteen, even if he has been on a House List for thirteen years, he still has to pass the Public Schools' Common Entrance exam. This is the only academic obstacle they have to overcome, and it is not too difficult for those at a good prep school. At one time, the majority of Etonians arrived through the House List system, which thereby favoured the established Eton families, but now the school limits them to fifty percent of the total intake – a figure which will probably decrease even more in the years to come.

The General List is in the main composed of people who apply later, any time up to the age of ten. All of them are required to sit Eton's own exam and everyone is graded A, B, or C. The A people are guaranteed a place, subject to passing Common Entrance, which should be a formality, for the As. The B people might be accepted, subject to availability and the Common Entrance. The Cs are told there's no chance.

You can also, of course, get in by winning a scholarship. There are seventy scholars at Eton who have their own house, or College, inside the school and wear their own distinctive gowns. They have their school fees partly or wholly paid for by the school.

When Eton was founded, in 1440 by Henry VI, it provided for these seventy scholars, poor boys who were given a free education. Henry VI saw it mainly as a religious foundation, part of a pilgrimage centre, and he lavished a substantial income from land on 'The King's College of Our Lady of Eton beside Windsor', and made plans for it to have the largest church in the kingdom. A year later he founded King's College, Cambridge, which would be supplied by scholars from Eton.

Henry VI was deposed in 1461, when the Yorkists took over, and many of his plans never materialised, but the core of the school today, the scholars' College and the Chapel, date from the fifteenth century. Fee-paying

Etonians talking to beaks during the regular morning meetings with staff known as 'chambers'.

'oppidans', or pupils lodging in the town, were encouraged from the beginning and as the school's reputation grew, so did their numbers. The school's buildings expanded, notably with the construction of Lupton's Tower in 1520 and the Upper School in 1694.

The earliest records of what life was like for the pupils date from the mid-sixteenth century. Boys slept two or three to a bed and were up at five o'clock, chanting prayers while they dressed, and were at work by six. All teaching was in Latin and it was virtually the only subject taught. One hour a day was allowed for play, but even as early as 1519, judging by a sentence for trans-lation in a school exercise, the Eton game was football. "We will play with a bag full of wynde."

There were only two holidays, three weeks at Christmas and three weeks in the summer, which divided the year in two halves. Despite the change to a three-term year in the eighteenth century, Eton still uses the word 'halves' to describe its terms.

At first, the oppidans lodged with Fellows of the school, or with landladies in the town, but in the early nineteenth century the system of Dames' houses arose, as it did in almost all the great British boarding schools. Gladstone boarded with a Mrs Shurey and Wellington with a Miss Naylor. By the end of the nineteenth century, most of these houses had been taken over by masters, though the last of the great Eton Dames, Miss Evans, did not retire till 1906. (Hence the name of the house I had first visited.)

During its five and a half centuries, Eton has seen many changes. It has been caught up in national events, as in the Civil War when Prince Rupert used the school grounds for an artillery attack on Windsor Castle, and it has suffered financial failures and periods of unpopularity when masters abused their responsibilities. In 1841 the educational standard had fallen so low that half the scholarship places were unfilled.

The most famous old Etonian is probably the Duke of Wellington, victor of Waterloo and later Prime Minister, though he was only at the school two years. His most famous saying, that the battle of Waterloo was won on the playing fields of Eton, was probably never said, at least not in those precise words. The comment he is later known to have made, when visiting Eton in 1818, was "I really do believe I owe my spirit of enterprise to the tricks I used to play in the garden."

Apart from Prime Ministers they have also produced stars in almost every field – writers ranging from Gray, Shelley and Fielding to George Orwell and Aldous Huxley; great explorers like Sir Humphrey Gilbert, founder of Newfoundland, and Captain Oates; scientists such as Robert Boyle, Sir John Herschel, Sir Joseph Banks. And did you know that Thomas Lynch of South Carolina, a signatory of the Declaration of Independence, was an Old Etonian? Over the centuries, they've also produced their share of baddies, pirates, highwaymen, murderers, and confidence tricksters. Just like anywhere else.

They've had strong Royal connections since George III, who spent most of his reign at nearby Windsor Castle and was closely connected with the school. The fourth of June, George's birthday, is still one of Eton's great annual celebrations. Several members of the Royal family have attended Eton, and they had two in residence the day I visited, the Earl of St Andrews, son of the Duke of Kent, and James Ogilvy, son of Princess Alexandra.

The ancient buildings, dating back to 1450, are all in excellent condition,

Head Master, Eric Anderson, lunching in College Hall with some of the Scholars.

expensively cared for, while there are modern facilities like computers and electronic equipment, and many new buildings, such as the Farrer Theatre, the Bekynton dining hall, the refurbished Library, which are the result of a twenty-year rebuilding programme, just finished.

The school has around 1,250 boys. The original College still houses seventy scholars, while there are now twenty-four separate oppidan houses with around fifty boys each. There are nearly 130 full-time masters, and a range of clubs, societies and facilities, from sporting to artistic, which would be completely impossible in any state-run day school. The fees in 1981 were £3,500 a year.

It must be a daunting task to take over such a school, such an institution, even when, as all good teachers will tell you, a school is only as good as its pupils. Little wonder that Eric Anderson, when he was first asked in early 1980 to become the new Head Master of Eton, didn't really want it, preferring to stay and finish the job he was doing, which was being the Head Master of Shrewsbury.

In teaching circles, Eton is known to be a tough job. Some heads have not had an easy ride. There's an important governing body which consists of a resident Provost, who is a Royal Appointment, at present Lord Charteris, formerly the Queen's Private Secretary, and ten Fellows, all eminent people in their own world. At the same time, on the other flank, each of Eton's twenty-five housemasters (counting the Scholars as one house), has traditionally been able to build up his own power and authority and there have been clashes in the past when a head has failed to take the housemasters with him on a new development.

Then there are the media. It doesn't matter which school you come from to Eton, however well-known, you will never before have had such constant press interest to contend with. You live your life in public from now on. One mistake can take years to repair.

Mr Anderson and his wife Poppy poured out sherry in front of the log fire in their large drawing room, part of the head's official quarters in the original fifteenth-century courtyard of the school. They were just recovering from the shock of having received a telephone call from a newspaper or T.V. or radio station every eight minutes for the last two days. They had only been at Eton a few weeks and still couldn't believe that so much attention could possibly be paid to such a trivial little incident.

It concerned the arrival of a French mistress at the school. Her pretty photograph with Ooh La La caption was in every paper that morning as Eton's first ever woman-teacher. In fact she was only filling in for one term and Eton already had several women-teachers working part time, but she happened to be French and pretty and seen and photographed running a stall at a school charity fête. The school itself had put out a notice with details of the fête, including the new teacher's name, for the local press, but on a dull day it had been picked up by the national papers. Just because it was Eton.

It was a harmless story for the new head to have to learn his lessons on, luckily for him. He'll have much worse in the years to come, when no doubt someone will be expelled for having drugs, or a titled boy is involved in some scandal. They still shudder at Eton, amongst the older masters, about the time when a group of Etonians on a school trip allegedly wrecked a hotel in Switzerland and the world's press had a field day.

Mr Anderson is forty four, rather young to be Eton's head, but then all his previous appointments happened at an early age. He first became a head at thirty four, of Abingdon School, before moving to Shrewsbury five years later in 1975. He hasn't got what one might call an Etonian background, and in fact refers to himself as an incomer. But then Eton, like so many British Institutions, prides itself on being able to appoint, when it chooses, from well outside the magic circle.

He's a Scotsman from Edinburgh, son of a kilt-maker, an old-established and successful firm of kilt-makers, but still very much bourgeois. He went to an Edinburgh day school, George Watson's, and then a provincial university, St Andrews, which was where he met his wife Poppy, or Elizabeth, who was also reading English. Mr Anderson's special subject was Walter Scott.

He went on to Balliol College, Oxford, which at last brings him into the Eton catchment area, though it was Balliol's Scottish connections which attracted him. He went back to Scotland for his first teaching jobs, at Fettes and Gordonstoun, during the time Prince Charles was there, before moving to England. He is Church of Scotland and the Eton rules have had to be changed by the Privy Council as it is a Church of England foundation.

He's tall and imposing, as a traditional head master should be, but he has healthy boyish looks and hair, a gentle if faint Scottish accent and an informal manner which makes him very approachable. He can look a patrician figure when required, but his style is classless, unforbidding, un-pompous. He is not a complete stranger to Eton as his son David was a King's Scholar, now at Oxford. He also has a daughter, Catherine, at school in Bath.

In the end, he couldn't resist the challenge of Eton, though he would have liked a few years longer at Shrewsbury. So far, he had been pleasantly surprised by how kind everyone had been to him, staff and pupils, much friendlier than he'd been led to expect.

He had noticed what most people immediately notice about Etonians, how self-assured and mature they are. Considering his own experience of top public schools, I was surprised he should find that remarkable. "No, they are

The Eton Wall Game.

different here, even more so than Shrewsbury. It's true what one previous head told me – that Etonians have the priceless art of putting adults at their ease." So that's why I had been so impressed at that Lit. Soc. dinner.

"It's partly to do with each one of them from the very beginning having his own room. They have to learn to talk to their housemaster when he comes round to see them individually. It also makes them very independent."

We then went for lunch in College Hall, where the scholars have eaten since 1450, which the head master promised would probably be more photogenic than gastronomic. He had no objection to photographs being taken, nor did the master in charge of the scholars, but the lady dishing out the food, Miss Johnstone, Matron-in-College, wasn't at all pleased. Despite the fact that the Head Master himself, and the master in college, had both given permission and were both standing there, she wouldn't be persuaded. She didn't like any interruptions in *her* dining room. I could see at once how formidable the Dames must have been in the old days. However, she relented when Frank Herrmann promised to be very discreet and make no noise, fading into the background.

It was like a huge baronial hall with a raftered ceiling and an enormous fireplace, lots of carved woodwork and coats of arms on stained glass windows. It rather dwarfed the seventy scholars who sat at long dark wooden tables. I was seated at the top table, which had violently blue chairs, and I noticed several black and oriental faces amongst the scholars, all of them dressed in their school regulation uniform of tail coats, striped trousers, high collars and white bow ties, plus their scholars' gowns. The main course was rissoles, cauliflower in white sauce and chips, more Blackpool than cordon bleu, but the sponge pudding afterwards was excellent.

On my right was a very polished and charming seventeen-year-old boy from Uganda, Harry Matovu, a classics scholar, something of a legend in the school, being a great all-rounder, academic as well as a good actor. He's lived in England since he was three, and went to a prep school before Eton. He said he was considering politics as a career, though probably not in Uganda, the way things were at the moment. (His uncle was prime minister after Amin, but was now under house arrest.) His concern at that moment was to get an Oxbridge scholarship, like everyone else at the top table. They'd already sat A levels – and everyone I spoke to at the top table had got four subjects, all As.

Opposite me sat Tom Bannatyne, Captain of the School, a small, rather pale young boy, whose job it was to say a few words of Latin before and after the meal. The Captain of the School is always the senior scholar. There is also a Captain of Oppidans, representing the 1,200 or so non-scholars. Just to confuse the issue, there is a third school 'captain' figure, the President of Pop, who is elected by the society itself and is in practice the most powerful boy in the school.

Tom Bannatyne comes from Kent and his father works for a garage, on the sales side. He was aged ten and at his local state primary school when the head called him in one day and told him about Eton's Junior Scholarship scheme. This has been created in the last ten years to broaden the net, to bring in clever but poor boys who otherwise might be missed and give them the chance of a highly academic education, suitable to their talents.

Tom and his parents thought it sounded interesting, and he went off to Eton for two days and sat some exams. "I got through those and Eton then paid for me for the next three years to go to a prep school, Ashdown House. Everything was organised by Eton."

At thirteen, he sat the Eton scholarship exam, and came out first, which is why he's Captain of School today, now that he is in his final year. Since the age of ten, Eton has paid all his educational and other expenses. Not even football clubs are allowed to scout talent as young as that. He's a scientist, having taken Maths, Physics and Chemistry at A level, and was trying for a scholarship to Queen's, Cambridge.

He said he's never felt socially out of things at Eton. His only unhappy period was his first year or so at the prep school, as the change from his primary was rather sudden and dramatic. By the time he arrived at Eton, he was used to the boarding system. Nor does he feel cut off particularly from his family and local friends. "I stay in bed most of the time during the holidays. I suppose I am better equipped than most people here to know how the other half live. They *think* they do, because they watch television, but they don't."

He had enjoyed his years at Eton and could only see that he'd gained by coming there. I suggested that someone as naturally gifted as he is would still have got to Oxbridge from his local comprehensive, but he wasn't convinced.

After lunch, I had a look round the school buildings. In the old parts, it's very much like a stately home or a very tasteful museum, with treasures everywhere, all beautifully cared for, and it's hard to remember that it's a working school. The smell is of furniture wax rather than sweat or antiseptic.

In the corridor outside the head's office is a collection of prints of people connected with Eton. The school also has a priceless collection of 'Leaving

Portraits' which include works by Gainsborough, Romney, Reynolds, Lawrence, Opie and Benjamin West. They originated with an eighteenth-century headmaster of Eton, Dr Barnard, who asked distinguished pupils on leaving to have their portrait painted, at the pupil's expense, and given to the school. It has been customary until then for a young gentleman on leaving Eton to slip £10 or £15 into the head's hands as a final thank you. For that same amount, Dr Barnard was able to obtain some of the best artists of the day, as even popular portrait painters charged little more than £10–£20 for a sitting. And so the tradition began.

Bobby Butler-Sloss, who was about to take me on a tour of the rest of the school, had been elected to Pop since I'd last met him, and had a large copy of the school rules on his wall, just to prove it. The Eton Society, as it is officially called, began in 1811 as a debating society and met in a local lollypop shop, hence its nickname. It eventually became the school's disciplinary body, a function it still retains. There are thirty members of Pop, elected by the members, and they are in effect the school's prefects. Traditionally, Pop has been dominated by the hearties, the sportsmen rather than the intellectuals, but Bobby (definitely not a hearty) says that more of the arties are now being elected, people like himself, interested in acting and writing rather than football. He hopes to read English at Cambridge and eventually become a magazine journalist. His mother is a judge and his father a junior barrister.

Members of Pop are allowed to wear fancy waistcoats, and lighter check trousers, which sounds a trivial privilege, till you realise how even the hint of a different colour or material can stand out when 1,200 boys, in their school dress, are entirely in black and white. They tend to flaunt their privileges, standing with thumbs in their waistcoats, displaying their feathers. Bobby is much more retiring and quiet, as members of Pop go, and divests himself of all school uniform whenever possible.

We walked round the various houses, going into rooms, talking to boys from different years and different backgrounds, ending up Messing – having tea – in the room of a friend of Bobby's.

Taking tea, the informal social high-light of the day for most boys. Bobby Butler-Sloss, pouring, is on the left.

A more formal meal in College Hall where the Scholars of Eton have eaten since 1450.

A more formal meal in College Hall where the Scholars of Eton have eaten since 1450.

Tea is in many ways the social highlight of the day as unlike lunch and dinner, which are served in the cafeteria for Oppidans, or in College Hall for scholars, they have it in one another's rooms. It usually ends up much the same, sliced bread toasted with jam, but the company and conversation varies as people come and go. There were about nine boys having tea.

A younger boy brought back some waistcoats, sent by a Popper from another house, and the conversation dwelt on the old days of fagging. Fagging had recently been officially ended and senior boys no longer have a specific smaller boy to run their errands. Bobby said he quite used to enjoy it when he was a fag, despite spending an hour every Saturday evening washing the football clothes and boots for an older boy. "He was nice to me and told me a lot about the school and let me play his record player. Fagging was open to abuse, but I'm rather sad it's gone."

In its place there is now a system of 'community service'. The idea is that senior boys like Poppers have a lot of extra duties in the school and do after all need assistance. They don't any more have a personal fag, but they can call on junior boys to run errands for them on school business. The effect seemed to me to be much the same. Instead of calling them fags, senior boys now refer to smaller boys, only half jocularly, as servants, short for community servants, when they get them to make toast or take messages.

They then discussed whether it was true, as Bobby had said, that the arties were becoming more accepted in the school. They agreed up to a point, especially since the success of some recent school plays, though the most *popular* boys in the school still tended to be the sporting all-rounders. People who were *only* distinguished by their academic success had little status in the school, so they all agreed.

We moved on to the room of Peter Barnes, Captain of the Oppidans, who has a collection of fifteen fancy waistcoats. He looks more the archetypal Etonian, tall and fair-haired, striding through the world like one of nature's prefects, with a deep imperious tone which he has carefully cultivated. He is well aware of his own pretensions but at the same time greatly relishes being Captain of the Oppidans, a figure to be reckoned with in the school, able to make small boys quake. His father used to be Director of Housing for Camden. Unlike many of his contemporaries I spoke to, he had no clear idea of a future career, apart from wanting to be a Figure in the Establishment. He smiled at his own choice of words, but I took it all the same to be a serious aim.

One younger boy, Adam McEwan, aged fifteen, said he was often rather bored when he got back to Eton at the beginning of each half, with the other boys and the school. After living in London with his London friends, everyone at Eton seemed rather narrow-minded. "But after a week, I become part of Eton again and I forget London." None of the others agreed. The school would appear to have become their complete life, even during the holidays. They approved of almost everything, denying it was an ivory tower, positive they were getting the best possible advantages to develop them as rounded personalities.

New girl at Eton, one of the 20 who now share lessons with the boys.

They all often moan about the rigid dress regulations, but they agreed that the alternative would be something boring, like dark suits, so they would rather have their own distinctive uniform and cut a bit of a dash, even at the risk of ridicule.

Most of them had suffered some sort of persecution for being an Etonian. One boy had been spat at in the street that morning by a young workman going past on his bicycle. The previous night one boy had been beaten up in Slough, when found to be an Etonian. It had been partly his own fault, trying to adopt a punk hair-style, despite his Eton clothes, which was asking for trouble. They were against such attempts at dressing down, or trying to affect a lower class accent, just to be fashionable.

They have to put up with a lot, being part of a tourist route. The school is itself a tourist trap, while Windsor and the Castle are only minutes further on, over the Thames. "The worst are the Germans. When a bus-load of seventy of them unloads, it can be frightful. Americans just stare, loving it all, but the Germans, they now seem to jeer."

The school these days cashes in on such attention, charging tourists 35p a time to tour the Chapel and other old parts of the school, making themselves £20,000 a year. They also sell booklets on Eton and even car stickers saying 'I've been to Eton', a development which isn't too popular with the more traditional masters.

The one thing they all missed was girls. "I still feel more nervous talking to a girl than a boy," said Bobby. Others thought that six months in the outside world would cure all that, but Bobby wasn't so sure. He's observed Etonians talking to girls and they always act a little differently.

The school does now have a handful of girls around, about twenty in all. Only four are permanently at the school, being daughters of masters, the others are visitors from local schools, spending a term sharing some lessons with the boys as a preparation for Oxbridge exams.

I met one later in the street, Clare Brooks, aged eighteen, from St Mary's Convent at Ascot, who was taking twelve lessons a week at Eton. She was the centre of attention, with about five boys ringed round her. She didn't think the boys in her classes were much cleverer than the girls, but they were probably better in discussions. When later I asked some boys what they thought of the girls, they all detected a lack of depth in their knowledge. Etonians are of course convinced that their own teaching and tutorial system is the best there is.

I then went for a drink in the school's own pub, Tap, which is open to any of the pupils over sixteen. It's ostensibly a private club, which is how they get round the licensing laws. Only beer and cider are served, plus sandwiches and rolls, but it is built exactly like a pub with the usual bar-room decorations. Everyone was on half-pints of beer or Guinness and munching food yet again, like teenagers everywhere, though it was only five o'clock and they'd just finished tea and were soon to get supper. I recognised quite a few of the scholars, such as Tom Bannatyne, I'd met at lunch.

On the walls were scores of photographs of recently-left Etonians, snapshots presented to Tap by regular drinkers. Leavers, as these photographs are called, are a direct descendant of the leaving portraits which were begun in the eighteenth century. It is the custom for every boy about to leave to have printed around 200 photographs of himself and give them to his friends and favourite masters, with his name and address on the back. So begins the Old Etonian network which can see you in free meals through life.

For those left behind, it becomes the smart thing to pin up as many Leavers on your study wall as possible, showing how popular you are. Even Tom Bannatyne, a first-generation Etonian, was having 180 printed. Some people do joke ones, pictures of themselves sitting on the lavatory or in funny clothes.

"Sock me a pint before you go," shouted someone. Socking someone is to give them a present, such as sweets or a drink. Masters are beaks and to say you are 'up to Mr Young' means you are in Mr Young's class. Tugs are the scholars. To 'mob' someone is to tease them or fool around. Oh, the list of Eton slang is endless, as in every closed institution.

P.B. means Private Business which is an informal tutorial all boys attend for forty-five minutes twice a week. You are assigned your subject teacher, and a lot of Eton sixth form teaching takes place in small groups, but for Private Business you can choose your own tutor. It means that popular masters are greatly over-subscribed.

I went to one later that evening run by a young master called Tim Young, an Old Etonian himself, once President of Pop, who is in charge of the school's association football team. In the summer he'd taken a school team around

Gentlemen of Pop, the exclusive Eton School Society, displaying themselves and their waistcoats.

America on a soccer tour. His team was a great success, apparently, especially with the girls.

About ten boys were slumped in easy chairs in formal school dress, as it was officially a school event, though Mr Young himself was in an American-style football shirt and canvas shoes and looked very American, tanned and blond with a square open face. His accent betrayed mid-Atlantic as well as Cockney overtones, which was strange, considering his own background, but he had taught in a comprehensive school before returning to Eton. His father is Brian Young, until recently Director General of the I.B.A., and formerly head master of Charterhouse.

I listened to them discussing their U.S. tour. Before I'd arrived they'd been arguing whether marijuana should be legalised. Any subjects can be discussed at P.B., though the tutor usually structures each one round a topic, such as a book, or a film or some slides.

They then asked for my impressions of my day at the school, and naturally, being well brought up, I said how impressed I had been by everything. Eton was certainly doing well what it set out to do well.

There was a pause. I then added that I didn't want to get into the morality of it all, whether such privilege should be allowed, as my visit was to look at Eton as a Great British Institution, a famous element in our national heritage, but nonetheless and notwithstanding, it did just strike me that it might not be preparing boys for the outside world of today.

To a man, they denied that they were cut off from the real world. In Eton, you had to mix and get along with people from all walks of life, from different backgrounds, different races, different temperaments. If you could survive Eton, you could survive anywhere. Comprehensive boys, after all, were cut off from people like them. They only experienced one part of real life.

Mr Young thought it was the boarding aspect that was most vital. If a boy had a particular problem, he could give him an hour after lessons were over, and talk it through with him, for as long as it took. In a comprehensive, that was impossible.

I said it was the home background that mattered most. In the end, middle-class children always end up dominating our Universities, whether they go through the state or the private sector.

Naturally, we didn't reach any conclusions, but I admired their pride in their own system, their lack of cynicism, of any real doubts. All day I had looked for some radical spirit, anyone who was against school, but if any existed, I couldn't find one. Literary memoirs are full of people unhappy at their public school, but perhaps they keep it quiet at the time. There is today such competition to get into Eton, and there is great reflected glory in every family with an Etonian, that you are bound to feel successful, just by being there. The feeling is justifiable, not just because of the competition, but because of all the marvellous facilities, excellent teaching, liberal principles, scholastic successes, historic associations and beautiful buildings which Eton has to offer.

Later that evening I went back to Bobby's room to thank him for the day. He put on his stereo a record of the 'Eton Boating Song', one of the best-known songs in the English language. The words were written by an Eton master for a Fourth of June ceremony in 1863, and then put to music by an Old Etonian, Captain Algernon Drummond, who read the words while serving with the Rifle Brigade in India.

I thought Bobby was doing it as a joke, to send it up, but although he laughed at some of the awful lines and the amateur singing (it was a live recording, made at a school concert) he was obviously rather moved by it. He often plays it to himself, late at night when he's had a draggy day and feels like something gently emotional.

He would miss Eton when he left in a month's time. He wouldn't say he was *proud* to have been there. It contained people he disapproved of. Eton had snobs and louts who could get drunk and become aggressive, just as they have in comprehensives, only they would be called vandals.

He never likes boasting in any way about being an Etonian, which is why he always gets quickly out of his uniform. During the holidays in London, having his hair cut, for example, he always hides the fact that he's an Etonian.

Thinking about it unemotionally, the word he would use would be 'pleased'. Yes, he was pleased to be at Eton.

Right. *The end of the Eton tails....*

12 Neil Kinnock

NEIL KINNOCK, M.P., divides his time between Wales and Westminster. At Westminster he has a room measuring eight feet by ten which he shares with his secretary, two desks and four large filing cabinets. Compared with American or German politicians, British ones have to make do with very few facilities and a modest salary.

Pinned to the curtains of the window beside his desk he has a few letters, choice examples of the loony letters all M.P.'s get. "Yours disgusted, a pensioner, R. Harrison," was the entire contents of one letter. "Why are you on T.V. so often? Less Kinnock and more Kermit." "Is there something fundamentally dishonest about the way you comb your hair, Kinnock?"

On one wall he had pinned two of his own favourite quotations. One was from an Indian restaurant-owner in his constituency: "I am worried about the split in the Party but Almighty God will help us to make the Party Strongest. With Regards and Gratitudes, Sabi." The other was taken from the words of Gandhi: "There seems enough for everyone's need but not for everyone's greed." Mr Kinnock is on the Left of the Labour Party and is known for his strong socialistic views on many subjects. (On education, for example, he would like to close places like Eton.)

On this particular Friday morning, he was leaving London to drive the 153 miles to his constituency in South Wales, a journey he does frequently, all through the year. He was wearing a smart two-piece grey suit and a duffle coat. His suit, and his red Austin Princess car and the fact that he does 23,000 miles a year, belting along the motorway between London and Wales, could make strangers take him for a commercial traveller. Salesmen, however, don't usually wear duffle coats. Duffle coats have student-ish, left-wing overtones and no salesman wants to be mistaken for such a creature.

He is aged thirty-nine, well-built, with only slight signs of podginess, receding red hair, a light, frecklish complexion and a deep, rather hoarse Welsh accent. He used to have a good singing voice but doesn't trust it for serious singing any more. Too many late nights in smoke-filled rooms. Too much shouting and arguing, impassioned speeches in crowded halls or open-air rallies. He also smokes a lot and is rarely without his pipe.

In his photographs, he can look serious and much older than his years. In the flesh he is young, bouncy, open, full of enthusiasm with no pretensions. Like most M.P.'s, from any party, his normal conversation carries far more expletives than is evident when being interviewed by Robin Day for some ponderous B.B.C. programme.

He has been M.P. for Bedwellty in South Wales since 1970. He refused office in the 1974–79 Labour Government but in 1979 became Labour spokesman on Education and in 1980 a member of the Shadow Cabinet. Many political pundits have tipped him as a future leader of the Labour party, which causes him some weary amusement. Despite what some may think, he doesn't look upon himself as a careerist. It has all happened almost by chance. He knows anyway that in politics the most tipped rarely make it.

He is regarded as one of the best speakers in the House of Commons. This is a generally held opinion, agreed upon by even his political enemies, and as a left-winger he has many of those. He was recently named in a book as the number one speaker in the House, top of a list of five people who can be guaranteed to bring people into the Chamber whenever it is known they are going to speak. (The other four were Enoch Powell, Edward Heath, Peter Shore, Michael Foot.) He does not deny that he is a good speaker, but is equally wary of such descriptions. He feels people hold his fluency against him, forgetting, or even ignoring, his underlying serious intent. He finds all speeches a strain and would be happy if he never had to make another speech in his life. So he says.

That morning *The Times*, and other papers, carried a long report of his speech in a debate on education in the House, in which he had led for the Opposition. The debate had not finished till ten o'clock at night and he had not got back to his home in Kingston until 10.45, but it was the first evening that week he had had a conversation with his wife. She had stayed up especially for his return, as it was Friday night, and she wasn't due at work next morning. She teaches in a comprehensive school. During the rest of that week, she had been in bed by the time he had got home.

He had been busy in the House every day and then had had evening speeches and meetings in London and various parts of the country, including a Cambridge University debate. Mr Kinnock, as a good speaker, and as a Shadow Cabinet spokesman, and as an expert on education, a topic on which most people have views, is constantly in demand. His friends fear for his health. They think he has been doing far too much these last ten years. When he's over forty, so they hope, he might slow down.

He gets about forty letters every day at the House, many of them requests for him to speak. He has to say his diary is full for the year ahead. He hates

Neil Kinnock, MP for Bedwellty.

saying it, as it sounds so ridiculous, but that is the case. All the same, in any week, he has five outside engagements and makes up to ten speeches. His wife says he's like a woman with sixteen children. He can't say no.

The weekend ahead was going to be purely constituency work, the humdrum duties which every British M.P. has to undertake, to a greater or lesser extent, regardless of how eminent they might be back in the Palace of Westminster. This is what they were elected to do, to represent all the people who live in their constituency, whether or not they voted for them. Every four years, the voters have a chance to decide whether he or she has done a good job. These days, come-uppance can occur even more frequently, especially in the Labour Party, if a group of activists on the local executive of the Party manage to stir things up.

Mr Kinnock goes to Bedwellty two weekends out of three. He holds 'surgeries' for anyone who wants to see him, every second Saturday, but there are other meetings and matters which require his presence. He has a home in the constituency, where he would be staying this weekend, which he and his family use some weekends and during holidays.

In the boot of his car he had packed a cardboard box with a bottle of milk, some margarine and a packet of crumpets, rations for a self-catering bachelor weekend. After a hard and exhausting week, it wasn't the sort of fun-filled weekend which many happily married men would willingly choose, but, if you are an M.P., especially one who cares as passionately as Mr Kinnock, there is no choice. It has to be done.

He had at least seen his two children over breakfast. Stephen, aged eleven, plays for his primary school football team and he'd gone through, blow by blow, their 8–0 victory the previous day. Rachel, aged nine, had played him a tune on her guitar, till they had argued about the fingering, as he tried to tell her the correct procedure. This had then been forgotten when Mrs Thatcher came on the radio and Rachel proceded to do her impersonation of the Prime Minister, much to everyone's amusement. Mrs Thatcher is not the favourite person in the Kinnock household.

During the two-and-a-quarter-hour drive from Kingston to Pontllanfraith, the little mining village near Newport where he has his Welsh home, Mr Kinnock usually plays his tapes, sometimes Beethoven, sometimes 1950s rock music, sometimes Welsh male voice choirs, depending on his mood. He hates the journey. He plans eventually to move nearer Central London, probably to Ealing, so he will be closer to the House, and near enough to Paddington to make his Welsh journeys by train. M.P.'s get free first-class travel to and from their constituency, one of their few perks.

They do get an allowance for having to run two homes, around £4,500, and in recent years they have also got an allowance for a secretary, up to £8,000 a year. Their own basic salary in 1981 was only £11,750 a year, far less than most business executives get, especially when you consider their hours, conditions of work and responsibilities.

For a few years after he became an M.P. he did try to have his main home in Wales, taking digs in London for the five nights a week he had to be in the House, but the strain was too much. It was a year after the death of his parents, within a week of each other in 1971, that he decided to bring his own family nearer to his main place of work. It is not surprising that the family life of so many M.P.'s is disrupted, and divorce so frequent, when

Neil Kinnock, one of the top five speakers in the House of Commons.

they have to live such split lives, on the road with their pathetic cardboard boxes, or dependent on suitcases and strange hotel bedrooms.

His father was a miner called Gordon Kinnock, but the Scottish connection is only in the name. They have all been Welsh born and bred, on both sides, for the last three generations. After twenty-five years in the pits, his father was invalided out with dermatitis, which at that time was not considered an industrial disease. He was unemployed for a year and then spent the next twenty-five years as a labourer in the steel works. His mother was a district

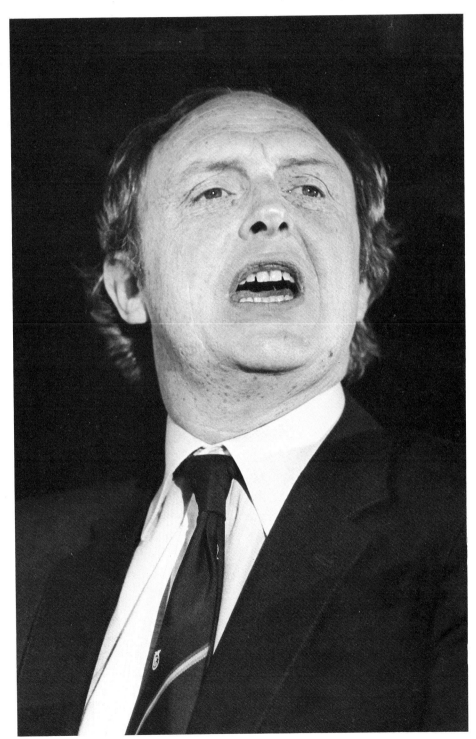

nurse, much loved around Tredegar, who knew all the local families and their history, but never indulged in any gossip.

Neil is much the same. He hates parliamentary gossip, never retailing any, refusing when possible to be told any. This sets him apart from most M.P.'s. There is no bigger hive of gossip in the whole country than Westminster. Together, the lobby press and the politicians live their lives in a constant state of gossip, obsessed by every rumour, every newspaper story, analysing every chance remark, turning straws into haystacks.

He was born in 1942 and lived the first years of his life in a colliery town, in a terrace row beside the pit, then in 1947 they got a move to a new council-owned prefab. "It was like moving to Beverley Hills. It had a fridge, a bath, central heating and a smokeless grate. It was on a mountain outside Tredegar and people used to come just to look at it."

He passed the eleven plus in the top stream and was awarded a place at Lewis School, considered the best grammar school in the district, thirteen miles away from his home. He could have gone to the local grammar in Tredegar but passing for Lewis, so he says, was to an eleven-year-old like being picked for Wales. You didn't turn it down.

"I hated it," so he now says. "I only liked one year, and that was my last year." He thinks it wasn't a matter of social distinction, although it was a very smart school where the prefects wore tassles on their caps. He feels one reason was that he was bolshie, against the system, and was always in trouble. One simpler explanation for his dislike of school was that he wasn't very good, either at sport – despite being mad keen – or lessons. He got only three O levels, failing everything except English, History and Geography.

"My disappointment was mixed with relief – it seemed the perfect excuse to leave school. I decided I could either go down the pit or into the army, but my parents were violently against it. They made me go back and re-sit."

He must have stuck in a bit harder this time, as he got A levels in Economics, History and English (2 B's and a C) and went on to University College, Cardiff to read Industrial Relations.

At Cardiff, he threw himself into the Union and the Labour Party where he met his wife Glenys, who was Secretary of the Socialist Society while he was Chairman. "I started doing a lot of speaking, as a way of trying to impress Glenys. There wasn't much else about me which would impress her.

"I liked winning debates against the Tories. It was an easy time to be a Socialist. There were so many big subjects, Cuba, Anti-Apartheid and a dying Tory Government. Things are more complex today. In the 1960s everything seemed possible. We thought Socialism was going to solve so many things. The Labour Government under Wilson missed its great opportunity between 1964 and 1970. Today, now that we've been through twelve years of Labour rule, nobody is willing to depend merely on the personality of the Labour leaders. The power of democratic government as a whole has been curtailed. Freedom of action has been reduced for all governments. The country is less hopeful today, less libertarian, more right-wing. Labour has got to be very, very tough to stick to its principles today, prepared to lose an election for them, if we are to maintain our essential integrity.

Despite his success in student politics, he never seriously contemplated it as a career. "When I meet kids at the universities today who say they intend to 'make a career' in politics, I want to kick their arses. People who think of politics as a 'career' are repulsive." Instead, he became a teacher for the Workers Education Association, working in his home area, for four years after graduating. (He graduated a year late as he failed a part of his final exams and had to re-sit a whole year, but his county, Monmouth, extended his grant, for which he has been eternally grateful.)

In 1970, when he was twenty-seven, some friends in the local Labour party in Bedwellty asked him to stand for the Labour nomination which had unexpectedly become vacant. There were three apparently more favoured, more experienced, candidates, but in the final selection meetings he was chosen by 76 votes to 74, much to most people's surprise, and his own. The tradition in the Welsh valleys, especially the Red ones, with massive Socialist majorities going back for decades, is of having a horny-handed M.P., one with long experience of either the pits or the trade union movement. At twenty-seven, Kinnock was looked upon as a young whipper-snapper, an airy-fairy arts graduate who had done nothing in life so far.

"I was asked at one meeting about the fact that I'd never worked with my hands. I had, during holiday jobs, but I knew that wouldn't impress anyone. I asked them to imagine me going to the manager of the colliery, wearing my cap and gown, and asking for a job, and told them that if I did that they wouldn't be nominating me, they would be certifying me. This got a big laugh. I felt that was the turning point in being accepted."

His first two years in London were not very happy. He felt lonely, having left his wife and baby son and daughter behind in Wales, and found West-minster procedure utterly confusing. He'd never been inside the House of Commons until he was elected. The Tories had just come to power, with a good majority, and nobody was interested in an eager, ginger-headed young Welsh Socialist.

"I arrived with a lot to say and I managed as best I could to say it, but they're used to articulate fellows and I was nothing special. The only real sense of purpose was in my constituency work. I could see there a multitude of injustices, but despite how hard I worked for people, I only ever seemed to kick one goal in twenty attempts. There didn't seem much point in being an M.P. It seemed to be all banging your head against a wall without even chipping the brick. I did consider getting out and letting someone else have a go."

It was the Miners Strike of 1972 which gave his life a focal point and provided a platform. As an M.P. for a mining constituency (one quarter of the work force is in, or associated with, mining), he was called upon to put their case, which he did with passion and fluency, speaking at public meetings all over the country and writing for *Tribune*, establishing himself as a new voice, one which the media were eager to use. They've been using him ever since.

We arrived in his constituency just after twelve o'clock, driving up the Rhymney Valley towards Bedwas. His constituency straddles two long valleys which stretch from Newport in the South up to Tredegar. In each there is that strange amalgam of impoverished industrial landscape, old mining and steel villages, depressed terrace houses, mean-looking chapels, side by side with beauty and greenery. You look up the steep slopes of the valleys, at the fields and woods and untouched mountain tops, while in the valley bottom there is all the detritus of man-made life, left-overs from the glacier of the industrial revolution which has now passed on. There were fourteen collieries in his constituency just seventeen years ago. Now there are only four. It's as if the Gorbals had been dumped in the Lake District.

He was due at 12.30 to visit Bedwas Bodyworks, the first of two factories he had agreed to go to that day. Both of them were thriving, which made a change. His normal reason for visiting a factory is when there's trouble, such as a strike, and he is asked to address the workers or reason with the management.

Bedwas Bodyworks had written to him some time ago, inviting him to see over the plant, look at their youth training scheme, and have lunch. No other reason was given. He'd never been there before and didn't know what sort of bodies they worked on, though he remembered the site when it had been owned by a previous company.

Was there really any point in touring a factory, like minor royalty, when obviously the management would be going to show him only the good things?

"It's the best way to find out anything. It always starts as a Fixed Smile Visit, but the management melt when you get to know them. As you go round, you ask to see everything and talk to random people on the way. I always ask to see the shop steward, although I don't know if this is a union firm."

It turned out to be a bright new factory, clean and efficient-looking. He was met by a very smart Oxford-educated man who had grown up in Kingston-on-Thames, where Neil now lives, who took him up to meet the managing director, a man with a strong Lancashire accent. They explained

the factory's business which is building security vehicles for people like Securicor (who now own the works), although they also work on refrigerated vans, ambulances and general re-painting jobs. They employ 120 workers and turn out about 400 vehicles a year. Their order books were healthy, with £750,000 worth of business lined up, but they were quite slack that week. Unlike most factories, they had avoided any lay-offs, and were determined not to be forced into any, if they possibly could. If they lost any craftsmen, when the recession turned they might not get them back. Anyway, they felt it was only fair that if workmen responded handsomely when they had emergency orders, as theirs had done, they had to play fair with them when things were slow.

The Oxford gentleman was very keen to ask Mr Kinnock what Robin Day was *really* like, and were the questions fiddled on 'Any Questions', which Mr Kinnock had appeared on the week before. I asked the two management men if they had a *specific* reason for inviting Mr Kinnock, apart from the pleasure of his company. They smiled and the Oxford gentleman produced a pamphlet entitled 'Government Contracts Preference Schemes' and asked Mr Kinnock if there was anything in it. The Lancashire M.D. said firmly that his firm had never had any favours, but if there were any going, well, they should know about them.

"Waste of time," said Mr Kinnock. "It's a cosmetic scheme. Absolutely toothless. I wouldn't bother with it." In theory, the scheme is to help firms in development areas get special attention when applying for Government contracts, such as Coal Board or Post Office work. In practice, according to Mr Kinnock, you have no more chance of getting the job, and there are many strings attached.

"Well, even if all it does is open a few doors," said the M.D., "it would help to get us on their tender lists." Mr Kinnock agreed that was possible.

After lunch, cold salad and beer in a mock pine dining room, Mr Kinnock toured the factory. He stopped to talk to a workman in the corner of a large and eerie warehouse who had a handwritten notice on his lathe which said 'I used to think hypothermia was a country in the Balkans until I discovered

Bedwas Bodyworks'. Mr Kinnock, and the management men walking round behind him, their arms folded, all thought it very funny.

He went into every department, and talked in passing to lots of workmen, asking where they lived, any problems, had they been on short time. Afterwards, he said he was impressed by both the management and the work force, and thought they did seem a good, happy team.

"Managing directors come in three types," he said as we drove on to the next factory. "Firstly, there's the Genuine Bloke, regardless of background or accent. I'd put the one we've just seen in that category. Then there's the Provincial Sod, who has a regional accent and is an unreconstituted Sergeant Major and a right bastard. Thirdly, there's the Public School Slob who doesn't know his arse from his elbow. They're dying out, thank God.

"Did you notice one thing about that factory? All the people but one in responsibility were non-Welshmen. They were either Lancashire, Oxford, West Country, Scotsmen. It's one of our problems in Wales. We don't have a management class. The people who might have been have all gone into teaching."

The next visit was to the Stuart Crystal glass works at Aberbargoed, a branch of the Staffordshire firm which opened in South Wales in 1967 with a work force of only six. Now they have 120 and produce hand-made crystal glasses, decanters and ornaments which are sold all over the world. Even the most senior craftsmen, delicately blowing and shaping frightening-looking lumps of molten glass, seemed to be no more than lads. The whole work force was incredibly young. It is of course a new factory, introducing a new skill into the area, and the craftsmen have been trained straight from school.

It was much more of a formal visit this time as Mr Kinnock was part of a bigger party, which contained the Chairman and Councillors of Rhymney Valley District Council. The star guest was another Welsh M.P., the Rt. Hon. George Thomas, a Labour M.P. in Cardiff since 1945, a popular and much-loved figure throughout Wales. It was announced on the radio that day, during his tour of the glass works, that he was going to resign his seat at the next election and therefore cease to be Mr Speaker in the House of Commons. There was much good-natured mickey-taking as he went round and people shouting 'Or-der, Or-der'. Since the radio started broadcasting parliamentary debates, most people in Britain can recognise Mr Thomas's accent.

A lot of the shouting came from the Council chairman, a lady called Cissy Powell, who tried without success to get Mr Thomas to say 'Or-der, Or-der'. She is a strong character, known through the Valleys for her colourful language and sometimes fiery behaviour.

In the glass works, Mr Kinnock talked to many of the young workers, and recognised several from previous meetings. Some were wearing red rugby shirts as they worked away at their bench. (Next day, Wales was playing France in Paris.) Afterwards there were tea and cakes and little speeches, and each Councillor and the two M.P.s were given some crystal in a handsome box. Three or four of the young craftsmen, whom we had seen earlier, working in the heat and noise of the furnaces, were present at the little tea party, cleaned up and spruce, watching the V.I.P.s, yet looking somehow smaller and more insignificant. They had seemed like giants in front of the furnaces, making magic at incredible speed.

After the glass works, there was a reception at some Elizabethan manor

Neil Kinnock in the Rhymney Valley:
how green was the valley, how busy it
once was. In some of the old mining
villages, male unemployment is now
32%.

house which the Council was rehabilitating, but, despite driving round various muddy farm tracks, Mr Kinnock failed to find the entrance, and so instead we went on to his final appointment of the day, a reception at the Council offices to mark the 75th anniversary of the Caerphilly Male Voice choir.

All the choir, with wives, were resplendent in their best evening suits and dresses. Later that evening, there was going to be a banquet for them in Caerphilly Castle, with Mr Thomas as guest of honour. The local press were taking photographs of the choir and guests, which now included three local M.P.s, plus Councillors. There was a lot of hearty banter between one photographer and Cissy, telling each other to shut up, to stop picking your nose, get into line when I bloody tell you, oh God, we don't want *you* in the photograph.

Various people came up to Mr Kinnock, congratulating him on speeches they'd heard him make, or just to talk to him.

"Hello, Neil, we haven't met, but I've seen you on the tele."

"That's what my wife says to me," said Mr Kinnock. Everyone laughed.

"Anyway, Neil, keep giving them stick, boy."

I talked to one choir member who said that he personally had never forgiven Neil for leaving the constituency to live in Kingston. I said that the majority of M.P.s had their main home near Westminster. That was the trouble, he said, they lost touch. Neil was now part of the Thames Valley not the Rhymney Valley. But wasn't it better that an M.P. had a stable home life, seeing as much of his own family as possible? He didn't seem convinced.

"But that's the only thing I've got against him. I am a fan. Neil Kinnock's got it. You can see that."

It was almost eight o'clock by the time he got to his home in the little mining village of Pontllanfraith, a modest terrace house in the middle of the row. I'd read an unkind report in *The Times* which had said it smelled of damp, but it turned out to be surprisingly warm and inviting. A friend had been in earlier and put on the central heating.

On the table was a pile of bills and letters, one of them an enormous screed from a Maltese who had written to say he was being unfairly deprived of

British citizenship. Mr Kinnock read it carefully, muttering and swearing oaths against the Home Office. There was also a note from a friend, Gwyn Evans, a member of his local party executive, who lives nearby and had put the heat on. The note said he'd see Neil in the club for a drink at ten, then they'd go to the Indian for a meal.

He took his duffle coat off at last, having read every letter, then started to unpack his cardboard box and make some tea, but very soon the 'phone started ringing, calls from constituents who knew he is usually in his house at this time on a Friday evening. Several of them were long-running sagas. One woman, whose child had died in hospital, was still blaming the medicals for neglect. She had got herself into the hands of solicitors, despite Mr Kinnock's previous advice and had run up a bill of £1,500. She was now contemplating selling her house to pay for further legal fees. He listened carefully and sympathetically, promising to write more letters, chase more Government departments. She wasn't even in his constituency, but he felt he couldn't hang up on her now.

Mr Kinnock outside his constituency home in the mining village of Pontllanfraith.

Below right: *Inside his Pontllanfraith home, a little bit of Habitat in the Welsh valleys.*

"I don't kid myself that I can do much good. The welfare role of the M.P. has considerably increased in the last few years, but I haven't got the space at the House to organise a real fight, or the staff to help me. If only I had a case worker, I could do so much more. I *know* that lady has a case about the death of her daughter, and I've heard of three similar cases in the same hospital, but it would need such research to build up the argument. You need an enormous dossier to make any authority investigate itself. I've tried the local and national press, to get them interested, and stories have appeared, but nothing's been done.

"I've never been delirious about politics. In fact I've been very depressed about it all for the last year. Well, there's Mrs Thatcher for a start and what she's doing. My constituents have been hammered. This area of South Wales is in a bloody awful mess. Unemployment is 17.29 and in Risca, where we were this afternoon, 32.3 percent of the male population is unemployed, in a village where there was only 5 percent unemployment just two years ago.

"I'm fed up with the disputes in my own party, the incessant clash of vanities between the so-called Left and so-called Right. There are some valid points to argue about, but we have much more vital things to do to bring about the advance of socialism.

"I'm depressed that it's so hard to get across alternative policies. The quality national press don't take 'Left' policy or 'Bennite' policy seriously. The populars have just turned us all into bogeys, filling their readers up with lies and rubbish.

"I'm tired because I'm doing too much. I'm buggering myself at the moment. I don't get a hell of a lot of enjoyment out of it. I haven't made any dents for a long time.

"And yet, I can't leave. M.P.'s have practically no power, apart from scrutinising proposals, but if I did get out, and then things got worse, I would feel guilty that I hadn't stayed and fought. I'd also be letting down a hell of a lot of people. If I could find a job with greater influence, where things can be changed faster and better, then I'd take it, but there isn't one.

"It's not a matter of personal advancement. I've had enough ego trips. The nicest thing is when people come up and say your speech gave them a lift, but the danger there is that you go round looking for audiences to applaud you. I've seen it happening with some of my colleagues. They search for a moveable gallery.

"You see a lot of dirty things as an M.P., but you meet a lot of good people. Most of these good people are in the constituencies, doing selfless work that no one hears about. The House of Commons is like a factory. That's where I happen to work. I have some close friends there, and some not close friends. Just because you work with people in the same party, it doesn't mean to say you like them. My unto-the-death friends are here, amongst the party workers. I can't let them down.

"I do enjoy a good combative argument, when you know what should be said and done, when you can see a chance to advance socialism, even in this complicated world when none of us can do very much.

"I never make notes before a speech. I've tried, but it doesn't work for me. You can't smell an audience until you get there and start speaking. Rhetoric these days has become a term of abuse. People who use colourful language or gesticulate with their hands are suspected, accused of putting on a show. In my case, when it happens, it is an expression of passion. If passion has no longer got any place in argument then by God, we're in a pretty sad state. I do try on occasions to make a speech which sticks only to the facts, going through the points analytically. It happened the other day, when I had something very serious I wanted to get across. The papers next day dismissed it as dull."

All the same, apart from his depression that evening about the state of the world, it was clear he is still proud to be serving in the House of Commons. "There is no cleaner or more honest national assembly anywhere in the world. A British M.P. is uncorruptible. There would be no point in trying to corrupt him, as the legislative and the administrative power is separate in the British system. It doesn't need money to be an M.P., the way it does in America. So you don't need wealthy backers, who then might try to influence you.

"There are pressure groups, trying to influence events, but they can't do it the way they can in America. Look how long their gun lobby has stopped the American gun laws being changed. It does happen now and again that some important British politician is revealed to be in the pay of some firm, but what they are after is the prestige of his association, of having him on the board, almost for social reasons, to open doors, but he can never *do* anything for them in the House. He can't change the laws of the land in their favour. We might not have much real power, but we are unbuyable."

The 'phone rang, at two minutes past ten, and it was his friend Gwyn to say he already had the pints lined up, where the hell was he?

The next couple of hours were spent in the club, talking to old friends, discussing local issues, Council intrigues, amid a lot of jokes and laughter, as if he had not a depressed thought in his head. It didn't seem like an act, a professional, turning on the charm. He is a gregarious individual, but he appeared sincere as he listened to people's stories and problems.

Finally, we reached his favourite local Indian restaurant, Moti Raj in Newport, where the owner is Sabur Ali Kahn, a Labour party supporter – the one whose letter he has on his Westminster office wall. It was empty when we arrived but by two o'clock in the morning, when we left, it was absolutely full. Every table was taken by young people, having a late-night meal after a night at the disco.

I was shattered by the time we got back to his home and eventually to bed, which he had arranged for me, with the electric blanket on, yet all I had done all day was observe. He had been giving himself for almost fourteen hours, non stop. On big occasions, during elections, he can keep it up for thirty-six hours without going to bed. I couldn't be an M.P. You lose too much sleep.

Next morning, Gwyn came round for breakfast and they continued talking about local Labour party politics. Gwyn organises an annual Chartist Rally in the constituency which began in 1977 and now gets up to 1,000 people turning out to hear Neil and other Left wing leaders. It's Bedwellty's version of a May Day Rally.

Gwyn works for I.C.I. but appears to live his private life for the party, along with half a dozen others in the constituency. They are the die-hards, the ones who will drop everything to deliver leaflets, or travel up to Westminster for a demonstration. He has great admiration for Neil, but can be critical, thinking that at times Neil lets his temper get the upper hand. On these occasions, one of the party faithful tries to steer Neil away from the confrontation.

At ten o'clock that morning, we arrived at the village of Cross Keys where his fortnightly surgery was due to be held in the Miners' Institute. There are notices throughout Bedwellty saying at what time and at what place Mr Kinnock will next be available. He half-expected nobody to be waiting, as it was a very rainy morning, but the entrance hall was full. One by one they filed in to see him as he sat in the corner of a large dance hall, still with last night's decorations up, the drums on stage and the lingering smell of stale beer.

A young couple came first, with the wife complaining that she was being refused the discount to buy her council house because the house had been in the name of her previous husband, even though she had lived in it for thirteen years. She maintained it was sex discrimination. Mr Kinnock said that was the law, alas. It was the person whose name was on the rent book who was the official tenant and therefore qualified for the discount. But he took down the details and, there and then, wrote a letter to the local housing department, putting her case.

Next came an old man, worried that his rent was going up after forty-eight years in the same house, a cottage without a bathroom or inside lavatory. He and his sick wife found it very hard to use the outside W.C., right at the bottom of their garden. They'd only paid £1.20 all these years, he said, but now it was going up by £3. Mr Kinnock again got out his pen and wrote a letter on his behalf, slowly explaining the law to him, saying he held out little hope about the rent staying the same, but at least the Council might force the landlord to make some improvements.

Then four people came in together, two young lads in their early twenties, and their mothers, with a long saga about police harassment, which they took in turns to explain, each picking up the story and taking it on. They alleged they'd been roughed up by the police, put in the cells for the night, after innocently coming out of a Chinese take-away. They maintained it was mistaken identity. The police had been called to the Chinese, because somebody had broken a door, and had just picked on them, as the first people they'd seen coming out. They had done nothing whatsoever, not even given cheek, though later one of them might have sworn back at the police.

"The police swore much more than I did. Can't I have them for it?"

"No chance," said Mr Kinnock. "You can't get the police for swearing, unless there happens to be a judge passing by. Next time you go to the Chinese, make sure you have a judge with you."

Mr Kinnock said he believed their story and that he would complain to the Chief Constable and to the Home Office, but they might as well give up any hope of getting damages for wrongful arrest. He'd failed on previous occasions to get that. He would try instead to get their charges dismissed.

The surgery was due to last till 11.30, but at one o'clock he was still there. In the afternoon he had other meetings with local Labour Party workers, but he did manage to fit in a look at the Wales-France rugby match on the tele in a local government workers' club. (Wales lost.)

Usually, he tries to drive home to Kingston early Saturday evening, in time to see his children before bed, but he had arranged to go to a retirement party for his favourite aunt, so, once again he was home very late.

"I had a nice old man of sixty-six in one surgery who said the police were following him. I asked how long this had been going on, and he said ever since he'd been a lad. It had happened again last week, he said. While walking in Risca a copper had come up and asked him the time.

"I arranged for a friendly deputy chief constable to write him a nice letter, thanking him for his co-operation, how the police relied on reliable people like him. His obsession then stopped.

"He was a normal bloke, really, apart from that one obsession about the police. He'd been moved into a home since his mother died and he was very lonely. I suppose about 20 percent of the people who come to surgeries are paranoid, but who is to say it is a result of madness or of a lifetime being pushed around?"

It might not be such a glamorous job, being an M.P., as it sometimes looks from the outside, or particularly powerful, or even very satisfying, but it is reassuring to think that out in the constituencies there are M.P.'s trying as hard as Neil Kinnock to make the British parliamentary system work, catering for the needs of the meek and not just of the mighty.

The week-end work that Westminster never sees – Mr Kinnock at a surgery in his constituency.

13 The Giant's Causeway

WHEN William Makepeace Thackeray visited the Giant's Causeway in 1842 he hardly knew what hit him. A dozen rough guides pounced upon him, arguing and fighting, pushing and pulling him. Then, before he realised what was happening, he was at sea.

He was on a tour of Ireland, in order to write his *Irish Sketch Book*, and had been looking forward to a quiet appraisal of one of the Wonders of the Western World, which was how the Victorians viewed the Giant's Causeway.

I was perfectly helpless. I wanted to walk down to the shore by myself, but they would not let me, and I had nothing for it but to yield myself into the hands of the guides who had seized me. We were up one swelling wave that came in a huge advancing body before I had the leisure to ask myself why the deuce I was on that boat, with four rowers hurrooing and bounding madly from one huge liquid mountain to another – four rowers I was bound to pay . . .

Poor old Thackeray. They insisted on taking him to a cove, though his stomach was heaving so much he could see nothing, protecting him from the spray with an exaggerated show of rough kindness, making him change seats all the time. Before they would allow him back to shore he was forced to buy 'boxes of specimens' from them.

The guide meanwhile was telling some story of a ship of the Spanish Armada having fired her guns at two peaks of rock – what benighted fools these Spanish Armadilloes must have been, it is easy to know that chimney pots do not grow on rocks.

"But where, if you please, is the Causeway?"

"That's the Causeway before you," says the guide.

"Which?"

"That pier which you see jutting out into the bay, right ahead."

"*Mon Dieu!* And have I travelled 150 miles to see *that?*"

Over the centuries, ever since it was first discovered, many people's first impression of the Causeway has been one of disappointment, just like Thackeray's.

How can a natural phenomenon be 'discovered'? It was discovered in the sense that it was not known to civilised man until 1692 when the Bishop of Derry came across it. The following year a paper about its discovery was read to the Royal Society.

The Giant's Causeway is in Northern Ireland, right on the northern tip of the Antrim coast, about sixty miles north of Belfast. (Thackeray had come up from Dublin.) It is still a wild and sparsely-inhabited stretch of coastline, but in the seventeenth and eighteenth centuries the few local peasants were so fierce and inhospitable that strangers were unwilling to travel that far. It was in the nineteenth century that it became a tourist attraction, once the coast road was completed in 1834, and gentlemen like Thackeray could travel there in coaches, even though the peasants were still not exactly civilised.

The attraction of the Causeway was part of that general fascination for the Romantic and the Picturesque which affected so many poets and artists of the day as they saw in such natural wonders a spiritual communion with God. So off they went on Grand Tours, ticking off each wondrous sight. Boswell tried to get Dr Johnson to go, but he refused. He said that the Causeway was no doubt worth seeing, but it was 'not worth going to see'.

It also fascinated architects who were enthralled and amazed that any landscape should contain such strange yet exact shapes, and the phrase 'natural architecture' first came into use. It led to the notion that perhaps the original inspiration for all architecture had been derived from natural forms.

Most of all, of course, it excited the geologists. In this short stretch of rocky coast, about five or six miles long, there are so many strange rock formations, apart from the most celebrated chunk, the so-called Giant's Causeway, with examples of almost every known rock formation, from every epoch. It is a textbook in stone.

It all began sixty million years ago when the area was being subjected to intense volcanic activity. There were no towering Etnas in Antrim but a series of gentler eruptions as molten rock was forced up through fissures in the limestone. It was in the cooling-down operation, apparently, that strange things happened. The lava flow which came out, composed of basalt, turned itself into hexagonal columns as it slowly cooled. Old geologists used to call this the 'starch trap'. Those who have watched starch cooling in a basin will know that, as it dries, the surface cracks into hexagonal shapes.

There are many different arrangements and shapes amongst these columns,

The Causeway coast.

up on the rocky cliffs as well as down upon the shore itself. It was the early guides, competing with one another to flaunt their knowledge, and fleece the innocent trippers, who made up the names which many of the rock formations still have, such as the Organ, the Wishing Chair, Chimney Tops, the Giant's Pot Lid, the Coffin, the Giant's Causeway.

The Giant who supposedly built the Causeway, which consists of a low terrace of these hexagonal shapes, flat enough to walk over, is said to have been the legendary Irish giant, Finn McCool. He wanted stepping stones so that he could walk over the ocean and keep his feet dry when he went to fight the legendary Scottish giant, Benadonner. (In some variations of this legend, he just stood and shouted at him.) The Scottish giant was living just eighty miles away, on the Island of Staffa, in Fingal's Cave – an area which has similar rocky formations.

Fingal's Cave was discovered later than the Giant's Causeway, by Sir Joseph Banks, the Old Etonian who became President of the Royal Society, on a cruise of exploration in 1772. "Compared to this what are the cathedrals and palaces built by men! Where is now the boast of the architect!"

Most nineteenth-century travellers, not just Thackeray, recorded the wildness of the Causeway characters, and this was made worse by the building of two hotels which competed for customers, employing rival bands of guides.

By the end of the century, local people from Northern Ireland had also started to come in their thousands to see this wonder on their own doorstep, catching the train on day trips from Belfast to Portrush and then a little tram from Portrush to the Causeway, in itself one of the modern wonders of the world. The trams, built in 1883, ran along a little track and were powered by hydro-electricity, the first trams of their type in the world. They ran until 1949, by which time most people were coming in their petrol-driven engines, but are still today nostalgically remembered by many.

One of the hotels has now gone, and so have the rather horrid-looking shacks which the old ragged guides used between the Wars. On its site is a new car park and a rather tasteful tea room run by the National Trust. The Trust took over the Causeway coast in 1961 and it is one of their proudest possessions in the whole of the United Kingdom, beautifully and lovingly cared for. You might have seen it on the Post Office's 22p stamps in 1981.

There is now little need for guides, and the boats have all stopped. Instead, they have their own little exhibition centre in the tea room, and their own printed booklets. Today's public, anyway, prefers to discover places on its own.

I parked at the Causeway tea room, having driven myself up from Belfast Airport, a delightful route along empty and exceedingly straight roads. Since the Troubles, the tourist industry in Northern Ireland has taken something of a battering. If and when the present tragic situation is ever resolved, it will still take many decades to repair the damage that has been done to the image of the Ulster people and their beautiful country. The rest of the world has been fed on Belfast's bombs and burning cars for so long that it is unaware that Northern Ireland is still a green and pleasant land.

I arrived in some trepidation, worrying that I might stumble into far worse terrors that Thackeray's wild-eyed guides, but apart from the enormous military barriers at Belfast Airport, I saw no signs of the Troubles whatsoever throughout my journey to the Causeway and back, neither wreckage, barricades

An example of 'natural architecture': a gateway through a column of stones.

nor even slogans on the walls. It was only when I was posting some postcards home and had trouble using the letter-box, thinking it was out of use, that I realised that the slit had been deliberately narrowed. A precaution against letter bombs.

According to the Northern Ireland Tourist Board's figures, they were getting 1,139,000 tourists a year in the Province in 1968. This fell dramatically when the present Troubles began, dropping to 435,000 in 1972, their lowest figure ever.

Surprisingly, the tourists since then have been *increasing*. By 1980, the numbers had risen to 710,000 (this is outside visitors who spent seven nights or more in the province). They weren't expecting it to rise any higher for a while, as unemployment and the economic recession generally is hitting everyone's tourist trade.

The Causeway has always been one of Ulster's major attractions, coming fourth overall, after Crawfordsburn Country Park, Ulster Folk Museum and Tollymore Forest Park. Everyone who visits Ulster, or even Ireland as a whole, still wants to take it in. You don't pay to walk the Causeway, or look at all the geological wonders, but the National Trust estimates, from the cars which park, that around 150,000 visit the rocks every year.

The National Trust warden who looks after the Causeway coast is Desmond Milling, a tall, gentle man of sixty-six. He was born in Southern Ireland where his father was killed by the I.R.A. in 1918, and the family then moved to Ulster. He was an Army officer during the last war and then joined the Colonial Service, spending most of his time in Africa. He was invalided out in 1954 and joined the National Trust, after applying to them several times for various posts. He has fifteen National Trust properties along the coast to look after, but his major concern is the twelve-mile-long cliff path, the North Antrim Cliff Walk, which includes the Giant's Causeway and the adjoining bays.

He's very proud of the path, which he says is the finest cliff walk in Britain, but it entails constant work as the fences are attacked by the winter winds, landslides and passing vandals. Since the Troubles, he has noticed that far more youths appear to delight in wrecking fences and breaking lavatories, for no apparent reason. He points out all the time to visitors that the National Trust is not a Government concern, so any vandals will not be making any anti-authority gesture. The Trust is a private charity, open to all.

He walked down the first section of the path with me, from the tea house up on the top of the cliff to the first few bays. Unlike many cliff walks, there is a lower as well as an upper path for most of the way, with several connections, so it is possible to work out round walks, from anything up to four or five hours, without having to retrace your steps. All the way he enthused about the joys of the Causeway coast, especially when the sun suddenly came out, after a morning which had been dull and hazy.

"I get so depressed when visitors come for the first time and it's bad weather. They go away disappointed, and so do I. Now, in the sun, they go away glowing. You should see their faces when they see the colours. You didn't imagine, did you, that there would be so many? Look at those primroses. Have you ever seen such banks before? They cover that cliff completely. And look here, now, this is the first of the wild orchids. And what about these dog violets and the wild thrift?

"You forget the Troubles, and your own troubles, when you come here. There's something for everybody – geologists, botanists, ornithologists, walkers and just boys with their girl friends."

His own particular delight is the bird life and he has watched with fascination the arrival in recent years of the fulmar petrel. They appeared to me, at first sight, to be just big seagulls, but under his tutelage I could see the differences. Their deep croaking noises echoed round the cliffs and as I watched them circling overhead and then swooping down I could see why the locals call them 'wooden wings'. They are heavier than seagulls and float in the air rather stiffly, with their wings stuck out.

"They remind me of stocky little fly halves. Don't go near their nests. They spit at you. It's a most vile, evil-smelling liquid which you'll never get off

The Wishing Chair, an arrangement of stones which make a perfect seat.

your clothes. They were first recorded nesting here in 1912, yet now look at them. They only lay one egg at a time. How do they multiply so quickly? I'm not an expert, you see. Just an enthusiast. Look, there's a stone chat. And can you see those two eider ducks in the water? I hope we can find you a chough, perhaps a peregrine, or even a buzzard.

"I was coming down this path one day and I saw a peregrine hit a rock pigeon in mid-air. Smack. Right into it, like a bullet. There was a flurry of feathers and the pigeon started to fall, but the peregrine had wheeled round and swooped below and caught the pigeon with its talons, just before it hit the water, and then flew off with it. It was a most amazing sight."

He pointed out, just off the coast in the distance, a dark, mysterious-looking rock called Sheep Island. There are many islands off the Antrim coast, the biggest being Rathlin Island which has a population of about a hundred people, plus the cave where Robert the Bruce saw his spider. Sheep Island is much smaller and uninhabited and belongs to the Trust.

Mr Milling first went on it ten years ago to have a look at the puffins which breed there, and found they'd all gone. The island was covered in a mass of little holes and paths, but not a puffin in sight. On investigation he discovered that rats had systematically eaten all the puffin eggs and their young, and had completely taken over the island.

Over the next year he made several boat trips, taking cans and then buckets of poison, trying to get rid of them, but with no success. In the end, with the help of a Royal Marines helicopter, over thirty milk churns filled with Warfarin were dropped on the island and eventually the rats were removed. Last year, on his annual trip to the island, he found that puffins had returned and were breeding once more.

I caught my first sight of the Giant's Causeway from several hundred yards away, looking down from the cliff path. I have to admit that, if Mr Milling had not pointed it out, I might never have known. From a distance, it looks no more interesting than lumps of rocks you see on many beaches round the world. As we drew nearer I could see that it is an odd shape, like a rather gnarled alligator which has crawled on to the shore and collapsed.

It is only on close inspection that you really begin to wonder. Is it perhaps a gigantic hoax, a trick dreamt up by some of those devious old guides? Each hexagonal column looks completely man-made, chiselled out by the thousand by some stonemason's magical factory. They might even be made of concrete, judging by the basic colour which is cement grey.

Mr Milling was upset by my reference to cement and pointed out just how numerous were the shades and colours, most of them caused by lichen, sparkling and gleaming in the bright afternoon sun. There are reckoned to be 37,000 of these columns on the Causeway, most of them hexagonal but quite a few pentagonal, plus occasional ones which have four, seven and even eight sides. In the old days, guides would offer to take you to where they'd personally discovered a ten-sided column, for an extra consideration.

The columns on the Causeway itself are not very high, from about three to six feet. (There are much taller ones in the other bays.) It is the mass of them that is so remarkable, all packed together like a monster Aero bar, a magical honeycomb, a child's Lego set which has gone mad and started growing. By being so neatly piled together, in a mound stretching about 200 yards across, you can walk all over them. The taller columns, elsewhere, are high up on the cliff face and impossible to clamber over. The Giant's Causeway is one of Nature's Adventure Playgrounds.

We found the Wishing Chair, an arrangement of stones which appears to make a perfect seat, with the main stone well polished by the bottoms of thousands of visitors over the centuries. Perhaps millions. Before the Troubles, the Causeway received as many as 250,000 visitors a year.

On even closer inspection, something more remarkable can be seen. Each column is in fact in layers, separated by ball and socket joints. Where stones have come loose and lie around, you can see a slight hollow, where another stone has rested on top. They are all too heavy for even the strongest vandal to steal, but the guides in the old days used to chip bits off and carve shapes out of them, producing their souvenirs, or Irish 'diamonds', which is what they told Thackeray they were.

I continued along the cliff path to explore the other bays. There are thirteen bays in all, each with different and equally amazing rock structures, though many visitors still think, as Thackeray did, that the Causeway is all there is to be seen. Mr Milling is very pleased that half of today's visitors explore the other paths. When he first came, only a tenth of the visitors moved further afield than the Causeway.

In many places the cliff path is a deep, iron red, caused by the laterite content. When there has been any sort of fresh landslide, the path turns blood-red. Mr Milling reports any serious falls to the Trust's two workmen, who repair and clear the paths, though they tend to dismiss minor slips as 'just a few crumbs, Mr Milling, just a few crumbs'.

In the bay next to the Causeway, Port Noffer, the architectural highlight is the Organ. (It is so easy to fall into the habit of describing the rocks as 'architecture', but this is to praise nature for its cleverness, not to demean it.) The Organ is high up on the cliff face, a group of tall hexagonal columns, like the pipes of a giant organ, with the tallest pipes being a hundred feet high. Some are gently tilting, like the pipes of Pan, or the fingers of a fan, or the spume of Niagara Falls which has been brought to an abrupt halt and then frozen in time and space.

I stood chatting for a while to an English couple I met along the path, and we all exclaimed over the wonders. They were both from London, but not strictly holiday-makers. She was an actress, Anne Aston, who was in rep that week at the Riverside Theatre in Coleraine, just along the coast. Her companion had come along to help, but really have a holiday. They'd been out every day so far, exploring the coast, and couldn't get over the beauty of Antrim, having expected a deprived and decaying community.

"The audiences are so appreciative," she said. "Many English companies who've been booked to play in Northern Ireland have cancelled at the last moment which has been very disappointing for them, so we've been given a great welcome." She had been worried when they'd got lost one day in their car, and wandered thirty miles further than they'd anticipated, and came across a village near the Border with two burned-out cars. Apart from that, everything had been delightful. They would definitely come again to the Causeway for a real holiday, when the Troubles were over.

The next bay, Port Reostan, is in itself a wonder, as the cliffs on all sides are completely covered with basalt formations and form a giant open air concert hall. It is known locally as the Amphitheatre.

The Giant's Causeway: thousands of hexagonal stones, a magical honeycomb, all made by nature.

I stood on the little path, looking up at all the towering columns and weird shapes, with only the sea to lend a sense of reality, to let you know that you are not either in some subterranean cave or high in the clouds. It's as if God had commissioned all his best rock sculptors from all over the world, let them loose in this open air theatre, and told them to carve their most fantastical shapes. I found the Amphitheatre the most amazing and impressive sight on the whole Coast, far more so than the Giant's Causeway which by comparison is homely and tame. In wild weather, however, I suppose these strange bays must be frightening. Thackeray, when he at last escaped his guides and managed to wander round the bays, was convinced that he had come to the end, or perhaps the beginning, of the Universe.

Does the sun ever shine here? When the world was moulded and fashioned out of formless chaos, this must have been the *bit* over – a remnant of chaos.

Amidst these terrifying rocks, Thackeray found an old beggar woman and imagined that she had been there for centuries, since the Creation. On a closer look, he found she was selling sips of whisky.

How do you dare to sell whisky there, old woman? Did you serve old Saturn with a glass when he lay along the Causeway here? In reply, she says she has no change for a shilling. She never has. But her whisky is good.

Then I met a large Irish family, mum and dad and young kids, plus two teenage boys who were struggling along in cumbersome motorbike gear, big leather boots and black leather jackets decorated with slogans saying 'Hell's Angels' and 'Los Angeles'. The parents were carrying a picnic and dad was promising the smaller children a drink, very soon, once they got on to the higher path. They said they came from Dundonald, just outside Belfast, and had a day trip, once a year, to look at the Causeway.

I was standing in the next bay, Port Na Spaniagh, looking out to sea, which was rapidly changing colour, going through all the shades of blue and green as I watched, reflecting the changing sun, when over the high rocks behind me whirred a massive helicopter. I thought for a moment it was a giant buzzard, as I'd been told by Mr Milling to look out for them, but it was an R.A.F. helicopter, with the number 65 on its belly. It circled round the Causeway several times. Surely there could be no terrorist lurking there. Perhaps it was a new commanding officer, being shown the local sights. Then it whirled off in the direction of Coleraine and I started to explore Port Na Spaniagh, a bay with a very interesting name and some historic connections.

Thackeray thought that the Spanish stories he had been told by his guides in 1842 were a load of rubbish. "A parcel of legends from the mouths of simple peasants," so he wrote, "a dullard who narrates them at the rate of sixpence a lie."

In 1968, a legend which had been kept alive for almost 400 years came true when the Belgian nautical archæologist, Robert Sténuit, brought from the waters of Port Na Spaniagh bay a treasure trove of guns, cannon balls, jewels, medals, ingots, silver, gold ornaments and coins. They had all come from the wreck of the biggest ship in the Spanish Armada, the galleass *Girona*. (A galleass combined the fire power of a galleon with the speed of an oared galley.)

The ship had been in trouble elsewhere along the Irish coast, where it had

One of the many bays along the Causeway Coast, each with strange rock formations, like mountains carved out of crystals.

fled after the Armada, but been successfully repaired. On October 27, 1588, it was in full sail, set to return to Spain with 1,300 men on board, although the vessel had been built for only 550, under the command of Don Alonso de Leiva, one of the most distinguished of the Armada commanders. She sank a few hundred yards off shore, after hitting a 'cruel talon of rock', so Robert Sténuit put it, just at the entrance to the bay which was later called Port Na Spaniagh. Had she mistaken some basalt columns, known as the Chimney Tops, for a real building, perhaps Dunseverick Castle? This castle is only four miles further on, beside a safe and sandy beach, Whitepark Bay. No one knows. She sank at once. Out of the 1,300 men on board, only five survived.

The finding of such historic items was a story that went round the world. They were eventually bought for the agreed price of £132,000 by the Ulster Museum in Belfast, where they are on show today. There may have been more Armada treasures washed up at the time, but they have long since disappeared. It is said that a favourite Irish prayer used to be: "May God be good and send a shipwreck."

The cliff path eventually comes out just past Dunseverick Castle, which is now a ruin, with only two walls standing, where the scenery changes and becomes lush and rather affluent, with smart-looking farm houses and rich fields. I admired a little harbour called Port Braddon, with four pretty white-washed cottages and some almost tropical-looking flowers and trees. The Causeway coast proper has no trees. If Thackeray had got this far perhaps he would not have wished he was back safe in his own home.

> There is that in nature which passes even our powers. We can feel the beauty of a magnificent landscape perhaps, but we can describe a leg of mutton and turnips better. Well, I am a Cockney. I wish I were in Pall Mall!

I retraced my steps back to the tea house, above the Causeway, and just as I was buying postcards, and examining the National Trust's little exhibitions of rocks and bird life, a rather strange Irish gentleman came up to me and whispered in my ear. He was carrying a paper carrier bag and had obviously had a glass of two of whisky.

"Would you like to come and see the Wishing Chair, sir. I can also show you the Organ. Even the Coffin, sir. Yes, sir, I can even show you the Coffin."

I explained that I had finished my sightseeing, thank you very much. I'd already walked the Causeway and the Bays. Very nice. He wasn't so easily dissuaded, so we sat on the steps of the tea house and had a chat. He said he was called Alex Martin and that he was sixty-four but I could call him the King of the Causeway. "Everyone calls me that, sir. I was born on the Causeway, sir, sixty-four years ago, sir."

That's funny, I said. I hadn't noticed a maternity hospital down there, or even a house, not amongst all those cruel talons of jagged rocks.

"I can tell you this, sir," he said, clicking his fingers which he did regularly all the time he talked, as if jogging his memory, leaning confidentially into my left ear. "There *used* to be a cottage down there, sir. That's where I was born. King of the Causeway. I've been on the television you know, sir. You can go ahead. Call me the King of the Causeway."

He said he hadn't got a job but he was always willing to help anyone.

"Just as long as there's an odd pound in it, sir." The previous day he had attached himself to five English motor cyclists, in Northern Ireland for some race, whom he'd met wandering round the Causeway. He'd guided them all day, then shown them various hostelries till two in the morning. "They were very good to me, sir. And now what about the Organ, sir? I can show you where that is. Even the Coffin."

He was not at all hectoring or aggressive, like the self-appointed guides who had captured Thackeray, but had adopted a courteous, gently persuasive manner. One felt rather privileged to have been chosen for his confidences, and of course his great wisdom and personal knowledge of the Causeway. All the same, I declined another walk over the rocks.

"Would you like to see my shop, Sir?" I agreed to see his shop and I stood up, expecting to walk to his establishment, but he told me to stay seated. He picked up his carrier bag which he had lain on the floor beside him during our chat. He opened it with great ceremony and brought out various bundles wrapped in greaseproof paper. Inside were bits of stones, carved in the shape of the Wishing Chair, and some sticks which he'd varnished and tied with a green ribbon. Along the side of the sticks was rather blotchily painted the word 'Shillelagh'.

I said I already had too many souvenirs to carry on the plane back to London. "No, no, they're *specimens*, not souvenirs, sir. All genuine specimens from the Causeway." I asked if my friend Mr Herrmann could take his photograph, and naturally there would be a few pounds for his trouble, and he graciously agreed.

Thackeray did little drawings all the way through his *Irish Sketch Book*, making the local beggars and guides look distinctly unsavoury, but in our photograph of the King of the Causeway he looks rather distinguished, don't you think, smart and quite well-dressed, even artistic, with a fleeting resemblance to Samuel Beckett. Business can't be that bad on the Giant's Causeway these days, despite all the Troubles.

Above: *The self styled King of the Causeway, Alex Martin.*

Right: *Sunset over the Giant's Causeway.*

14 Hardy's Wessex

LITERARY Britain is one of our great invisible exports. Some invisible exporters, invisible in the sense that they have no concrete product, no factory you can point to where the stuff is actually made, do bring in a lot of real money, like the Stock Exchange, even though they are simply providing a service, trading in bits of paper.

When bits of paper go out round the world from Literary Britain, the immediate effect is mental and emotional. Not a lot of hard cash is generated by the hundreds of thousands of schoolchildren and students who are at this moment sitting in some foreign land studying Shakespeare, or Dickens, the Brontës, Wordsworth or D. H. Lawrence. One hopes the result is not heavy boredom, and a lifetime's antipathy to the English language, but some successful intellectual flag-waving for the British way of life.

Many of these people, as adults, do decide that they will come to Britain, just to look at Shakespeare's Stratford, Dickens's London, the Brontës' Yorkshire, Wordsworth's Lake District, and the result is then apparent over the counter. An invisible export becomes real.

The statue of Thomas Hardy in Dorchester, unveiled by Sir James Barrie in 1931.

One of the more surprising of our literary exports in recent years has become Hardy's Wessex. Surprising, because there is no such place on any Ordnance Survey map as Wessex and because Hardy, the writer, has always struck many British people as rather dull and heavy. Could it just be the result of all those glamorous films and T.V. productions?

He does appear to have become very fashionable amongst our own students, even more than D. H. Lawrence. In 1980, Antonia Byatt, the novelist and lecturer in English at University College, London, did a survey of the reading habits of 500 prospective English undergraduates. Counting up the mentions for individual writers, Hardy was top with 194. After him came Jane Austen 165, D. H. Lawrence 158, Dickens 124, the Brontës 106, Orwell 105, George Eliot 69, James Joyce 66, Graham Greene 65, Evelyn Waugh 62.

Ah well, you say, he is bound to be popular with English students. But I have in front of me a report by Mamoru Osawa, a Japanese Professor of English Literature, about the Japanese Hardy Society which was founded in 1957. In it, I discovered that Hardy has been studied in Japan since 1890, when reading circles were first set up to discuss his work. This was before *Tess of the d'Urbervilles* was published.

When they got round to establishing the official Hardy Society, in 1957, there was a total of 1,614 items of Japanese Hardyana. That means published books, articles and theses, written in Japanese, all about Hardy. It is now quite common to find professional Hardy scholars in Japan who devote themselves full-time to such things as the study of the Dorset dialects of the nineteenth century, or the problems of Wessex husbandry.

The first and obvious sign of the success of the present-day Hardy industry, back here in England, is that suddenly you find the name Wessex appearing all over the place. The regional tourist boards and planning people now stick the term Wessex on their publicity maps and literature, and hotels and resorts boast they are in Wessex. It is assumed that most people are familiar with the term and that they will know where it is, well, give or take a few hundred miles.

Basically, Wessex is Dorset. Hardy Country is taken to be an area of about fifty miles across, centred on Dorchester. Hardy was writing about his native Dorset, but called it Wessex to spare too many blushes, though pushing out the county boundaries when it suited him. It was of course the name for an ancient region of England, though one defunct since Anglo-Saxon times. After centuries, it is now understood by everyone. Try saying you had a holiday in Mercia and see how people react.

Thomas Hardy was born in Higher Bockhampton near Dorchester on June 2, 1840. His father was a self-employed stonemason and builder, just as his father had been before him. Their family home, which had been built by the grandfather in 1800, was a simple, thatched cottage with cob or mud walls, about three miles outside Dorchester in rather wild, isolated heathland. The family was humble but not impoverished, with a tradition that in times past they had had a higher social station. Hardy was very interested in his own pedigree and was pleased to think the family was descended from the Le Hardys of Jersey and that Admiral Sir Thomas Masterman Hardy, captain of Nelson's *Victory* at Trafalgar ('Kiss me, Hardy'), had been a relation.

He went to a local village school and then to school in the town of Dorchester which he left at sixteen to become articled to a Dorchester architect, John Hicks, who specialised in church restorations. He continued to live at home, still basically a country boy, playing the fiddle in church, just as his father and grandfather had done before him. His two other teenage interests were Greek, which he was teaching himself, and girls, whom he admired from afar, almost obsessively, but without much success. He was small, shy and

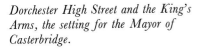

Dorchester High Street and the King's Arms, the setting for the Mayor of Casterbridge.

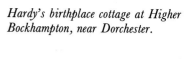

Hardy's birthplace cottage at Higher Bockhampton, near Dorchester.

introverted and had a dislike of being touched. He watched girls when he was in church sitting in his pew, in the street, or at dances when he was playing his fiddle, and romanticised over what would happen if ever he really got to know them. He once witnessed a public execution in Dorchester of a woman who had murdered her husband, and his memory later was of how well her body had looked in its gown, silhouetted against the sky, as it swung from left to right.

An older pupil in the architect's office used to tell him tales of life in London, doing little dances round his desk, humming a quadrille which he'd heard in one of the London dance halls. The tune stayed in Hardy's head, but he was unable to find its name. In 1862, he decided he would move to London, getting work with a firm of architects at Adelphi Terrace, beside the Thames, where he remained for the next six years. He failed to track down the dance tune, despite going round all the dance halls, nor did he make any serious relationships with any young ladies, as far as is known. It sounds a rather melancholy period in his life, alone in the Big City, with his strong Dorset accent and country ways, having few friends and his health beginning to suffer from the London smog in the winter and the stench from the Thames in the summer beneath his office window.

He came back to his old firm in Dorchester in 1867 and to his parents' home at Higher Bockhampton, now a confirmed agnostic, having been brought up Church of England, and with a longing to write. He'd already written some poetry for his own amusement, but without any success, and now thought he would try fiction, though architecture was still his full-time profession, and only conceivable means of earning a living.

His first attempt was turned down by Macmillans but his second novel, *Desperate Remedies*, was eventually published by another firm in 1871, though he had to pay them a guarantee of £75 against any losses. In the end, he got only £60 of his money back. He'd tried to write what he thought the public of the time might want, a rather lurid crime novel, with unbelievable characters and plot, and it was poorly received.

In 1872, sitting at his bedroom window, back home in his own family cottage, he conceived *Under the Greenwood Tree*, writing this time about people and feelings and countryside he knew at first hand, setting it amongst the fields he could see from his window and about village people he remembered from his childhood. It had a simple, uncomplicated love story, with a sub-plot about the church choir and orchestra.

Hardy's cottage is still much as it was, with the thatch intact, though the basic mud core walls now have a covering of brick. You are not allowed to drive up to the cottage but have a ten-minute walk through a path in the woods, which makes a charming arrival, though a trifle muddy if the weather is wet.

It was bought by the National Trust in 1948 who have an excellent, and erudite, tenant, Anne Winchcombe. The cottage is open to the public from April to October each year and you can inspect the interior, as long as you make an appointment first.

Mrs Winchcombe is against anything that smacks of commercialisation, which is why she prefers to have an appointments system. That way, she says, over ninety percent of the visitors to the cottage are Hardy-lovers. You get very few people simply coming in out of the rain. By comparison, Shakespeare's Stratford is like Blackpool. "Naturally, if someone hasn't booked and says they have come all the way from Utah and it's their life's ambition to see Hardy's cottage, then I wouldn't be so rude as to turn them away."

I did ask to buy a Thomas Hardy biro, when mine ran out, thinking they would sell that sort of discreet little souvenir, but she was rather shocked at the thought. All they do is sell Hardy texts, cards and booklets. Their space, she says, is limited. They don't even stock a certain two-volume biography of Hardy, recently published to good reviews in the serious papers and written by a distinguished author. Some Hardy lovers, apparently, consider it has a slanted view of Hardy's personality.

Mrs Winchcombe is Scottish by descent, took a degree in English at Cambridge, and has written a couple of novels and worked for a time for

Melbury Osmond, known as Great Hintock in 'The Woodlanders'.

the B.B.C. She took over the tenancy in 1970, having seen the house advertised. She and her late husband decided it would make a suitable spot for retirement.

Roughly half of the annual 12,000 visitors are from abroad, mainly from Japan and America. The Americans, she says, love Hardy's minute descriptions of nature and accept Dorset as being part of their own country. The Japanese love the tragedy in Hardy. She took me to a corner and pulled out copies of Hardy in various foreign languages – a Japanese *Under the Greenwood Tree*, a Greek *Mayor of Casterbridge*, a Korean *Tess of the d'Urbervilles*.

None of the furniture or possessions in the house belonged to the Hardy family, which is a slight disappointment. They had all gone by the time the National Trust arrived. But the present furnishings are of the correct period, many of them, such as the grandfather clock, donated by Hardy-lovers.

She took me upstairs to the room in which Hardy was born. As all Hardy-lovers know, the doctor who delivered his mother put the baby aside, leaving him on a window-sill, believing him to be still-born. It was only the quickness of the nurse in attendance, who noticed the baby was breathing, which saved his life. There's another oft-quoted incident a few months later when his mother came in from the garden one hot afternoon and found him asleep in his cradle with a large snake curled upon his chest. One can well understand Hardy's belief that tragedy was never far round the corner.

A double bed is still set in the birth-room but there are two window-sills, one either side (the house is very narrow and the three rooms upstairs are the width of the house), and Mrs Winchcombe didn't know which one he'd been dumped on and left for dead. But in his own smaller bedroom, next door, there is only one window, so this is without doubt where he sat and wrote *Under the Greenwood Tree*. I examined the sill carefully, but found it a bit low to sit at in comfort. Hardy was only five feet five inches high, so perhaps he found it easier. Outside, I could see the greenwood trees and in the distance, around ten miles away, there was a statue on a hill. Mrs Winchcombe said it was Blagdon Hill. By a nice coincidence, the statue is of his famous if distant relative, Admiral Hardy.

Under the Greenwood Tree was published in 1872 and this time it earned him some money, though not much, as he was paid just £30 for the copyright. The following year he was asked by Leslie Stephen, editor of the *Cornhill* magazine, to write a new novel which he would publish in parts as a serial. The commissioning letter, which was to change his life, almost never reached him. It was entrusted to some local children, on its route from Dorchester to his cottage three miles away, who dropped it in some mud and lost it. But for the sharp eye of a farm labourer who happened to be passing that way and saw it lying in the mud, Hardy might never have received it. The novel which resulted was *Far from the Madding Crowd* and it was the first of his books to bring him national recognition.

Not long afterwards, he married Emma Lavinia Gifford, having courted her for some four years. He'd had girl friends before her, for instance two of his cousins, but nothing had ever come of the relationships. He'd met Emma when his employer asked him to go down to Cornwall to look at a church on which some restoration work had to be done. He refused at first, not wanting to go all that way on what sounded a rather boring job.

On March 7, 1870, a day he never forgot, he arrived at this remote church, after a long train journey and a sixteen-mile ride by horse and cart, still wishing

Melbury Bubb Church in the Blackmore Vale, a favourite walking place for Hardy.

he'd stayed at home and got on with his writing, to be greeted at the door of the vicarage by a young lady in brown. The vicar was ill in bed. She said she was his sister-in-law and offered to show him round the church while he made his plans and drawings of the work to be done. He had some papers sticking out of his pocket, which she presumed to be architectural drawings, but on their tour she was delighted to find it was a poem he'd been working on.

They were both, on this first meeting, nearly thirty years old. Emma was from a genteel middle-class, clerical family, but her hopes of an interesting husband must have by then appeared slight. Hardy's own background was more artisan, but he was an architect, with the glamour of a London training, and the added attraction of wanting to be a writer. It was as much a surprise to her, stuck away in remotest Cornwall, to open the door to such an exciting stranger, as it was to him. He stayed several days, spinning out his drawings, and they had long walks on the cliffs and sea shore and into the nearby little town of Boscastle. It was a most romantic courtship, in beautiful surroundings.

Four years later, he was able to give up architecture, thanks to the success of *Far from the Madding Crowd*, and this doubtless made him think he was now secure enough to be married. For the first ten years of their marriage they moved around like gypsies, partly in London, but mainly in Wessex, in a series of rented houses, both on the coast and inland, all the time turning out more novels, till eventually Hardy designed a large house for himself in Dorchester, Max Gate. It was built for him by his younger brother Henry, who had followed their father into the building trade. Thomas and Emma moved into Max Gate in 1885 and lived there for the rest of their lives.

By this time, alas, their marriage had become little more than a shell. Neither took another partner, though Hardy's interest in a series of young, beautiful and talented ladies had caused Emma to grow jealous and withdrawn. He conducted long relationships with actresses who appeared in stage adaptations of his novels, or with young ladies who illustrated his books, but all of them were apparently platonic. Even his recent biographer failed to prove any sexual liaisons, though he gave a few mild hints.

Emma and Thomas lived separate lives in their big new house, not speaking to each other, though keeping up appearances when entertaining the quality, which included most of the contemporary great names as Hardy became a national figure, perhaps the most respected writer in his day England has ever known.

One of their local neighbours was T. E. Lawrence who often popped in to see Hardy. When later his exploits with the Arabs were all over the newspapers, Mrs Hardy was asked what she thought of him. She said she was surprised. She had always considered him the sort of man who was useful to have around when the blinds got stuck.

The breakdown of Hardy's marriage to Emma is well attested, clearly evident in their private letters, and even Mrs Winchcombe in her little monogram on Hardy, *A Wayfarer*, writes of the 'tensions', but she offers few explanations. "I think Emma was rather eccentric. It ran in her family. And as the marriage went on, they also began to differ on matters of morality and religion."

In *Far from the Madding Crowd* Hardy wrote that 'all romance ends at marriage', something he appears to have believed in his own case. This greatly

Hardy country: looking south from Suttonpoyntz, a setting used for 'The Trumpet–Major.'

upset Emma, having such things made public, even if it was supposedly in a work of fiction. But it was *Jude the Obscure* in 1894 which is thought to have bought their marriage finally to a standstill. She considered it too autobiographical, especially her husband's pessimistic attitude to marriage, and she called it 'Jude the Obscene'. She tried to stop its publication, even going up to London to bring pressure on literary friends. It had to be expurgated in the serial version, as it was thought too strong for the times, and on publication in book form it was roundly condemned by the Bishop of Wakefield who threw his copy in the fire.

The general reaction to *Jude* made Hardy give up writing novels. He was greatly depressed by the criticism, unable to see why people could not face or believe his form of rural realism, knowing he could have described much more sordid yet true stories of country life. He was at the height of his international acclaim, with his books being quickly translated and read abroad, from those writing circles in Japan to America. *Tess of the d'Urbervilles*, the novel before *Jude*, had even been serialised in a Moscow magazine at the same time as it was being published in London and was admired by Tolstoy. From then on, till the end of his life, Hardy devoted himself to poetry.

Emma died in 1912 at Max Gate and two strange things happened. Although he had ignored Emma for so long and had grown to regret his marriage, he was suddenly filled with terrible remorse and guilt that he had treated her so badly, ignoring her own illnesses and loneliness, thinking only of his own work and pleasures. His mind went back to that romantic first meeting in Cornwall, and their early passionate years, and he started writing some beautiful love poems, some of the most moving ever written about married love.

Then, just fourteen months after the death of Emma, he married Florence Dugdale, a lady some forty years younger than himself who had been working as his secretary. For the first three years of their association he had kept her secret from Emma, though they had eventually become close friends and it would appear Florence felt sorry for Hardy's treatment of Emma. Hardy's continued obsession with the memory of his lost love for Emma made his marriage to Florence far from happy as she was dragged round the houses and scenes of his first courtship, over forty years previously.

The story of Hardy's personal life is intriguing rather than dramatic. Compared with the lives of many writers it was decidedly dull. Even Wordsworth had an illegitimate child. Walter Scott suffered a spectacular bankruptcy. Dickens had several affairs. Thackeray's wife went insane. Oscar Wilde was put in gaol. Coleridge was on drugs. Keats and Shelley had tragic ends, and Byron's whole life was a scandal.

There was something faintly dried up about Hardy as a person, though his admirers can point to examples of his love of young people. His nature was melancholy and fatalistic. He had no children, from either marriage, and his blood line has finished. Neither his younger brother Henry, who became the builder, nor his two sisters Mary and Kate, who became teachers, ever married. It is almost as if those portents at his birth finally came true.

But those thousands of Hardy fans round the world like him for his work, not for his person. It is precisely his pessimistic approach to life, which comes through in his major novels, that proves to be one of his attractions. The tragedies and deaths, with the rural characters of Wessex looking on like a

Woolbridge Manor beside the River Frome where Tess of the D'Urbervilles had her honeymoon.

Greek chorus, while the heroes and heroines come to grief, have a wide appeal. In Japan, apparently, judging by the many learned books about him, they even see in him reflections of Buddha and carefully analyse 'the Buddhist outlook underlying Hardy's renunciative tone of thought'.

Most of all, it is his description of nature and country life which gives such pleasure. He is by far the most topographical novelist there's ever been in the English language, confining his novels to that little fifty-mile stretch of Dorset. Every place he mentions can be easily identified, even when he changed the names of towns and villages, such as Casterbridge for Dorchester, Upper Mellstock for Higher Bockhampton.

This is a bonus for all Hardy fans as it is so easy to organise marvellous tours of Hardy country, either on foot or by car. By car, you can get round the whole circuit in a day, armed with the many pamphlets on sale at Hardy Cottage, and elsewhere, which take each of the major novels and exactly locates the scenes and places. You've read the book, now see the original.

The film and T.V. adaptations of Hardy's novels owe a lot of their success to having such strong rural characters and dramatic events, and to the use of authentic locations. *Far from the Madding Crowd*, John Schlesinger's film, might have taken a few liberties with the characters, but it was a marvellous film to *look* at. Roman Polanski's *Tess* in 1981, the most recent Hardy film, was completely faithful to the book, and to the Wessex accents, despite being shot in France. Perhaps the most popular adaptation in recent years was the B.B.C.'s *The Mayor of Casterbridge*. They used the village of Corfe for the major scenes, not Dorchester, as it was easier to block off the traffic, though Corfe does appear in many of the books.

I went into Dorchester to have a look at the heart of Hardy land, crossing Grey's bridge over the River Frome, near where Henchard (the Mayor of

Casterbridge) contemplated suicide, and then up the main street to the statue of Hardy unveiled in 1931 by Sir James Barrie. It was turning slightly green and Hardy's head, which makes him look like Clement Attlee, seemed a bit small for his body, but it is a fine statue with an imposing situation and every year on his birthday, June 2, the Thomas Hardy Society (G.B. branch) lays a wreath and organises a lecture.

Going back down the main street, I went into the Dorset County Museum which for lovers of Hardy is probably next in importance to the birth cottage. This is where many manuscripts and Hardy memorabilia are kept. It is an amazing building, recently refurbished and the winner of several awards, and is worth a visit just for its architecture. It was built as a museum in 1883 by the local architect Crickmay. (Hardy worked with Crickmay and it was he who sent Hardy down to Cornwall on the church job.) The main feature is an enormous cast-iron hall with a mosaic floor, brilliantly lit from above by natural light, which is like a highly ornate Victorian Railway station.

At one end, they've re-created Hardy's study at Max Gate which you can peer into through a large plate-glass window. His books are all there on the shelves, his cloak and hat hanging up, his magnifying glass and pens at the ready (one pen has the word 'Jude' scratched on it), and his violin waiting to be played in the corner. On his desk is a wooden calendar, turned to Monday, March 7.

I had arrived late in the day and the caretaker was soon jangling his keys, waiting for me to leave. I asked him if the date had any meaning, or was it just a random date, left by the last person who had turned the little wooden knobs? He didn't know. He wasn't personally interested in Hardy, though he couldn't get over the scores of American and Japanese visitors who were. "They're more took up than what our English people is. They're full of it."

St Peter's Church, Dorchester's oldest church, is just a few doors down the street. The Rector in 1606 was the Rev. John White, later the founder of the Colony of Massachusetts in New England, who is buried in the porch. I opened the church door and was greeted by the sound of organ music and by an old tramp, who'd been asleep in a back pew, who came up and asked in rather slurred but very posh tones if he could help me. I said I was looking for a drawing of the church, done in Hardy's hand, which was supposed to be on one of the walls. He'd obviously never heard of it, but he followed me round as I searched, offering to find me a nice hotel, a nice place for a drink, and I thought for a moment I was back on the Giant's Causeway, but I declined his kindness.

I found the drawing inside a chapel in the south aisle, framed and hanging on a wall, beside the effigies of two knights. Hardy had drawn it while learning the business of church restoration in Dorchester. It is dated August 4, 1856, so he must have been just sixteen at the time. It was probably one of the first architectural duties he was given.

Further down the street I went into the King's Arms Hotel, made famous by *The Mayor of Casterbridge*. This was where Henchard, the Mayor, had many of his meetings and banquets, all carefully re-created in the T.V. serial. I asked a lady at the reception desk if there were any Hardy mementoes.

"There's the Casterbridge Room and the Hardy Room upstairs," she said. "Japanese gentlemen are always writing to book the bedroom above the Casterbridge room, saying they'll pay any price, just as long as they can sleep

Overleaf: Sturminster Newton, the view from a house where Hardy and Emma lived when they were first married.

Left: *A gentleman on a road north of Dorchester collecting food for his rabbit, a left-over from the world of Hardy.*

there. It's number 18. Sorry, it's occupied just now, so you can't see it. Personally, I couldn't sleep there. It's a beautiful room, but right over the street and very noisy.

"I think you either like Hardy or you don't. I don't. I'm a short cutter and I don't like all those long descriptions. Bit boring I think and he sounds a sour character. The T.V. crew stayed when they were filming, which was nice. Actually, we've got very strong connections with Queen Victoria. She stayed here in the stage coach days. Would you like to ..."

I went up the stairs to their Hardy Room which was small and sparsely furnished and obviously used as the residents' T.V. lounge. Next door the Casterbridge Room was bigger and more handsome with enormous bow windows overlooking the street. It is used for private functions, as it was in Hardy's day, and modern equivalents of Henchard's banquets still go on.

I stopped for a coffee at a snack bar in South Street, on the way to the railway station, without realising, till I saw a plaque, that this was the site of the architect's firm where Hardy had worked for so long. It's called Terry's Café and Terry himself was busy frying hamburgers and chips but said hold on a moment, and he'd take me down into the basement. Hardy worked here from 1850–62 and, although the ground floor café part has changed somewhat, the basement and upper floors are much the same as they were, with bare brick walls.

"There's an American who comes in every evening," said Terry. "He's been here for two years, doing research on Hardy the Architect. He *always* eats here. Would you like a meal?" I said I was sorry, I had another appointment. "Oh well, some other time. He's just heard he's got his grant renewed for another two years, so at least he'll be coming back ..."

My last visit was to Stinsford, Hardy's Mellstock, to the church where he worshipped as a boy and where his family played the violin. Hardy's mother Jemima, to whom he was devoted, and who was a strong influence on his life, always said she had first seen her husband when he had played in the little church orchestra. They had fallen in love at first hearing, not just first sight.

Hardy died on January 10, 1928, at Max Gate, the house he had built. Like the cottage, it is owned by the National Trust, but let to a private tenant and not open to the public. Hardy had always said he wanted to be buried in Stinsford Church, along with his parents, but Florence, his young widow, bowed to pressure and allowed his body to be buried in Westminster Abbey where it now lies, next to Dickens, not far from Tennyson and Dr Johnson.

However, to keep to the spirit of Hardy's wishes, his heart was removed from his body and buried at Stinsford Church, in the same tomb as his two wives, with Emma on the left and Florence on the right. The graves of his Hardy forebears are all around him. Recently, they have been joined by another English poet, Cecil Day Lewis.

On the way home I thought how apt it was. His body resides securely in our capital city, but his heart will lie for ever in Wessex. It also struck me at last why that calendar in his re-created study should be turned permanently to Monday, March 7. That was the day, back in 1870, when he first met Emma. After her death, he kept the calendar at that date for the rest of his life. A fictional-sounding fact, which all true Hardy-lovers will immediately spot when they visit Hardy country.

15 The Derby

AND SO to Epsom to watch the Derby. People who know nothing about horses or gambling put a bet on the Derby and the Grand National every year and their life pauses for a moment, then they forget all about racing for another year. But their memories live on, often passed through families, of the year a long-forgotten horse won the Derby, or nearly won the Derby, or they nearly put a bet on a horse which nearly won the Derby. People can date years by their Derby fancy, remembering it was the same year they got married, or had that holiday, or gave birth.

The Derby is traditionally one of the classic races, though I'm not sure what that means, knowing nothing about horses and never having been to the Derby before, or to any other race course. It's a race for the world's best thoroughbreds, so that naturally makes it classic. The classiest horses with the best form usually do well in the Derby, whereas the Grand National, being longer and over fences, not on the flat, can often be a lottery.

It's also a classic race because it's gone on for so long. It celebrated 200 years of unbroken history in 1979, and shows every sign of managing another 200 years. It's now part of the language, part of our culture, part of our heritage. It has inspired the works of artists like Stubbs, Frith, Degas, Munnings. Dickens was a regular attender and Derby scenes have been used in countless books, plays, musicals and films.

The first Derby was held in 1780 and took its name from Edward Stanley, the 12th Earl of Derby. The field is always limited to three-year-old colts and fillies who race over a 1½-mile (2,400 metres) course. The name 'Derby' has been borrowed by many other big race meetings round the world, so that there are the Irish Derby, the Japan Derby and the Kentucky Derby. It has even infiltrated other sports and any keenly contested occasion, such as a football game between two rival teams, is known as a 'Derby'.

In the world of racing it still reigns supreme, attracting the biggest crowds for any race and providing rich prizes for the owners. The prize money that day, according to the programme, was going to be £129,060 for the winner, £53,314 for the second, £25,876 for third and £11,894 for fourth. The breeding value of any horse winning the Derby is at once astronomical, making the prize money seem almost incidental.

Epsom is in suburban Surrey, executive commuter country on the edges of real countryside, just seventeen miles from Central London. The Epsom Downs, where the race has always been held, are common land. This provides one of the many unique features about the Derby – you don't have to pay to see it. Anyone can picnic for free, right beside the finishing stretch, though you have to be there very bright and early indeed to get a place. Naturally, the Grandstand and other enclosed bits require entrance fees, but the vast

Culture clash at the Derby.

majority of people who attend the Derby pay nothing. According to the radio, as we drove down, 500,000 people were expected, with the bookmakers expecting to take £30 million in bets.

We eventually managed to park on a bit of grassland, quite near the Grandstand, tipping the attendant £2, which was what a traffic warden had suggested, out of the corner of his mouth, and put our little car beside a large black Daimler. A group of race-goers was getting out of the Daimler, all in the proper Derby gear of grey topper and tails, fussing over their hampers and champagne in the boot. They set off carrying the hampers by themselves, leaving the chauffeur to guard the car, his chamois leather immediately out, wiping away the dust.

Frank Herrmann and I were in ordinary summer clothes and felt sorry on such an incredibly hot and steamy day for the toffs in their heavy morning coats, but at the same time we were a bit worried about not being allowed in certain places. We had Grandstand and Paddock tickets, which don't require formal dress, but we hoped to insinuate ourselves into the other enclosures.

My first view of the 201st Derby was rather breath-taking. I managed to get across the track and climb up into the photographers' scaffolded stand by the red winning post. On the left, were the Grandstand buildings. On the right, the full extent of the Downs, already a human sea, a techni-coloured multi purpose fairground with stalls, open-top buses, bookies' stands, tents, pavilions, coaches and hundreds of thousands of half-naked people. Almost all of them seemed to be doing the same thing – eating. It was just after mid-day, and the cameramen were waiting for the procession down the track to the

The Royal Cavalcade arrives.

Grandstand of the Royal Party – but even they were obsessed by their stomachs, worrying about whether they could grab a hamburger and a coke, or would they get stuck on the other side of the track and miss the Royal arrival. Frank said really, what he fancied, but was there time, was jellied eels. Such decisions.

I could hear music down the track and in the distance the red-coated Band of the Welsh Guards was approaching in stately rhythm. I counted fifty-four of them, plus a gentleman in yellow in front. I felt sure one at least would collapse, under all that uniform and heavy bearskin, but they marched beneath us in perfect order. The turf was lushly green, no signs of grey or wear and tear which the rest of England's lawns were suffering from that hot June day.

In the far distance, towards Tattenham Corner, where the Royal Train had arrived exactly on time at 12.45, I could make out five large black beetles crawling down the track. The sounds of sporadic clapping, from either side of the track, preceded the first proper sight of the Royal cars. The clapping exploded like little bursts of gun-fire, carried towards us by the speed of sound and what little wind there was.

The Band below, who had been entertaining the crowd with *The Sound of Music* and *Oklahoma*, stopped in mid-tune and burst into a sprightly selection of Welsh airs, 'Men of Harlech' and 'The Ash Grove', just to let us, and Her Majesty, know their origins. An attendant jumped out of the first car, before it had come to a halt, raced round and opened the door on the Grandstand side, and out stepped the Queen and the Queen Mother. The Queen looked stern at first, in her yellow hat and matching yellow dress, with gloves

and a black handbag, but gave a genuine smile when the race officials came forward to greet her. The Queen Mother, as the country has come to expect, emerged smiling, looking round cheerfully and unaffectedly, obviously pleased to be there. She had a large purple hat which didn't quite match the lilac of her flowered dress and summer coat. She seemed incredibly sprightly and healthy. From her walk and general demeanour, she looked at a distance no older than the Queen. Below the Queen Mother's right knee was a large elastoplast. I hoped no photographer would be unkind enough to capture it.

There was at once some restrained clapping all round at the Royals' arrival, which continued politely for the emptying of the next four beetles which contained, amongst other notables, Princess Alexandra and her husband Angus Ogilvy, Prince and Princess Michael of Kent. They were more fashionably dressed, especially Princess Michael. The Queen and her mother are beyond fashion, preferring a dateless, strongly-coloured, garden fête style. It does at least make them very easy to spot.

Frank insisted on finding a tent and buying *two* tubs of jellied eels, now he'd got his first shot. I couldn't face such slimy things, so Frank ate mine as well. The queues in all the beer tents appeared to be turning manic, everyone pushing and struggling to get served, or to ward off the gypsies aggressively trying to pin lucky white heather on to any likely jacket. As so many men were now stripped to the waist, it was making life hard for the gypsies.

We then did a walk over the Downs, pushing our way through the lines of bookies, past the Pearly Queen, sandwich board men warning that Christ was Coming, and endless stalls offering palmistry, fortune-telling, cockles, whelks, mussels. Many of the stalls were being manned by Indians and Pakistanis, a new breed of traders to take advantage of the Derby crowds,

The Royal Party in the Paddock.

just as others have done in the last 201 years. They were selling carpets, rugs, jeans, dresses, vests and large cushions. Who on earth would want to go to the Derby and then lumber themselves with carpets or large cushions to carry home? Sun glasses at £1 each were selling briskly but girls' nighties, price £1.99, seemed to be sticking. A man selling toys was shouting that he would serve nobody over 118.

Beside the race track, sharing the best views with the bookies, were some strange-looking chopped-off buses. About a hundred of them take up these traditional places every year, providing a sight which has hardly altered in 200 years. In the old days, it was open-top horse carriages.

All of them appeared to be taken over by works parties, office and factory clubs who had organised themselves for the day, hiring the bus and outside caterers. Their food was every bit as lavish as the top-hatted fare due to be eaten across the track in the Grandstand boxes. Tables were being prepared in and round each coach, laden with huge hams, roast beef and salads. One bus contained an enormous fresh salmon, artistically decorated. In each bus, the bar took up almost as much space and every sort of drink was being lined up for the thirsty punters, with the whisky and gin bottles being professionally fixed to the measuring taps. There wasn't much champagne to be seen, the traditional Derby drink for the toffs, but a lot of wine. Most of all, it was beer that was being laid out. Many of the men had already had quite a few, and were stripping down for further exertions, swapping suggestive remarks with the office girls who were already giggly, half out of their summer dresses, some even in bikinis, coyly balancing their glasses of sweet Martini and Cinzano. It all seemed extremely good-natured, but one wondered if the goodness would last till the final race.

There were over a thousand bookies, with their names and towns showing they'd come from all over the country, Mansfield, Blackpool, Leeds, Sheffield. I'd asked my family that morning what they fancied and had agreed to put £1 on for each of them. I went up to one bookie, because he looked so like a Derby bookie, with large check trousers, an enormous belly and a big red face, just as bookies should. Behind him was a dusty but new-looking Rolls Royce, with his assistants, two very scruffy gypsy types wearing vests, sitting in the boot swigging beer. I could see from his board that the price for 'Blast Off' was fifty to one, so I asked to put on 50p each way. My seven-year-old daughter had chosen that because she liked the name. It reminded her of an ice lolly. I was given a little yellow ticket which didn't appear to have 'Blast Off's' name on it, just a complicated-looking number and the bookie's address in Portsea, London E.9. Beside him, an older man had a huge book laid out in which he was busily writing. It seemed a very cumbersome arrangement, having one's bet taken. I peered over his shoulder, which somewhat alarmed him. "You're not a V.A.T. man, are you?" I could see several pencil columns and in one he'd written my number and bet under the heading 'Blast Off'. Not many people had bet on 'Blast Off' so far, but then it was a rank outsider.

I went on to the Tote, the government-run betting system, all concrete and wood, like a football turnstile, just to spread my largesse, and put £1 each on my six other chosen horses. My teenage son had chosen 'Master Willie' because he always follows Scotland at football. My teenage daughter had chosen 'Hello Gorgeous' because she thought it was a funny name. My

Left:
The Band of the Welsh Guards.
Above:
The Queen Mother in the Paddock.

wife had chosen 'Noble Shamus' because I used to have an uncle called Shamus. My mother-in-law chose 'Monteverdi' because she thought it said Mantovani and she always likes his music. I chose 'Nikoli' because I saw the owner was Lord Iveagh and we live near the Iveagh Bequest. My father-in-law chose 'Henbit'. His was the only choice chosen on form, or so he said. The rest of us might just as well have stuck in pins.

I fought my way back across the track, up the concrete steps of the Grand-stand and eventually found a few feet spare where I stood, trying to work out the hieroglyphics in the race programme and the morning papers. A yellow notice in front of me announced, "A Ring Official will visit this point after each race to assist in disputes between Bookmakers and Backers." How civilised, I thought, but if that bookmaker disappears with my 'Blast Off' bet, how will I ever find him?

The man next to me looked knowledgeable, scribbling on his paper, so I started chatting to him, explaining it was my first ever race meeting. To my surprise, he turned out to be an economics lecturer, from the University of Kent at Canterbury. I'd already observed, from wandering around both sides of the track, that it's the upper and lower classes who are united in their passion for racing.

I hadn't noticed many obvious members of the professional middle classes. People at leisure soon give away their class, by their picnics, their clothes, their accents, their children, their reading. I couldn't see one person studying the *Guardian*'s form pages. The professional classes are usually too mean, or too sensible, to go gambling.

My university friend said he came racing about six times a year, mainly for the atmosphere. He'd been to courses all over the country, from Aintree to Ascot, and to Longchamps near Paris, but in his opinion there is no other day in the racing year like Derby Day. He liked its old-fashionedness, the open-top buses, the huge crowds of jolly Cockney families on the Downs who watch for nothing. He also admired the course and its exacting gradients, having walked round it himself, just to try it out. It starts with a climb, rising 150 feet in the first half-mile, then a gradual turn at Tattenham Corner, into a downhill bit on the straight, finishing on a considerable rise to the winning post. A true test of any thoroughbred's stamina.

He pointed out that it was unusual to have the Paddock so far away, not right beside the finish. It was well worth seeing, but I'd probably never get there and back in time to see the race. I set off at once.

I had to push my way there, but managed to arrive before the Royal Party. and saw the trainers in their top hats carrying out the saddles. It was such a strange sight, the perfect mixture of the two cultures in racing – the nobs playing the part of the stable boys. I felt as if I was cheating, peeping in the wings before the main characters were ready to take the stage.

Once saddled, the riderless horses then gradually appeared in the Paddock, all twenty-four of them, going round and round in the circle, each led by a stable boy, the horse's name and number on his left arm. I worked my way into a corner, near the Paddock fence, just beside the entry from the track. I could almost have touched each horse by leaning through the fence, should I have been overcome with a desire to touch horses. Their flesh rippled, making little waves up and down their bodies, exposing different patterns, revealing where they'd just been brushed and in which direction and what

Tick-tack polka at the Derby.

shape and design of horse brush had been used. They were thoroughbred, thoroughly bred: no fat, no ugly lumps, elegant and refined, all high-quality muscle. The boys leading them seemed decidedly lumpen and commonplace by comparison. There was something majestic, and at the same time rather troubling, even obscene, that any animals should be raised to such a peak of brilliance, to be worshipped with such awe by human beings.

The Royal Party entered the arena led by the Queen and the Queen Mother, followed by owners and stewards, all in their top hats, all looking terribly tall and aristocratic, carved noses and chins, hereditary rulers of vast estates, or so they seemed from their lordly demeanour, till one or two peeled off to guard the entrance and it became apparent they were probably security men, subjects rather than masters, but looking equally impressive. Clothes maketh the man, but it must be tough at the Derby if you're small and fat, however well-bred, however big an owner.

Of the ladies in the magic circle, only the Queen and the Queen Mother appeared word perfect in their parts. They immediately scanned their pro-

gramme, looking back and forward as the horses circled round them, checking numbers, checking form, checking chances. The favourite, 'Nikoli', had given his trainers some worry just before the Paddock entrance, as his heart had started to beat unusually quickly, so they'd given him a quick bath to cool him down. Doubtless the highly knowledgeable Royal eyes were observing any tell-tale drips, give-away marks, signs of nervousness.

One of the circling horses, number two, which I looked up in my programme and found to be 'Bozovici', suddenly reared up on its front legs and started kicking out. The crowd around me gave a loud and nervous 'ooh', but the boy holding on to him seemed completely unperturbed. The Royal party also took little notice. Horses kicking obviously means nothing, not to experts, but I could see why the Royal Party remained standing in the centre of the stage, well beyond kicking distance.

Then, almost with a bang and crash of drums, enter stage left, unleashed like hounds, here they come, bring on the dancing jockeys. It all happened so suddenly that I had to refocus my eyes. Their colours were so startling after the grey toppers, a mass of red, green, yellow, blue and black silks, most with vivid patterns, stars and stripes, dots and bands. They were all so small, little old men, clockwork jockeys who had just been wound up, the trick of some mad Hong Kong toy manufacturer, samples for us all to watch doing their tricks.

The jockeys were also well-rehearsed, going at once to their respective masters, quickly passing up final bits of information, receiving down good luck messages from the stooping owners. The Queen didn't have a horse in that Derby, which was a shame. I would have put 50p on it. Together, the tall, grey top hats and the miniature men then observed the horses circling in silence, while we all held our breath, not wishing to disturb the final rites, ruffle the mysteries, spoil the pageantry, waiting for the unseen ringmaster to bring on the next delight. But that was it. The Queen and Queen Mother

Overleaf: *half a mile out on the back straight in the 1981 Derby. The leading horse is Silver Season with Riberetto on the right and behind, half hidden, is Shergar (in green), the eventual winner.*

Left: *Time for drinks on the roof of a topless bus.*

slowly exited, still talking earnestly to their respective top-hatted attendants, then everyone else followed, still at the agreed distance.

I only recognised one of the top hats, though judging by the Derby programme they included such distinguished racing people as the Earl of Derby, Major General Sir James d'Avigdor-Goldsmid, Major the Hon. Sir John Astor. The face I picked out belonged to Willie Whitelaw, the Home Secretary. Others in the crowd recognised him at the same time and he received a polite little clap as he left the Paddock. He beamed and his lower jaw shook merrily. I hoped he had a bet on 'Master Willie'.

The Queen Mother got a lift in a royal limousine back to the Grandstand, but she showed no signs of tiredness, which was remarkable, considering her age, the intense heat, all that standing and presumably some sort of pain in her right leg. The Queen, and the rest of the Royal party, walked back along the track, and I raced almost parallel with them, pushing through the crowds to the Grandstand. I got back just in time.

Then it all happened so very quickly that I'm not quite sure of the details, though they will be in all the racing records by now. It takes only about three minutes to get round the Derby course, and with the dry, firm going, this Derby turned out to be a very fast one, only 2 minutes, 34 seconds, the third fastest in history. They set off in a blur of noise and movement when I was looking elsewhere, though I did hear one commentator announce that at the halfway stage 'Blast Off' was leading. I wondered how I would ever find that bookmaker to collect my 50–1 winnings. Then there was a torrent of names from the loudspeakers, none of which I recognised, and a great crescendo of shouting as they entered the straight and flashed past us. The roof of the stand practically came off, reverberating to the vast crowd shouting out their favourites. It was at least as noisy as a goal for England at Wembley, though perhaps longer-drawn out.

I had to wait for the official announcement to discover what had happened, though all around me there were long faces, people stamping on plastic beer glasses, tearing up their programmes, muttering obscenities about Lester Piggott. A very bad day for the Irish, so one little group was muttering. I suppose at any race meeting, and most of all at one with half a million backers, most people are bound to lose.

The winner turned out to be the second favourite, 'Henbit'. So my father-in-law had won. 'Master Willie' was second, so my son Jake's fancy had come off. (And Willie Whitelaw *had* put a bet on it – £1 each way.) Out of my seven horses, two had turned out lucky, which wasn't a bad record for an absolute beginner. I went later to collect my winnings and received back £6.85 for an outlay of £7. A day's betting had cost me only 15p.

Immediately after the race, I rushed round the Grandstand to get into the enclosures, flashing various tickets I'd borrowed from the photographers, and found myself outside the jockeys' room. I obviously wasn't allowed in there, but I stood outside and realised I was standing near the winning owner, judging by the questions being thrown at her by a bevy of gossip columnists. She was Mrs Arpad Plesch, a wealthy Hungarian-born lady, who was wearing a veil. She had won the Derby before, in 1961, when her husband was still alive. She was obviously very excited.

"What's it like to have a horse now worth £6 million?" asked one journalist. "What's it like to have a horse worth £5 million?" said another. That was quick, I thought, even in these hard economic times. A drop of a million in a second. Mrs Plesch laughed and introduced the press to her daughter, Princess Bunny Esterhazy, formerly the wife of Dominic Elliot, and then in turn her grandson, Alexander Elliot, a young man in a topper, looking very mature, but only a teenager and due back at Mr Peake's house at Eton by ten o'clock that night.

She then rushed off to greet other friends inside the private enclosure and the journalists started checking their notes with each other. Nigel Dempster, of the *Daily Mail*, was telling his fellow scribes the owner's family pedigree and marriages, putting them right on the spellings, when he noticed that her young grandson was still within earshot.

"Why are you not as tall as your father?" said Nigel Dempster.

"I'm still growing," said Alexander, politely but smartly.

Pearly Queen.

Members Enclosure.

I followed a couple of American T.V. cameramen from N.B.C., to see what American cameramen do at the Derby, and was beside them when they managed to grab Willie Carson, the winning jockey. It was the second year running that he had ridden the Derby winner. The previous year on 'Troy' he'd won by a bigger margin, which therefore had to be called a better victory, so he explained in his soft Scottish accent. "But all Derby victories are good victories." There had been one particular problem this time on the finishing stretch, though until then he'd had a fair and easy ride. 'Henbit' was now lame, and would be unable to run again that season. Just a furlong or so from home, the colt had fractured a bone in a foot.

I stood around a bit longer in the saddling enclosure, spotting Lester Piggott, taller than every other jockey, but physically very worn and weary, his eyes almost hidden by bags and lines. A lot of people were saying, "Hello, Eve," and I looked around for some lady, but they were talking to a little man in a lounge suit, looking very smooth and sophisticated, who turned out to be Yves Saint-Martin, formerly the French champion jockey.

Back at the car, I waited for Frank. The same Daimler was still parked beside us, the chauffeur still doing his polishing. He must have been there since 11.30, almost seven hours previously. No, he hadn't watched the race. "It's so dirty over there," he said, giving a little shudder towards the Grandstand and Downs. "Even your finger nails get dirty. I can't stand being sweaty and dirty."

He was waiting for his top-hatted party to return, a group of advertising Executives, taking out some important clients. They were all on expenses, he said, so he knew there would be no big tips at the end of the day. That was why he'd let them carry the champagne themselves. "They asked me to carry it over, but I said it was no use, not unless they had Grandstand tickets for me to get in as well, which I knew they wouldn't have. Of course I could have helped them over, but I wasn't going to, was I."

It was his own Daimler which he hires out for £90 a day. It had been a very slow spring, but he was booked up for the rest of the summer. He was worried about various political problems affecting the season. He'd been

told the Saudis might not be coming, after a T.V. programme they'd objected
to.

"I had one Saudi last year and, do you know, till then I'd never really
seen money in my whole life, not *real* money. I had him for eight weeks and
every day for eight weeks our first stop was at the bank where he drew out
£10,000 in cash. Each bleeding day. We'd go first to Harrods and he'd spend
at least £1,000 on suits and clothes. Then to Bond Street to some jewellers.
It had all gone by each evening. It's very easy to get rid of £10,000 a day,
when you know how.

"But there's still a lot of money around in England. Especially on Derby
Day. That's when you see it coming out. It's the biggest day in the racing
calendar, innit?"

16 The Thames at Cookham

I STOOD on the bridge at Cookham, looking along the lush green river banks at the affluent riverside houses and behind them the olde worlde village High Street with its ancient buildings, all beautifully kept, even if most of them now seem to be antique shops or twee restaurants, and it seemed such a picture post-card version of the Heart of England, beloved by the tourist authorities, and enjoyed each year by thousands of visitors. It all felt so safe, confident, self-assured. What a surprise they would get if the Danes suddenly returned in their long boats and started raping and pillaging all the bijou residences.

The Thames is now a place for pleasure, and it is hard to realise what a vital part it has played in our turbulent island history. It is our principal river, on which our capital city rests, and it has been navigated since time unknown – the perfect way into the soft underbelly of England, as the Romans realised. Julius Caesar called it Tamesis, when he arrived in 55 B.C.

The Danish hordes, some 800 years later, actually got as far upstream as Reading, till Alfred the Great, who fought them right along the river, drove them out and established some sort of peace. It then eventually settled down as a working river, used for commercial transport, with barges going up as far as Oxford. After the seventeenth century, they managed to go even further when new locks were installed which improved navigation.

It's a very little river, when you consider its long history and great importance. The Thames is only 210 miles in length, just a trickle, really, compared with a 4,000-mile monster like the Amazon.

Along the tow path near Cookham.

It rises in the Cotswolds, about three miles outside Cirencester. From Lechlade, where there is a statue of Old Father Thames beside the lock, lying down holding a spade, a memento of the Irish navigators who originally worked on our waterways, there are a series of forty-four weirs and locks all the way down to Teddington, a distance of some 123 miles. This is the fresh-water Thames, navigable all the way, carefully looked after by Thames Water and now one of the country's most popular pleasure grounds. The working days are over on this stretch. The 30,000 or so registered boats which use the River are all pleasure craft.

In theory, all of this route is also walkable, if you could follow the old towpaths which the bargemen used. In practice, though, the towpath frequently crossed the river, using ferry points which no longer exist. However, the Ramblers Association have mapped out a 156-mile-long Thames Walk, from Lechlade down to Putney, using nearby country paths when the old towpath runs out. In the next few years, this will be improved even more, with new paths and new ferry facilities, and it could become one of the most popular long walks in Britain, rivalling the Pennine Way, if not nearly so arduous.

The fresh-water Thames, whether you follow it by boat or on foot, goes through some very historic and beautiful towns and villages on its journey from the Cotswolds – Oxford, Dorchester, Reading, Henley, Maidenhead, Windsor, Hampton, Kingston and Teddington.

Below Teddington, the Thames is tidal, for a distance of around ninety miles, depending on where you decide the Thames stops and the North Sea begins. There are still lots of pleasure craft, right through Greater London, from Teddington to Greenwich, and a river trip is one of the delights of any visit to London, but by this time the river is again a working river, once you reach the docklands.

Cookham is about halfway up the Thames, a very pretty stretch with artistic and literary associations. Stanley Spencer lived here, and painted river scenes, and so did Kenneth Grahame, who wrote *The Wind in the Willows*. Choosing just one mile of river, out of a possible 200 miles, is bound to be a bit arbitrary, but it seemed as suitable a place as any to watch people messing around with boats.

As I stood on Cookham Bridge, admiring the rich views, I noticed beside the bridge an old building called Turk's Boat Yard, a rather battered wooden construction, painted white, though peeling badly. By concentrating my eyes, I could make out the wording on the side: "Watermen by Appointment to Her Majesty the Queen."

I rang and asked for Mr Turk from the 'phone box in the village High Street, thinking it might be too impolite just to arrive, as he is a Royal appointment, and he said he could spare me a few moments. I went back to the boat yard, as directed, and found him jammed in the corner of an attic room, with a secretary and a calor gas stove, surrounded by ancient files and dusty drawers.

Frederick John Turk is sixty-seven and his family have been boatmen on the Thames since 1760. He was in the merchant navy for twenty-five years before he came ashore in 1954 and took over his father's business. He has a white beard and looks like an old sailor, rather gruff and world-weary, but then he does have to put up with strangers knocking at his door from all over the world and asking him silly questions about his Royal Watermanly duties.

Part of his business is renting out rowing boats, of which he has six, price £3 an hour, from Easter to September. He does a bit of boat building, but not much these days. No one wants wooden boats any more. It was in 1963 that he took over his father's position as Keeper of the Royal Swans.

Mute swans are our native British swans, the ones we normally see, all white with a deep yellow beak. There are other varieties, such as Whooper Swans and Bewicks who are mainly in Scotland and the North and they are migratory. It is an offence to catch any swan, or to interfere with it, but you could be in worse trouble if you touch a mute swan. Traditionally, they are Royal birds.

Mute swans, despite their name, do make a bit of hissing and grunting, though they are the least vocal of all swans. They're also the biggest, and the adults can weigh thirty pounds, which makes them the heaviest of all flying birds.

There are around 200 mute swans on the River Thames between Sunbury and Pangbourne, a distance of some seventy miles, which is the stretch Mr

Boats moored near Cookham.

Turk looks after on behalf of the Queen, a stretch which for centuries has become something of a swan sanctuary. He is responsible for their welfare and is constantly being called out by the police and the public to help some poor swan in distress. How often? He seemed irritated by the question. He didn't know how often. In the end, his secretary said 'very often'. About two or three times a week, night and day.

Last winter he had been called out to the M40 where a swan had landed on the main carriageway in fog and, in trying to avoid it, three cars had smashed into each other. The swan was still there, in the road, when he arrived. He caught it with his bare hands, as he always does, and then tied its wings and legs, put it in his car and took it back to the river. It's a regular occurrence, picking swans off the motorway, as both the M4 and M40 are nearby.

However, fishermen are a bigger danger to swans than motorists. They will leave their lead pellets, bits of nylon line and old hooks all lying around, and the swan population is at present on the decline. There is also the problem of the Thames being such an active river, with those 30,000 pleasure boats to compete with, that it's hard for them to find a quiet spot to breed. Then there's the danger from pike, who will eat whole cygnets if they get a chance, or rats who take the eggs, or foxes who attack young swans, if given half a chance. If they survive all that, swans will live for around twenty-five years.

The big event in the swan calendar is Swan Upping which happens each

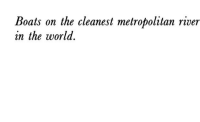

Boats on the cleanest metropolitan river in the world.

year in early July. Although mute swans are considered Royal birds, it so happens that on the Thames around half of them belong to two livery companies, the Worshipful Company of Vintners and the Worshipful Company of Dyers. In the old days, swans were kept for eating, and were looked upon as a great delicacy, so it was necessary to differentiate the Royal swans from the Company swans. For over 700 years, the swans on the Thames have been rounded up every year and the young appropriately marked. The Queen's swans have no marks but the Vintners' have two nicks on their beak and the Dyers' one nick on the beak.

It takes a week for Mr Turk and eighteen other Watermen and helpers to move up the Thames in six boats and catch and mark all the swans. The cygnets are easy to catch, as they can't fly, but the adult swans can give you a nasty bruise with their wings. It just takes experience and confidence to know how to handle them.

Mr Turk wears special clothes for Swan Upping, a jacket of scarlet and white trousers, so you know he is the Royal Swan Keeper, not to be confused with Dyers' Swan Keeper, who wears blue, or the Vintners' Swan Keeper who wears white and green. Even the ordinary swan markers and boatmen have their costumes. No wonder it is such a hit with tourists right along those seventy miles of the Thames. Look out for details in the local papers each July.

Until the last ten years, Swan Upping always made a front-page photograph in *The Times* and the *Daily Telegraph*, and often the B.B.C. T.V. news, but for some reason the media are not as keen as they once were on such ancient customs, however colourful. Mr Turk did, however, make *The Times* in 1981, mainly because so few swans were caught, only about fifty.

It is today mainly a ceremonial duty, but the week-by-week job of protecting swans, keeping records of them, looking after their welfare, is still worth doing and Mr Turk is very proud of it. He is responsible to the Lord Chamberlain and receives an emolument, which he won't reveal, plus his expenses. Yes, he has met the Queen, but not on the River. It was a Royal garden party.

I then had a look around Cookham Village, starting at the ancient Norman church which seemed very prosperous, both inside and out, with a rich magnolia in full bloom in the churchyard and some thick carpets inside on parts of the floor. They have a Stanley Spencer on the wall, 'The Last Supper', a rather weird painting, like something from a Ken Russell film.

There are many, and more attractive, Spencers to be seen at the Spencer Gallery in the High Street. The building was once a Methodist chapel, where Spencer was often taken as a boy by his mother. He was born in 1891 a few doors along the street, in a modest terrace house called Fernlea. The gallery boasts that it is the only art gallery in Britain devoted exclusively to an artist in the village where he was born and spent most of his working life.

It is a light, airy building and has a nice collection of mementoes, as well as paintings, such as his pencils, brushes, easel, knives, spectacles and an extremely battered old pram in which he used to push his painting tackle around the village. There's an old notice beside the pram which says:

> As he is anxious to complete his painting of the churchyard, Mr Stanley Spencer would be grateful if visitors would kindly avoid distracting his attention from his work.

The biggest painting on show is an enormous one, about twenty-two feet long, which covers almost one wall and is his unfinished canvas, 'Christ Preaching at Cookham Regatta'. He was still working on it at his death in 1959 and you can see in the unfinished third where he has drawn in the bits to be done later in oil. It is of great interest to all art students, and for visitors generally, since the success of the Stanley Spencer exhibition at the Royal Academy in 1980. The little gallery in Cookham noticed an immediate increase and now gets over 10,000 visitors a year.

I then set off down Mill Lane to start my walk along the River, heading downstream in the direction of Maidenhead. This stretch of the Thames is called Cliveden Reach and the Cliveden estate is on the opposite bank, a place with two notorious associations, with the pre-war so-called "Cliveden Set" and with the Christine Keeler–Stephen Ward scandal of 1963. You can often hear guides on the pleasure cruisers pointing out where the high jinks were supposed to have taken place.

The banks on either side are lush and meadow-like, then the land starts rising on the Cliveden side till eventually there is a chalk cliff as the river cuts deeply into the bank, making it look almost like a Rhine gorge. I wondered if the name of the estate originally came from these cliffs – Cliff Den. Over the centuries this could have become Cliveden. Or was there a bloke called Clive and this was his den? One's mind does tend to meander on a river walk. The fields don't necessarily always look greener on the other side, but they can usually appear more interesting.

I passed several islands in the middle of the river, which made it difficult to work out which was the far bank and which was another island. I was surprised how wide the river was, estimating it must be around fifty yards across. The water was rather muddy, so I could see no signs of fish, or of any fishermen, though the Thames today is teeming with fish.

The fresh-water Thames has always been relatively good for fishing, rich in bream, carp, chub, dace, roach, perch and pike, but it is the fish in the tidal Thames, from Teddington through London to the sea, that have seen the most amazing change in recent years.

In my lifetime, I have witnessed with my own eyes, and ears and nose, two dramatic improvements in London life. One has been the end of the London smog which as recently as 1960 filled every lung every winter. The other is the re-birth of the tidal Thames. In that same year it was so polluted that it had become a *dead* river, and no fish whatsoever had been recorded in the London Thames for over forty years.

For centuries, the Thames had been famous for its fish. In 1688 James Chetham wrote that the salmon from the Thames were 'the best in Europe'. In the eighteenth century more than 3,000 Thames salmon every season were being sent to Billingsgate market. There were forty boats between Wandsworth and Hammersmith fishing for flounders, eels, whitebait, smelts and lamperns. Between them, they caught 50,000 fish a day.

It was the Industrial Revolution which did most damage. From 1810 onwards, thousands of new factories started pouring their waste into the river and at the same time the arrival of domestic water closets meant that millions of homes were emptying their effluent through the drains into the Thames. The River became a stinking and poisoned sewer which was soon killing people, not just the fish. No wonder Thomas Hardy felt so ill every summer when he worked in that architect's office overlooking the river. (Whenever anyone goes on about the good old days in London, remind them of the smog and the poisoned river.)

The clean-up campaign started in 1953. By 1977, a total of ninety different species of fish had been found in the Thames between Kew and Tilbury, thanks to £200 million being spent on sewage treatment.

Today, Thames Water claims that the Thames is the cleanest metropolitan

Boulter's Lock: Boats in the lock. Left: *The Hotel.*

estuary in the world. Routine samplings at a London power station reveal 10,000 fish on every tide, including over thirty species, which are then returned live to the river. Salmon have been re-introduced, and have survived, for the first time in 150 years, though it has not yet been decided whether to start a major re-stocking programme. (Salmon are euryhaline, able to live in fresh and salt water, and they return from the sea to their river of origin to spawn, so it will take some time to get the full cycle going again.)

Not long after Cliveden, several houses started appearing along the banks, some of them very gracious, red-brick, castellated villas, as well as some brand-new ones, part of the suburban sprawl, spreading out from Maidenhead.

I was passing the gardens to one of the new houses, which was for sale, according to a Giddy and Giddy notice board, when an elderly man in wellington boots and shirt sleeves came out on to the tow path and said good day. I admired his house and he said, come in, have a look around the garden. "See that patio, that's where I sit and look right up the river to Cliveden."

He was retiring from business, so he said, and had just sold six shops which he'd built up from nothing.

"I won't miss the bricks and mortar, how can you miss bricks and mortar? I'm going to tell you something. This has been a *home*, not just a house. I'll miss that. My family's now grown up so we're going to move nearer London. The price of petrol, my God, have you seen the price of petrol.

"I used to have my own boat, tied up outside my own house, but I sold it. Vandalism! Who needs it? Vandalism is everywhere these days. You can't even protect your own property. And the river, it's so crowded. The boats are so big. What do you do? You spend half a day sitting in the boat, waiting to get through Cookham lock. Who needs it? This is all mine, you know, this bit of the tow path. I don't cut the grass. People just fetch their bloody dogs if you cut the grass."

He pointed to a very expensive-looking catamaran, long and black and sleek, with dark glass. He'd heard that it had cost the owner £33,000. "He's an intellectual. I don't know what he does. He works with his head. He's not your average bloke, is he, but he's got the money. I'm going to tell you something, who *has* the money these days? You don't know. Someone on £10,000 may have his little fiddles and pay no tax while someone on £30,000 pays all his taxes and has nothing to spend.

"I'm above flood level, you know. Oh yes, above flood level. See that house over there. You watch them run when the river rises. Oh yes.

"I came out of the army with fourpence. I work, I sweat, and now I have this nice house. You want to buy it?"

He laughed, looking at my dirty boots, and asked me where I'd been. I told him about my walk round Cookham and the Spencer gallery.

"It's what you like, isn't it? He was that old man who went round with that old pram. Yes? He had all that talent and he went round with an old pram. I don't like his stuff. At all. There's your Lowry, isn't there? People love that Lowry. I can't see it. I just can't see it. All dots and dashes, that's all."

He wouldn't tell me how much he wanted for his house. I had to guess. I started at £75,000, then tried £100,000. From his nods and winks I decided it must be around £150,000. He then invited me inside the house for tea, but I thanked him for his chat and said I must get on.

Boulter's Lock is just on the outskirts of Maidenhead, at a bulge in the River which contains three little islands, linked with bridges. It's like a harbour village, boats and buildings nestling round a large and rather affluent-looking hotel and restaurant, Boulter's Inn. The hotel has been a famous and fashionable social spot for many years. It was at its height in the Edwardian period when bucks came out from London with their ladies for a naughty night or two by the river. Like Skindles Hotel, which is on the river at the other side of Maidenhead, it still has a discreet if rather chintzy charm, and you wonder what sort of assignations are now being made, how many thrusting young executives have taken their secretaries out for scampi and fillet steak and intimate discussions.

I found the lock-keeper's cottage and knocked at the door. As I was standing there, the lock-keeper himself arrived. "I've got your knickers back," he shouted through the doorway, handing his wife a plastic carrier bag full of lady's clothes.

Bill Stacey and his wife Jill have been resident at Boulter's Lock for three years, after ten years as a relief keeper, being sent up and down the Thames as a permanent holiday relief. He comes from the Windsor area and was in the accounts department at Ford's motor company before he decided, he says, to leave the rat race. He suffers from chronic bronchitis, which was another reason he wanted an outdoor job.

He is large, bearded and jovial. Not all lock-keepers are as approachable. Having to deal with the public all day long, especially the dopier varieties, makes most people in his position rather wary, but he loves his job, and is amused by the public rather than irritated by them. Every week, on average, they get someone falling in the lock, or 'swimmers' as he refers to them. They always have a spare set of male and female clothes, just in case, though it is not part of his duties.

"It happened last Monday, Wednesday and Sunday, three swimmers in the one week. We had no spare clothes left, so this woman had to take Jill's best. She was on an outing with six publicans in a private boat, and they got a bit merry. She had no idea how she fell in. They rarely do.

"What normally happens is that they grab the sides, then the boat moves back, and they fall in. Or they start to step off, and the boat moves away, and in they go. They don't get the tuition they should get, but it's to be expected. Some boat yards are sending out seventy hire cruisers every Sunday, so they haven't time to teach everyone.

"I shouted to one bloke the other day 'Go astern'. He was about to crash into the wall, so I thought that was a pretty obvious instruction, meaning he should go into reverse. Boats don't have brakes. What this bloke did was walk round the boat and sit in the back! Naturally, the boat crashed. Walls can't move.

"I'm always telling people to 'Make your boat fast', and there's always someone every year who turns *up* the engine, instead of tying up the boat. The other day I was walking beside a bloke who was in the lock and having trouble and I said 'Hand us your line'. He completely untied the whole rope and threw it at me. As he drifted away he shouted, 'Now, look what you've made me do . . .'

"There's been no serious accident, luckily, but I've seen a few fingers lost. It happens when they're untying from a bollard. As he's struggling with it, some-

Sunset from Cookham Bridge.

one on the boat starts up and it moves off while his soppy fingers are still stuck·in the rope. I saw one bloke have three of his fingers severed, just like that."

As lock-keeper, his main professional duty is to get safely through the lock over 40,000 craft every year. Boulter's Lock is one of the busiest on the Thames. It's a big lock, $199\frac{1}{2}$ feet long, and can take around ten boats at a time. Normally, he can get each batch through in under fifteen minutes, as the lock these days is worked by an electric motor. (In the evening, after seven, when he is officially off duty, the lock can be worked manually.) But, in the height of summer, there can be queues of up to two hours, waiting to get through.

His other duties include reading the water levels every three hours, which are phoned through to the local Thames Water headquarters at Reading, and regulating the weir, raising the weir gates to get rid of extra water and so avoid flooding. There is constant communication up and down the Thames, between the forty-four locks, which means that news of any floods or other river problems is passed on quickly and action can be taken.

He considers himself well-paid and well-looked after, privileged to have the job. "It's all the noes which make my job so good – no travel to work, no rates, no rent, no repairs." He doesn't seem to mind having people banging on his door at all times of the day and night, to tell him some boys are shooting air guns at swans, which had happened the previous night.

The single most frequent question he gets asked is "Where's the nearest boozer?" which at least is easy to answer. "I was asked yesterday by a woman if she had to come back this way to return to Windsor. People have funny ideas about the Thames. They think it must be a circular river."

I then went over a little bridge beside the lock to the local offices of the Conservancy Division of Thames Water. I had seen some of their distinctive blue and white launches going up and down the river since I'd left Cookham.

Peter Bowles is the District Navigation Inspector in charge of Division Three, a twenty-one-mile-long stretch of the river which contains eight locks. He and his inspectors patrol the river, checking the locks and lock-keepers, water levels and weirs, landing stages and boats. All boats have to be registered and they spend a lot of time in riverside boat yards, making sure the boats are not dangerous, with their kitchens about to explode.

They don't like being looked upon as policemen, though they are continually stopping boats, the way policemen stop motorists, to make sure their permits and fittings are in order. Thames Valley Police have their own patrol boats for any criminal work. They are simply taking care of the river, for the public's good. A landing stage, for example, which is badly built, or left to rot, can float free and end up blocking a weir which can result in serious flooding. Someone speeding, which means going above eight knots (or seven miles an hour), can set up a wash which can damage other boats and landing stages as well as the banks of the river. A badly-built boat can be a floating bomb and could explode in a lock and do untold damage.

Mr Bowles has been a navigation inspector for twenty-five years. Before that he was at sea for ten years and holds a Master's Certificate. Many of the inspectors are former naval men. The biggest change he has seen in the last quarter of a century is the *speed* at which danger can happen, though he likes to think that they have kept pace, thanks to their improved scientific methods. An inch of heavy rain twenty-five years ago would make little difference to

the Thames. It would soak gently through the surrounding fields and only gradually get into the river. Now, so much of the land near the Thames is concrete, with modern roads, motorways and new housing estates. The rain comes straight off the concrete and into the river, and up go the levels.

In the London area, millions of pounds are being spent on flood preservation schemes, as there is now a real danger that a freak tidal wave could flood many square miles of central London. Such dangers exist, though in a milder form, right up the Thames. He was in the process that day of taking someone to court who had allowed an old boat to drift free and block a weir. It had made the water rise by six inches in a matter of hours.

One of his inspectors was just setting off in a launch and I was allowed to go along for the ride, back up to Cookham Lock where I'd started. He gently chided his boatman, a young man also in uniform, for leaving the landing stage without the red flag flying. Thames Water's official flag must be flown, whenever an inspector is on board. They do have standards, these river men.

We cruised along slowly and sedately while the inspector scanned the banks, telling me the history of various landing stages and boats as we went past them. They did seem like crawling cops, slowly driving through their manor.

It was strange to be actually on the river at last, three men in a boat, having been walking beside it up to now. It gave a completely new dimension. I felt *in* the river, rather than on it, part of its flow, not just a surface passenger. The boat was lying so deeply that the water appeared to be at eye level, which had a mesmerising effect, free-fall floating, as if in a dream. Even the water seemed different, so thick and rich and dense and full of life. I felt I could get out and walk on it with safety. The river appeared much bigger and broader, stretching for miles in every direction, as if we were on the lower Mississippi, not miles inland up the little old Thames.

We passed Cliveden and they both said how surprising it was that all the inspectors had gone up and down beside that house, day after day, year after year, and yet not one had realised what was going on inside. Makes you think, doesn't it?

That's the thing about the River. There's something going on somewhere, all the time.

Three girls on a boat.

17 The RSC

THEY WERE rehearsing in the basement of a church hall, Notre Dame, near Leicester Square, all standing around in their jeans and jumpers, a rather untidy-looking bunch of people in a large, cheerless hall. Ronald Eyre, the director, in shirt sleeves, was taking them through the last scene of *The Winter's Tale*. It was the fourth week of rehearsals, but they were still easing themselves into their parts, and into working with one another. There were a further six weeks yet to go. Other plays were being rehearsed at the same time, but even so, the R.S.C. likes to give its artists ample rehearsal time.

Sheila Hancock, who was playing Paulina, still felt a bit strange, having such time and space in which to rehearse. In the commercial theatre, in the West End or Broadway, where she has spent most of her acting life, you get only four weeks to rehearse. This was to be her first Shakespeare. She had been asked several times over the years to appear with the company but the dates had never fitted in with her other work. She was wearing trousers and a waistcoat and large spectacles. Considering she was new to the company, and new to Shakespeare, she didn't appear overawed, taking part in all the discussions, even when it didn't concern her part.

Gemma Jones, an equally distinguished actress, though known mainly for her T.V. work, was playing Hermione. She had just re-joined the company, having done many Shakespeare plays in the past, with the R.S.C. and other companies. She seemed much more hesitant and self-effacing, prefacing her few comments with 'Excuse me', or 'Don't you think ...' She was wearing jeans, jumper and a headscarf.

The two leading men, Patrick Stewart (Leontes) and Bernard Lloyd (Camillo) are both experienced R.S.C. actors, who have been long with the company. It was strange to hear them discussing the text. They still *sounded* like Shakespearean actors, even when they were talking amongst themselves, while Miss Hancock managed to sound like an ordinary person.

Around the side of the hall, while the seven actors and the director rehearsed, sat two assistant stage managers making notes and the director's assistant who was working on the schedules for the week ahead. The R.S.C. is a large and complicated repertory company. Most of them that day were working on two Shakespeare plays at the same time, so arranging the scenes which the director next wanted to rehearse, fitting in with available rehearsal rooms in London and Stratford, was as usual proving a difficult task.

The floor had two sets of markings, one in yellow for the set fittings and a larger one in white, marking the perimeter of the new Barbican theatre, the one which the R.S.C. is due to move into in the early summer of 1982. It was planned that *The Winter's Tale*, if all went well, would be one of the opening plays.

Trevor Nunn, artistic director of the Royal Shakespeare Company, at the Barbican.

"I think the word 'magic' has a wider connotation than you realise," Ron Eyre was saying, stopping them in the middle of the statue scene, a scene where Gemma Jones as Hermione has to stand still as a statue, supposedly having been dead for sixteen years. She had been standing dead still for a good half-hour already, without speaking, her face motionless, while around her the others argued over their lines.

"Is it not a witch sort of magic . . .?" said one of the actors.

"Is it more a drawing us out sort of magic?" suggested another.

It took them a good ten minutes to decide on the meaning of the word magic, then they started the speech again, but three men in overalls came into the room, wheeling a boxed-up piano which they noisily put into place at the end of the hall, getting it ready for a jazz concert that evening.

"Oh, bloody hell," said Annie, the assistant director, as the men proceded to hammer the piano apart. Ron Eyre lowered his voice, moved nearer to the actors, and went over a minor detail, till the workmen had finished. They had just started again on the King's long speech when one of the stage managers happened to rustle his papers as he was turning them over.

"Could you *not* fiddle about with that . . ." said the King, quietly, but very firmly.

"Okay, kids," said the director. "Go on."

This time the King managed to get to the end of his speech without interruptions, the speech in which he remembers he was responsible for the death of his wife. As he finished, he collapsed to his knees, uttering the most piercing, orgasmic screams. It was the first time they'd got right through the scene, and the first time Patrick Stewart had been able to act the lines properly.

"It's an Oedipus scream," whispered Annie, the assistant director, a large girl with a strong Yorkshire accent. "It's the scream when eyes get gouged out. Or the scream in *Lear* when Cordelia dies in his arms. Or *Macbeth*, after the murder of Duncan. I love hearing that scream. You hear it in all Shakespeare's tragedies. It's the cleansing scream, the end of a journey, making rebirth now possible. The pain of it is purging, yet it's the ultimate pleasure. Hmmm . . ."

The actors were now gathered round the King, to help him slowly up, and the scene moved on till the end, then they discussed it.

"Should I really walk towards him?" asked Bernard Lloyd. "After all, I'm supposed to be sixty-four . . . I'm a little confused."

"What you're really saying is, I want you to bugger off out of my sight . . ."

"Excuse me," said Gemma. "Could I make a comment? The noise of the King is so startling, the Patriarch collapsing, perhaps his daughter would find an ally in her own generation . . .?"

The director thought this was a good idea, and accordingly instructed the young actress playing Perdita, the King's daughter.

"Haven't we finished with me holding this bleeding curtain yet?" asked Sheila.

"No, not yet, Sheila, but don't hold it like a pantomime queen. It's not fairy wand time."

"I would like to put back that one line," said the King. "I know you hate it, Ron."

"No, no, I love the way you do it. Miraculous," he said, smiling. "Why people cut Shakespeare around, I don't know. You find he's always right in the end."

One of the actors had been going through his part with his text stuck in the top of his jeans. Most of the others held their rather battered versions in one hand, shoving it under their arms, or laying it on the floor, referring to it when necessary. There was a mix-up in two speeches as both actors got their words wrong, and Ron admonished them, bringing them to a halt.

"As we're now approaching this scene properly, perhaps from now on you could know your words."

"Oh," said the King. "Slap on the wrists time."

"Well," said Ron. "It has become a bit like a travelling library."

Mr Eyre is fifty-one and comes from Barnsley. He has been in the theatre since he left Oxford, and has directed many Shakespeare plays, for the R.S.C. and the National Theatre, as well as writing and presenting *The Long Search* for B.B.C. T.V.

"Everyone is working hard," he said during the lunch break. "The rehearsals are going very well. Nobody has buggered it up. In my time, I have worked with one well-known actor who insists on literally *every* line being analysed.

"Rehearsing is a process of going up any number of blind alleys so that when you finally decide to go up one, you know why you've chosen it. In some commercial plays, they often have as little as two weeks to rehearse. Directing then becomes little more than flower arranging. The director tells them where to stand, and lets them get on with it.

"We have so much more time. The danger then is a director can begin to think that he is the axis of the universe, that there is no product unless he makes it. But we all share in it. Some days you don't know how to do it, but it still moves on, very slowly, all the same.

"This scene we've just been doing – a statue comes to life – we're not in the world of *Z Cars*, but we have to make the audience believe it happens. We are in a different world, a different age, a time full of wonder, which is not some-

Rehearsing 'The Winter's Tale'. Left to right, *Gemma Jones, Patrick Stewart, Sheila Hancock, Ron Eyre.*

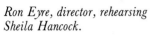

*Ron Eyre, director, rehearsing
Sheila Hancock.*

thing that makes much sense in the world of today. The most important line in the play is, 'It is required you do awake your faith'."

Over in a far corner of the hall, sitting on her own, Sheila Hancock was eating a sandwich and reading the *Guardian*. The male actors had gone off for a drink. Gemma had gone out to buy something from a health food shop.

"It is all so bloody amazing," said Sheila. "At this stage in a commercial play, I would have a stiff neck and a pain in the back. The pressure would be so great by now with the management breathing over you, the backers coming in and out, everyone getting worried, doing endless little press interviews and photographs, just to get the show publicity, of any sort.

"Here, well, the only concern is the text. Nothing else matters. There is no other pressure. It's wonderful. They have their own voice teacher, and I go to her. I couldn't believe such a thing. I've learned so much, about metre, how to say half-lines, how to change, how to interpret. I came to the Company determined to speak the lines well, so that everyone would understand it, but not demean Shakespeare. To make it accessible, yet cherish it.

"There's also a movement class, can you believe it? I go to that before every rehearsal. Have you seen *Nicholas Nickleby*? That's an example of the R.S.C. at its best. They use their voices and bodies better than any other group of actors in the whole world.

"I still feel a slight outsider. The experienced R.S.C. actors do talk differently, in sort of broken sentences. I thought at first, what the hell are they talking about? All they're doing is looking for clues. It's a wondrous experience.

"I don't *have* to say the iambic pentameters in the tum ti tum way. I've been

Patrick Stewart (Leontes) and Sheila Hancock (Paulina) in 'The Winter's Tale'.

told, if I feel strongly, I can change the rhythm. I have done it my way now and again, but then I've come back. The way they do it *is* right.

"There's a lot of hard work in a half-hour comedy show for T.V. You put a lot more in as an actress than you often get credit for, making something out of very little, which happens most of the time. A lot of padding is needed to make it work. It's so nice to do something that is *good*. That doesn't need padding.

"I've joined for the season and I'm also doing a part in *Titus* but I might not wait for the Barbican opening. I have an option to get out before then, if I want to. I'm loving it at the moment, but I still don't know if I can really fit into a company like this. It's so new and different for me. I'm an anarchist at heart. I may revolt against things. I can be rather disruptive at times. I joke a lot. Here, I have to submerge myself in the company.

"At the same time, you don't fear to make a suggestion. There's no time in the West End for such agonising. You can even make suggestions about *other* people's parts. Imagine some minor actor suggesting how Rex Harrison, for example, should play a line. You'd soon be told to mind your own bloody business. Here, every one can have their say.

"I'm hoping actually to do some directing myself, eventually. I've had a half-promise from Trevor that if I stay on to the end and all goes well, I might be allowed to do some ..."

Gemma Jones came back with her lunch, a vegetarian pasty, and proceeded to munch her way through it. "I asked the Company to take me on. It's a long time since I played with them and I've been after it for a long time. My ambition to be in the company has now been realised. Unless I misbehave, I hope to stay here. I will try to be a good girl. The money doesn't matter. It's a living wage. Enough for me and my family.

"It's easy to sound platitudinous about Shakespeare. It is simply the most rewarding thing an actress can do. It's only in Shakespeare that I realise, in brief flashes, why I am in the profession. It is a spiritual experience, a reward in a very tough world."

She hadn't said much all that morning, though of course it happened to be a scene where she was supposed to be a statue. Hadn't her mind wandered while they were endlessly discussing their own little lines?

"I admit I did once or twice think about what I'm cooking for supper. You just have to concentrate harder. The discussions are complicated, but the depth of analysis is supremely valuable.

"I don't say a lot in discussions. I am afraid of making a fool of myself. I store up my thoughts. I'm never quite sure. I don't want to appear arrogant, but I don't feel any 'awe' being here, working on this play. We all started out together on it, on the same day. But I feel the company as a whole is rather sort of awesome. The most creative talents in the profession are here at the R.S.C."

The youngest member of the cast, Leonie Mellinger, hadn't spoken all morning. She too was sitting alone during the lunch hour, watching the assistants getting ready. She is just twenty-one, a year out of drama school, with only T.V. experience so far. "It's my first theatre job. I'm now a member of the R.S.C. Well, for sixty weeks I am. That's my contract. I go to everything they lay on, voice tutorials, sonnet classes, movement, everything ...

"They asked me if I would audition for the part of Perdita. Somebody must have seen me on T.V. in *Sons and Lovers*. They called me back for a second audition. It was on the stage of the Aldwych, in front of Trevor and all the directors. I was very nervous. I still feel a bit in awe, working with all these experienced actors. Ron is very good at giving me confidence. I never let my mind wander, even when it's not my part. It will take a bit longer before I actually *say* anything in rehearsals ...''

Trevor is Trevor Nunn. That day he was sitting not far away in his rather unprepossessing office up fifty stone steps at the Aldwych, working on plans for the 1982 season. *The Winter's Tale* was just one of thirty productions which the Royal Shakespeare Company would be doing in the year ahead.

It is always hard to believe that someone so young and boyish should have been running such an enormous company for so many years. He was appointed artistic director in 1968, at the age of twenty-eight, a job which he did alone for ten years before Terry Hands was made joint artistic director in 1978. Although he now shares the artistic load, he is still in effect the company's chief executive, responsible for the ultimate organisation, as well as the artistic direction.

Under his leadership, the R.S.C. has become the world's biggest theatre company, producing more plays every year than anyone else. They have an acting staff of over a hundred, an overall staff of 500, and each year their productions are watched by more than one million people. They operate from four permanent theatres, two in Stratford and two in London, plus a winter season every year in Newcastle. They do new plays as well as Shakespeare, many of which transfer to the commercial, West End theatre or are turned into films and T.V. shows.

Their audiences on average are 95 percent filled to capacity, yet they still have endless money problems, relying on film and T.V. sales and sponsorship to keep them alive, as well as their annual Arts Council grant, always a source of great contention, as they argue that it is never enough. Their Arts Council grant, the only public one they get, sounds an enormous sum – in 1981 it was around £2 million – but it represents only 35 per cent of their total costs.

Trevor Nunn in the foyer at the Barbican.

They maintain it is a considerably lower proportion than any other State-aided company receives, either in Britain or abroad.

Their eminence as a company is comparatively recent, when you consider that Shakespeare was writing his first plays around 1584. It wasn't until 1879 that a Shakespeare Memorial Theatre was opened in Stratford-on-Avon, then in 1926 it was burnt to a shell. The present Stratford theatre, beside the river, dates from 1932. It will therefore be celebrating its fiftieth birthday in 1982.

It was in 1960, under their artistic director, Peter Hall, that they first acquired a London home, taking over the Aldwych Theatre, and in 1961 they changed their name to the Royal Shakespeare Company. Peter Hall created a pool of actors and directors on three-year contracts and built up an ensemble company, a system copied by the long-awaited National Theatre Company, set up in 1962, which finally moved in to its brand-new London premises in 1976.

After over 400 years since the birth in Britain of the world's greatest playwright, without ever having a British theatre company, we suddenly ended up with *two* national companies. The R.S.C., at the moment, appears to be the more fashionable, loved by all the critics, while the National often receives adverse criticism and poorer publicity, but we are indeed lucky to have two such companies, reinforcing London's claim to be the world's greatest theatrical centre.

Trevor Nunn was Peter Hall's own choice as his successor, to the surprise of many outsiders. Like Hall, he comes from a working-class, Suffolk background (Nunn's father is a cabinet-maker, Hall's a railwayman), and went to Cambridge where he directed thirty-three student productions. He then went to the Belgrade Theatre in Coventry for two years before joining the R.S.C. as a director in 1964. He is married to the actress Janet Suzman and they have a baby son, Joshua, already a paid-up member of the Ipswich Town Supporters Club, according to the rosette on his nursery wall at their Hampstead home.

Since 1964, he has directed many great productions at the R.S.C. and has become in his time the single most important influence on how Shakespeare should be played. In 1981 he did his first major outside production, the musical *Cats* in the West End. (All R.S.C. staff are allowed to do outside work.) Perhaps his most spectacularly successful production in recent years has been *Nicholas Nickleby* in 1980 which opened to mixed reviews and half-full audiences, but then became a sell-out. By popular demand, nay acclamation, as Vincent Crummles himself might have said, they were forced to bring it back twice the following year. Then in 1981 it was invited to New York.

The idea for Nickleby goes back seven or eight years, partly to a holiday Nunn had with his wife Janet in a remote cottage in Corfu. He started reading aloud from *Little Dorrit* to her every evening as a holiday amusement.

"I realised then how amazingly theatrical Dickens's words were, but I didn't do much about it. A year or so later I was in Russia, talking to the director of the Gorki Theatre, and I happened to ask him what his next production was – and it was an adaptation of *Pickwick Papers*. I thought, that's ridiculous. The *Russians* doing our novels.

"All the elements came together in 1979, a time of financial crisis when we thought we might go out of business completely in London. We needed one big epic production to concentrate our resources. We decided to take the plunge. It was a very dangerous decision. I won't feel like taking it again for many years. We could have done ourselves such damage, if it had failed."

They spent the first five weeks of rehearsals improvising from the book, letting the sixty or so actors who were available choose the characters they fancied doing. They decided not to cut out a single sub-plot, to use almost all the 157 named characters in the 900-page novel, to create on stage the sort of labyrinth Dickens created on paper, so that the audience would lose itself in a huge narrative adventure.

David Edgar, the playwright, had watched the initial workshop period and when he came to write the final script, he realised that it would need a play *nine hours* long to get everything in. So this was what they did. The play was divided in two parts which could be seen either on separate evenings or in one all-day sitting. Anyone who saw it, as I did, will never forget the experience. There can hardly have been a *bigger* play ever put on anywhere in the world. The 43 actors played between them 271 different characters. Only Nicholas (Roger Rees) and Smike (David Threlfall) played one role each. Many played six. One actress had ten costume changes.

There were so many costumes that John Napier, the designer, didn't have time to draw any of them. The actors queued up and each one went through the racks of a costumier with Napier trying clothes on them for their various parts, then he photographed them in character with a Polaroid. An album of 271 different Polaroid snaps was then presented to Trevor Nunn and John Caird (the co-director) for their approval. Only two costumes were changed.

"I remember when we moved into the Rainbow Theatre for the first time, for the final rehearsals," says Trevor. "It was like a mad house. There were between eight and nine rehearsals going on in the same theatre at the same time. There were moments when I felt we were leading an army of lemmings over a cliff."

In the end, it all ended in triumph, winning awards, the most for any British play in living memory. The production was acclaimed in New York and was filmed for T.V., the first major drama project for the new Fourth Channel.

The Winter's Tale, by comparison, would appear to be just another Shakespeare play. The reason for it cropping up at that moment in the repertory was indeed very prosaic – it was its turn. Under their charter, they are a *Shakespearean* company, and so they have to get through the entire canon of thirty-seven plays at regular intervals. The most popular ones come round every three years or so, while the less popular, like *The Winter's Tale*, take around five years to re-appear. It was previously done in 1969 and 1976.

It happens to be Trevor Nunn's own favourite Shakespeare play, which I discovered when I asked him to arrange the thirty-seven plays in order of his personal preference. *The Winter's Tale* was followed by *Twelfth Night, Henry IV, Part Two, King Lear, The Tempest* and *Hamlet*. I was surprised to see such popular favourites as *Macbeth* at 16, *Othello* 17, while *Romeo and Juliet* was right down the list at 25. Last were *Titus Andronicus* and *Henry VIII*.

"Along with *The Three Sisters* by Chekhov, I consider *A Winter's Tale* the most perfect play ever penned. The first part is a tragedy, of a man destroying himself, his friends, his family, ending in utter blackness and despair. The second part is pastoral, about young people, about love and faith and hope and resilience. The final part is one of reconciliation and rejoicing as the children bring the parents together again.

Youngh Love: Leonie Mellinger (Perdita) and Peter Chelsom (Florizel) in "The Winter's Tale".

"The end of the play is a miracle. No ordinary dramatist would even dare attempt a miracle on stage, but Shakespeare not only does it, he brings it off. You work on a knife edge with the statue scene. I have seen school productions make it hilarious. I've also seen it so wonderfully staged that I've burst into tears."

He was very pleased with the casting of the play, and the choice of the director. He had offered Ron Eyre several times the chance to be one of their nine associate directors, to make him throw in his lot with the company. And he was very pleased that Sheila Hancock had at last agreed to play Paulina.

Not all the R.S.C.'s Stratford productions come into London. It depends on many things. The production might not be good enough. Leading actors and actresses might leave, one of the many headaches for the artistic directors, as

Left: *Gemma Jones, making up for her part of Hermione in The Winter's Tale*. Right: *On stage*.

Equity only allows them to sign actors on a sixty-week contract. "At the end of the first sixty weeks, they can listen to the offers for the second year, and say no. Then I can get held over a barrel." However, it was hoped by everyone concerned that *The Winter's Tale* would be a success at Stratford then come to London in 1982 as part of the Company's opening season at the Barbican.

For the past thirteen years, since Trevor Nunn became artistic director, not a week of his life has passed without some decision having to be made about their move to the Barbican Centre, the massive arts and conference complex near St Paul's built by the City of London at a cost of almost £200 million. The two main elements are a 2,000-seat hall, to be the London home of the London Symphony Orchestra, and a 1,200-seat theatre for the R.S.C., plus a smaller theatre, The Pit, seating 200. The Centre also contains three cinemas, an art gallery, sculpture court, library, trade halls and restaurants.

Mr Nunn had decided not to organise any spectacular opening productions, but to carry on much as normal. The National Theatre's arrival at their proud new home had been rather spoiled by delays and over-expectations. The two plays he himself was about to start directing, *Henry IV, Parts One and Two* might well be suitable. "You would have to search a long way to find two other great plays which actually take place in the City of London. Falstaff lived in the City, after all. But, if *The Winter's Tale* turns out terribly well, and there were no serious cast changes, then it might have the honour of being our opening play."

Later that day, Nunn went round to the Barbican to see how work was progressing. The final shape of the theatre was now apparent, and most of the seats were in place, though there were dust and workmen and noise everywhere. From the very beginning, back in Peter Hall's day, the architects have involved the R.S.C. in every decision, from the design of the W.C. cisterns to the building of the stage.

As a large company, with many actors, a large repertory and constantly-changing productions, they needed a larger storage space than a normal theatre and more quick-change areas. All the dressing rooms (and there is space for eighty-eight, including twenty-one individual dressing rooms with baths or showers) have quick access to both sides of the stage, by lifts and stairs.

"The heart of every Shakespeare play is the soliloquy – when an actor stands alone and talks to the audience, when Shakespeare does his double think. He has to come forward and address the audience, in character, and say to them, 'Listen, at last I'm alone, these are the issues facing me, I can do this, or I can do that, what do you think . . .?'

"If you have a theatre in the round, with a wrap-around audience, then he can address only part of them while he has his back or his side to the rest. We worked out a Point of Command, the most important point of the stage, where soliloquies usually take place, and drew an arc of 120 degrees, the angle of human vision. The entire design of the theatre was built round one man being able to look out, at 120 degrees, and see everyone in the auditorium."

The strange thing is that the theatre *looks* like a wrap-around, because of the ingenious design. Unlike the endless galleries of the Victorian theatre, each piled straight on top of the other, up to the gods, there are only three narrow circles, containing just two rows of seats, which jut forward, one above the other, but *towards* the stage. There is a feeling of intimacy, yet with a total seating of 1,166, it is just bigger than the National's biggest theatre, the Olivier,

Gemma Jones and Patrick Stewart in The Winter's Tale.

which has 1,160 seats. The Shakespearean point of command has not been lost. Every seat in the theatre is within sixty-five feet of the stage.

Nunn sees the Company's arrival in the City of London as the beginning of a new community life. In Stratford, or on tour in, say, Newcastle, they have always gone out of their way to be part of the community, involved with educational and social projects, unlike their Aldwych life where they have been just another part of the West End, in an entertainment not a residential area. He hopes that in the City they will prove a focal point for people living in the East End. The aim is to work on the area, using all the facilities of the Barbican, and link up with local residents. The Guildhall School of Music and Drama is already part of the Barbican site, and it is planned that the School will have direct connection with the R.S.C., and with the London Symphony, all three institutions working for the benefit of all, making one big creative and educational centre.

In the summer of 1981, *The Winter's Tale* opened at Stratford-on-Avon to a warm reception, with Patrick Stewart particularly getting good reviews. The famous statue scene was considered by most critics to be a big success. (Frank Herrmann, taking photographs at the dress rehearsal, was almost in tears, even though he was supposed to be concentrating on his lenses, not his emotions ...)

It was still to be decided whether the play would be part of the opening season at the Barbican in 1982, but it was obvious to everyone by then that the move to the Barbican was going to be the most important development in the Royal Shakespeare Company's history, their first purpose-built home for fifty years. It might even prove a major development in the general artistic life of London, heralding a movement East, away from the West End.

Trevor Nunn, outside the Barbican.

18 The Stock Exchange

MEANWHILE in the City, it was just another day, doing what the City has been doing for the last 400 years, shifting money around.

It began for Mr Charles Telfer when he left home just after seven o'clock in the morning to catch the train to Waterloo. Mr Telfer is a stockbroker and he lives in Stockbroker Surrey near a village called Frensham, some forty-two miles from London, though he is at pains to point out that his house is *not* mock stockbroker but *real* Tudor. He is forty-nine years old, an amply-built, rather florid gentleman, whose bulky frame and jovial manner can often mislead strangers into thinking he might not be quick on his feet, or in his mind. When it comes to action, of either sort, Mr Telfer happens to be exceedingly alert.

Carol Davidson left her flat in Kensington High Street, which she shares with another girl, rather later and went by tube to Cannon Street whence she walked through Popeshead Alley and St Swithin's Lane, narrow and very ancient City streets, now surrounded by towering office blocks. Miss Davidson is twenty-three, a well-brought up young lady who went to a convent boarding school in Tunbridge Wells and left at eighteen with three A-levels. She works as a Stock Exchange guide. She got the job two years ago when she heard through a friend that the Stock Exchange was looking for a tall girl. She's not *really* all that tall, just five foot nine.

She arrived at the Stock Exchange about 9.30 and said hello to Rex and Eric and Paul, three of the Waiters, which is what the Stock Exchange calls their official attendants. She was wearing a smart grey flannel skirt and jacket, bought from Harrods, her winter uniform which, like the other three girls in her department, she will wear all winter, from September to April.

Mr Telfer's train ride from Frensham to Waterloo took him about one hour during which time he read the morning papers. He was particularly interested in one story about problems in the House of Fraser, the group which owns Harrods. There had been a running row for several weeks between Tiny Rowland of Lonrho, whose firm had acquired nearly 30 percent of the Fraser shares, and Sir Hugh Fraser, the chairman. They had fallen out and Mr Rowland had decided to sell his Fraser shares. The stockbroking firm for which Mr Telfer works had been instructed accordingly. Then, almost overnight, they had become friends again and the sale was off. Today, there was going to be a board meeting at the House of Fraser. Even Mr Telfer, whose job it is to make intelligent predictions about such things, was not sure what the day might bring.

At Waterloo, Mr Telfer changed to The Drain, the express tube which goes direct from Waterloo to Bank station in the City, a four-minute run which it does all day long, back and forward.

Overleaf: *The City at Night, with the Nat West Tower on the left.* Left: *Charles Telfer, stockbroker, at work.*

He was wearing a smart pin-striped suit, like many of the 300,000 people who come into the City each day. Bowler hats have long since gone out and even toppers are few and far between, except on formal business occasions for people like the Government brokers.

There is a certain glamour in the hurrying City masses, in their clean shirts and smart suits, but in essence they are simply going to work, about to clock on at their particular factory, put in the hours till the whistle blows and the City is denuded as the 300,000 bodies pile out into the streets again, rush to the stations and home. Most of them work in surprisingly cramped conditions at crowded, narrow desks with incessant noise all around as people shout into telephones or machines splutter out the latest information. Most of them have no more privacy or peace than many a factory worker.

Mr Telfer arrived at his office in Ocean House, Little Trinity Lane, before nine o'clock. His firm is called Carr, Sebag and they are one of the bigger stockbroking firms with around 300 staff, including fifty partners. They are the result of an amalgamation between Joseph Sebag and Co. and W. I. Carr in 1979. He was educated at Pangbourne College and Pembroke College, Oxford, coming down after two years when his father became seriously ill. His father, a Scottish accountant, had been a partner in Joseph Sebag, though he had died by the time Charles arrived in the firm. He admits it was a help getting in but thinks it was a hindrance when he was working his way up through the firm, as he felt he had to try harder to prove himself.

He is now a senior Partner, the Dealing Partner in charge of their Stock Exchange work. The majority of people who work in stockbroking firms rarely go near the Stock Exchange. The actual dealing is the tip of the iceberg. Behind the scenes, back in the office, the main activity is analysing the market, acquiring and passing on information and advice about what has happened and what might happen. Only the Dealers physically go out into the market place.

Mr Telfer had a quick look at his morning post, read a few messages, made a few 'phone calls, had a few words, then left his office and walked to the Stock Exchange, ready for opening time at half past nine, when the day's trading begins.

The London Stock Exchange is a monster modern block, twenty-five storeys high, in the heart of the City, just round the corner from the Bank of England in Threadneedle Street. It was opened by the Queen in 1973, on the site of the original Stock Exchange, a building they had used since 1802, though the selling of shares has been going on in this area of the City since the sixteenth century. Most of the business, like many other ancient City institutions, was originally conducted in coffee houses. They used the waiters to convey messages, which is why the attendants are called Waiters today.

The first share dealings were done to finance the merchant adventurers on their sixteenth-century explorations to the far corners of the globe. It is said to have been Sebastian Cabot's suggestion which led in 1553 to three ships being equipped for a voyage to Russia by gathering the necessary money together in £25 portions, till they had reached the total of £6,000, which is what they thought the voyage would cost. The idea of sharing the financing of the expedition was 'lest any private man should be too much oppressed'. Only one of the three ships survived, but it led to the formation of the Muscovy Company, the world's first joint stock company.

The arrival of share-holding companies, with shares which were easily transferable, provided an outlet for people who might have some spare cash. Until then, there had been few opportunities. There were no banks or building societies, back in the sixteenth century. You either bought land with your savings, lent it at interest (though this had formerly been illegal and usury was still not considered moral or respectable), or you hid it in the garden or under the bed. When Samuel Pepys fled before the Fire of London in 1666, he buried his gold and valuables.

With the coming of the Industrial Revolution, the idea of sharing the risks in a new venture, which had been developed for trading expeditions abroad, was applied to all sorts of new industries, most of all to the Railways. The coming of Railway mania in the 1840s created the world's first large-scale boom in shares, with all manner of people, from all classes, rushing to buy railway shares, many of which later collapsed.

Carol Davidson, Stock Exchange guide.

With shares changing hands in private enterprises, and in loans to the Monarch and Government, there had arisen by the end of the seventeenth century a race of people who handled these deals. There were brokers, who were the middle-men and on the whole respectable, and jobbers, who were not so respectable. In those early decades, swindles were frequent. It was over a long period of time that the Stock Exchange formulated its own council to control the dealing in shares.

Today, it is so highly regulated that it can take volumes to explain the different rules, but the process is very much the same, and so is a lot of the language. To help strangers, they have a bookstall inside the Visitors' entrance to the Stock Exchange, where you can also buy souvenir pens and badges.

Over 200,000 people a year visit the Stock Exchange and its Information Department likes to think that it's now the best free show in town. You can arrive any time, from 10 to 3.15, Monday to Friday, and watch the trading take place, without having to book, and go up to the Gallery, where you can see a twenty-minute film, be taken on a guided tour and have your questions answered.

Carol Davidson was on the microphone, in her role as a Gallery Guide, explaining what was happening to a crowd of students and schoolchildren who were milling around her, staring through the glass at the floor of the Exchange below.

"Our ten-minute talk is basically the same every day," she said during a break, "though we add on any company announcements. The announcement today is about the House of Fraser. I don't know the details. Just that today the House of Fraser is due to make some announcement.

"I couldn't wait to get on the microphone in the first few months, now I'm more used to it and it's just part of the job. We do the talk seven times a day, sharing it among the four of us. Sometimes the visitors are a bit noisy, when you get certain sorts of school parties. I started my talk one day and I could hear one boy saying loudly, 'Stuck up old cow.'"

As well as helping visitors, the four Gallery Guides also go out round the country, showing films and slides about the Stock Exchange. The previous day Carol had addressed sixty men at a Rotary Club luncheon in Newhaven. She was quite nervous at first of such groups, but now takes it in her stride. They also appear at Stock Exchange receptions, given by the Council for important visitors, where they act as hostesses.

Around 90 percent of the population has a stake in the Stock Exchange, even if most of them are not aware of it. There are $2\frac{1}{2}$ million individuals who directly own stocks and shares, plus many more millions whose pensions, bank savings and insurance policies are invested on the Stock Exchange. Most of our major firms, from British Rail to I.C.I. as well as the big unions, put their members' pension funds into shares.

Over £700 million change hands every day in 25,000 deals, which makes the London Stock Exchange the largest in the world, in terms of shares handled, but not the most valuable. It now ranks third in value, after New York and Japan.

The Stock Exchange, in London and in its provincial exchanges in Manchester, Glasgow, Birmingham, York, Belfast and Dublin, is different from the other major stock exchanges in the world in that the job of dealing in shares is divided. In Britain, the stockbroker never owns the shares. He is merely the agent, an intermediary, instructed by his client to either buy or sell shares. He makes his income from his commission on the sale. The stock jobber, or jobber, on the other hand, is dealing only for himself. He buys from brokers, and sells to brokers, and during the time that the shares are in his hands, he owns them. He has no contact with the client, and gets no commission. His income comes from making a profit on his dealings. The jobber is in effect the wholesaler, dealing in enormous amounts of shares, hoping that if he does make a loss on some shares, having paid too much and being forced to sell for a lower amount, he will make a profit each day on his total trading. The jobber is the one taking the risks. The broker is not risking any of his own money, though naturally he too can come a cropper, if his clients don't want to use him any more, or if they don't pay, leaving him with their debts.

In America, the system is simpler, with only one group, the brokers, directly engaged in matching up a buyer with a seller. The British defend their system on two grounds. It limits the possibility of frauds, as the broker is always there to protect his client. It is also, so the British maintain, a quicker system, ensuring a constant flow of business. Jobbers have to keep buying and selling

The floor of the Stock Exchange.

to survive. At any one moment they will always quote a price, regardless of the state of the market.

Only stockbrokers or jobbers who are Members of the Stock Exchange are allowed to trade on the floor of the house. In the old days, before 1968, you could buy your Membership, once you were approved by the Council, without having any qualifications. Naturally, it was often a home for younger sons. Today, Membership of the Stock Exchange has been turned into a profession, with exams to be passed, which can take five years, before you can be elected.

The public is not allowed on the floor, so you have to watch the action from above. Strangers, therefore, need Guides to explain what on earth is going on. I looked down and there seemed to be thousands of people buzzing around. They couldn't all be brokers, could they?

Carol explained that some were Blue Buttons, wearing the names of their firms on a blue metal badge, who are the apprentices, learning the business. They are not allowed to deal and mostly observe or run messages. Then there are the Yellow Badges, senior clerks, people long experienced in dealing, who have been given the authority of their firms to make deals, but without the status of being a Member. Finally, there are the Members themselves. They wear silver grey badges.

Government Broker in his topper.

At first sight it was like looking into a mill pond in early spring and finding a mass of writhing tadpoles, all struggling for survival, slipping back and forward, in and out of the throng, never appearing to get anywhere. Once your eyes start focusing properly, you can see pattern in the movement, shapes appear, like iron filings under a magnet.

Across the floor are fifteen hexagonal booths, like stalls at a fairground, displaying lists of prices, amidst a mass of telephones and flashing lights. These contain the jobbers who remain around their booths waiting for the brokers to come up and do business. Jobbers in the same line of business are grouped together. British Government stock is in a row at the back, as you look down from the Gallery. In the middle are those jobbers dealing in British companies. Nearest the front, it's foreign and mining shares. A trained eye can therefore look down and see exactly which area is having most of the excitement. The first hour and the last hour of trading are normally the busiest every day.

You can't hear what's happening down below, because of the plate glass window, so the effect is rather eerie, but it *looked* noisy, with all the rushing around, getting the day's business started. Most foreigners, even those in finance, find it very confusing. Why, for example, does a broker have to rush back and forward from jobber to jobber, finding out their prices, when a computer could work out the best prices at once?

The British maintain that what matters is being able to look the other chap firmly in the eye, negotiating in the flesh, sealing the bargains as gentlemen, in just a few words. Later on, the respective offices have all the paper work to do, but nothing can be altered. 'My Word is my Bond', so runs the proud motto of the Stock Exchange.

When a dealer approaches a jobber he at first gives very little away, simply asking, "What's Marks and Spencer?" The jobber then quotes a double price, 116–118. At this stage, he doesn't know whether the dealer wants to sell Marks shares or buy them, so he is saying that he'll buy them at 116p and sell them at 118p.

In quoting his price, the jobber has to reflect the past prices, how he thinks the market is going. He has to guess from perhaps previous deals whether the broker in question is trying to unload or buy a large amount. The broker then moves round other jobbers and selects the price which suits him best. He might eventually reveal what he is doing, perhaps getting a special price made when he says he wants to buy £1 million Marks shares.

The dealers are in permanent touch these days by walkie-talkie radios with their colleagues, either those in special 'Boxes' round the outside of the Stock Exchange floor, (unseen from the Gallery above), or in their main offices, supplying them with all the latest information and advice. Like link men on T.V. programmes, they have voices constantly in their ears, giving instructions, while they are conducting their negotiations.

As lunchtime drew near, the trading floor began to clear. Jobbers could be seen leaning back or sitting down on ledges round the stall, resting their legs. There were far fewer dealers around and those left were chatting in little groups of two or three. One was doing a silly walk, to the amusement of his friends. It's not that most dealers have rushed off to big business lunches, neglecting their work, but that the rest of the country has gone to lunch, and so orders from clients dry up. When times are really slack, impromptu games of cricket take place, paper darts get thrown, rude notes are pinned on the backs of unsuspecting people and other jolly pranks. During the skateboarding craze, someone introduced a board and several elderly Members had a go. All boys at heart.

Up in the Gallery, Carol came back from her lunch break to take her turn sitting at the information desk, ready to answer questions from visitors. A young American in a beard came up and complained to her about the film, saying that they'd missed out one vital factor in extolling the virtues of the Stock Exchange. "What about the risk factor? You don't tell people you can lose a lot of money."

"You have a point," replied Carol politely, "but it is meant to be a simple introduction to the Stock Exchange, about its history and how it works." He didn't look convinced.

At least once a day, someone appears in the Gallery and looks completely confused, blinking in amazement at the plate glass, as if they've staggered into a human zoo. She can now recognize such symptoms at once. They think they're in the Post Office. That's the next-door building.

Down in the Stock Exchange Boxes, something approaching pandemonium had broken out in the firm of Carr, Sebag. After a fairly quiet start to the morning, Charles Telfer was now shouting into various telephones, jumping up and down, rushing to teleprinters and T.V. screens, grabbing bits of paper, yelling instructions.

There were about three dozen people in his firm's Box, seated on either side of long narrow desks, as if they were all playing complicated electric organs, their lights and screens flashing in front of them. At one end was a raised dais with two telephonists working a switchboard. On one wall was a board with the latest prices, put up by hand, and below it nine T.V. cameras sending the latest prices, by closed circuits, to their major clients in London and elsewhere. It was very much like a bookmaker's office, cut off from real life, without daylight or fresh air, except that the floor was much cleaner.

"I haven't had lunch," said Charles. "What a bloody day. Would you believe it. Not a bite. Won't be a sec." And he was back to his machines,

Dealers on the floor.

pulling handles, pressing buttons, as if working one-armed bandits, hoping his luck would change.

From his figure, it didn't look as if Charles had missed many lunches in his life, so this must be serious. While I waited for whatever his panic was caused by to subside, I moved into a relatively quieter corner of the room and was offered a plastic cup of coffee by a couple of the firm's senior members, one of them a rather aristocratic-looking gentleman.

"Capitalism is a dead duck," he said. "The Tories are no better than the Socialists. They've ruined the market. I tell you, capitalism is dead. All these rules and regulations, what rubbish. If only we could get back to the days of free trade, when one could get on with one's bloody job without all this interference."

"But small shareholders have to be protected," said the other broker.

"No, they don't. The small people are now a minor part of the equation. All that happens is that the inevitable is prolonged."

Charles was at last off the 'phones and his colleagues were able to hear the latest excitement. It was all to do with the battle between Tiny Rowland of Lonhro and Sir Hugh Fraser of the House of Fraser.

That day at 1.10, just as Charles was going off for lunch, the news had come through from the Fraser board meeting that Hugh Fraser had been chucked out as chairman of the House of Fraser. Rowland had then immediately reversed his whole policy. Instead of selling his Fraser shares, as he'd announced a few days previously, he now said he was going to buy up the whole of the House of Fraser, offering 150p a share.

On the face of it, this was good news for Charles Telfer and all at Carr, Sebag. As Lonhro's brokers, it would now be their job to buy up Fraser shares. They knew, for example, exactly where to buy half a million pounds at a bargain price of 144p a share, which would have brought them in a commission of around £10,000. But, alas, for Carr, Sebag. There is a Stock Exchange rule˙ which states that no firm can take over another firm of a quarter its own size or more without the permission of its shareholders. So, until an emergency meeting of Lonhro shareholders, the brokers could do nothing. Their hands were tied. In the meantime, the Fraser shares were rising, so their clients would have to pay more money. Even worse, the delay might bring out a rival bidder, and they could be left with no shares to buy after all.

The senior Partner who had been moaning about all the rules had had his prejudices confirmed. Everyone agreed that Lonhro shareholders, when they met, would back Rowland, so the inevitable would still happen. Only it would take longer.

Charles made a few more 'phone calls passing on the Fraser news to his various departments and contacts, and then at 3.30, when trading on the floor stopped for the day, walked back to his office in Little Trinity Lane. They have five floors of the building, plus the basement, which includes their own printing press and a giant computer which takes up a whole room.

Charles pressed the button for the lift and it opened immediately, much to his surprise. Although it is a modern building, the lift had been playing tricks recently. "Hurrah," he said, as it opened. "The cleverest bloody thing I've done all day."

He went up to his own rather lavish room, complete with antiques and velvet-covered couches, which he shares with two other senior partners. Their secretary sits in a separate room. The language of brokers, talking amongst themselves, is very much like a school changing room. His secretary keeps a swear box in which she deposits 5p for every 'bloody' she happens to hear.

Charles made several 'phone calls and talked to various of his partners who walked in and out of the room. One of them came in and sat down at a desk, sighing for the old days. He too had had a rather unsatisfactory day. The City does seem to be full of either absolute pessimists or raging optimists.

"We lived on the fat of the land in the Sixties," said the broker, putting his long legs up on an antique desk. "And I mean fat. There was so much money around and shares were jumping. Macmillan was right. We never had it so good. It's been bloody awful since 1974. I'm an equity partner and there was one year when I earned nothing at all. The firm was very lucky just to break even on that year's work.

"In the old days, in the Sixties, we had a much higher social status. At a party, after they'd talked to the doctor, to tell him all their symptoms, they would make for the stockbroker to ask his advice about their Marks and Spencer shares. We were considered pretty smart people. Now, at parties, no one wants to talk to stockbrokers. We rate pretty low. They'd rather talk to some poofy antique dealer about their furniture than us. Who can blame them? Shares have been a rotten investment for many people in the last seven years.

"I believe it goes in cycles, seven fat years and seven lean. The fat ones really were fat, and the lean have been lean. I detect this year for the first time a little bit of flesh. Let's hope seven good years are coming up. In the

The floor of the Stock Exchange, seen from the Visitors' Gallery. The hexagonal boxes contain the jobbers who wait at their booths for the brokers to come and do business.

The following text appears in the image on the board:

BLACK...
BRIDON
BRIDPORT·C
CARLTON INDS.
DOWN BROS.
FRANCIS IND.
HAWKINS & T.

N RUBBER   Use a four-letter word today!
LTD.
. INT.
. GROUP

HAWTIN IND.
HESTAIR LTD.
LON. & MID. INDS.
MACFARLANE GROUP
MARTIN BLACK
MOSS, B.
PLYSU LTD.

NDELL PERMO

SMITH & NEPH.

REX

STEWARTS

NY DIT.
NLDEN

REVERTEX

PAINT
N IND.
ND PAINT
PHERSON D.
RS

FIRMS TAKEN OVER
WHITE CHILD & B.
ALBRIGHT & W.
R. MCBRIDE
W.W. BALL
FER CHEM HLDS.
VISCOSE DEV.

The floor of the Stock Exchange. Out of the 4,200 Members, only 38 are women.

meantime, we've had to adapt, to amalgamate in our case, and trim all expenses. I would say that the City as a whole is now carrying very few passengers. There are no old boys using the City as their club. Everyone counts. You are out, if you don't perform. No one can afford idlers."

Charles was eventually off the 'phone, still his beaming self. He had done a little bit of normal business during the day, selling £100,000 worth of shares for a pension fund, and getting 1½p a share more than he had expected, so that had pleased him. Altogether, despite the Fraser pandemonium, he had bought or sold £500,000 worth of shares. His best day ever, in dealings, came to £20 million. He had also found time in the morning for some Stock Exchange business. He is on the Council and involved in various of their committees.

"The pleasure is in the uncertainty. You can't plan your day. You think what future events might take place, you read all the analyses, read the papers, work out a strategy, then you have to wait and see if it all works out. At the end of each day, you know whether you were right or wrong. We would all like to know tomorrow's share prices today. Clients always have the benefit of hindsight, when they tell us what went wrong. We can lose our fees completely on a day like this. *And* I've had no lunch.

"I think some people here think I just hang about the Stock Exchange all day, talking to people, but when things happen, I act quickly. That's what I like doing. I really enjoy take-over bids. We were involved in the Racal offer for Decca, which meant fighting off G.E.C. and Arnold Weinstock, and we worked for Charles Clore in many of his take-overs, and for Beechams, and others. It's good to have the ball at your feet. Very good for the ego. But even when the other fellow has the ball, it's good trying to get in the middle and take it off him. That's the spice of life to me, being at the centre of an exciting deal."

But wasn't it all really just a game? The really creative decisions were being taken out there in the sticks, by industrialists actually *producing* the goods. The brokers were just playing with monopoly money.

"Let me tell you about Nimslo. I was introduced last year by a client to an American called Jerry Nimms who had a new invention, a three-D camera. He had failed to get enough money to develop it in America and was passing through London en route to Switzerland, hoping the Swiss bankers might put up some money. He never for one moment expected anybody in Britain would raise the money. He was literally passing through. I had a quick meeting with him and two of my corporate finance partners, listened to his idea, and within a few weeks we had helped to raise several million to develop his new camera. Here in Britain. It's now being manufactured up at Dundee in Scotland. The money all came from here, in the City. Now, isn't that exciting and constructive?"

He got his umbrella and around 6.30 made his way across the street to the Bank tube station, to get the Drain back to far-flung Surrey, smiling to himself at the thought of tomorrow's excitements.

Carol Davidson's work as a Guide finished not long after trading ceased, which means she always gets home before the rush hour. That day she was going to Harrods to do some shopping. One can't shop in the City.

She doesn't mind that the Stock Exchange and the City generally is such a male society. She doesn't have to go out at lunch, as she and the three other girls have their own little dining room. "I wouldn't go to the pubs anyway. They're just full of sweaty men. Who would want to be taken there?"

They get lots of offers of course, and find it quite easy to refuse, but like most of the women who work in the building they have to put up with a bit of teasing. Out of the 4,200 Members of the Stock Exchange only thirty-eight are women, though there are a few hundred female secretarial workers in the various broking firms.

"It's awful the names some girls have to put up with. I heard one today being called Martini. 'Anytime, anywhere.' I know others who are called Spanner, Sweaty Betty, the Israeli Gunboat, the Grimsby Trawler. It's frightful. I don't think I'd like to work down in the Boxes.

"The brokers themselves are very nice, terribly highly qualified people. You wouldn't believe the research that's done. I don't think I could do it. I'd resent working out all that advice, then the client doesn't take it.

"I love working in the Gallery. It's so nice. We organise our own lives, between the four of us. There's a constant stream of new faces. Every day is different."

Then she went home to Kensington, another day over, another £700 million of paper money having changed hands.

19 The Proms

GOING to the last night of the Proms is probably the most uplifting communal experience anyone in Britain can have. Wem-bu-lee is wonderful, but it can turn out a poor match and fifty percent of the crowd will always be slightly disappointed, having wanted the other team to win. Everybody wins, at the Proms. It's not just a matter of enjoying oneself, or even enjoying others enjoying themselves, but enjoying the fact of being British.

They began in 1895 and though they're always called the Henry Wood Promenade Concerts they weren't strictly his idea. It was Robert Newman, the manager of the newly-built Queen's Hall in Langham Place, who decided to put on concerts where the public could walk about and enjoy themselves. "I am going to run nightly concerts and train the public by easy stages. Popular at first, gradually raising the standard until I have *created* a public for classical and modern music." It was he who appointed Henry Wood, then aged twenty-six, to be the first conductor.

Six years later, during the 1901 Proms, this was the impression of a Prommer, Thomas Burke, after he had gone to his first concert.

"I had seen a poster announcing 'Promenade Concerts at the Queen's Hall; Smoking permitted; Admission One Shilling'. I wasn't sure what a Promenade Concert was; the words probably brought an image of a seaside promenade and its band; but I soon discovered what a Promenade Concert wasn't. It wasn't a concert at which, except in the interval, you could do any promenading. The Promenade floor was a jam, mainly of young men wearing straw hats ... We were young, and the majority was, I imagine, in my own condition; that is keenly responsive to music, but knowing little about it."

In 1926 the B.B.C. took over the sponsorship of the Proms, still with Sir Henry Wood as sole conductor. They lost their original home, the Queen's Hall, when it was destroyed by enemy action in 1941 but, despite a World War going on, the Proms managed to continue.

The B.B.C.'s Controller of Music is today responsible for the Proms, for their organisation and their content, and it is now an enormous exercise. In 1980, there were 22 orchestras, 42 conductors, 33 solo instrumentalists, 75 singers and 18 choirs who together performed 57 Proms in eight weeks. The total musical man power involved was 2,903 different artists. Despite the expense of such an operation, the cheap tickets were still amazingly cheap – only 90p to be a Promenader, if you could get a ticket.

The B.B.C. does of course get a lot of mileage out of the Proms. Nine of the concerts usually appear on T.V., while Radio 3, in wonderful stereo, broadcasts every one and Radio 4 does some of the more popular ones. Prom concerts, both live and recorded, constitute the major music on the World Service programmes and, in 1980 twenty-one of the concerts went live round

the world. The B.B.C. estimates that each year there is a world audience for the Proms of around 150 million.

The basic aim is still much the same as it was back in 1895. The public is being carefully educated. Each season, the programmes include a proportion of new or relatively-unknown music, some of it specially commissioned for the Proms, along with the all-time favourites.

Mozart was the most popular composer in the programmes for the 1980 Proms, with 12 works to be performed, followed by Beethoven 11, Richard Strauss 8 (though that includes five songs), Stravinsky 8, Tchaikovsky 6, Brahms 6, Handel 5. At the same time, there was a total of 74 works which had never before been performed at any Promenade concert.

The Last Night, the best-known night, for which all 7,500 tickets are now allocated by ballot, has retained its traditional format since the last War. The first half is serious and the second half, after the interval, is much lighter.

The famous 'Sea Songs' have been included since 1905 when Henry Wood put them together for a concert celebrating the Nelson Centenary. They were so successful that Wood played them on the last night for the next forty years. Sir William Glock, when he was the B.B.C.'s Music Controller in 1969, decided to drop them, but there was a national uproar, headlines in the newspapers, and they had to be recalled.

Henry Wood from the very beginning realised what enjoyment the 'Sea Songs' gave to thousands. "They stamp their feet in time to the hornpipe – that is, until I whip up the orchestra in a fierce *accelerando* which leaves behind all those whose stamping technique is not of the first quality. I like

Queuing for the Proms: some sleep outside the Albert Hall for up to ten days for the Last Night.

to win by two bars, if possible, but sometimes have to be content with a bar and a half. It is good fun and I enjoy it as much as they do."

During Sir Malcolm Sargent's reign, as the leading conductor of the Proms, it was felt that the programmes were becoming too safe and traditional. Since 1959, when William Glock became the B.B.C.'s Music Controller, there has been a larger element each year of new and experimental music. All the same, despite what some musical purists might say today, the Proms under Sargent were immensely popular and for several years even managed to make a small profit. In 1980, the B.B.C. had to subsidise a loss of about £50,000 – though this is small compared with the total budget of around £600,000. (In 1981, the Proms cost £850,000.)

Writing in the 1980 programme, Sir Michael Tippett, now seventy-five, recalled many of his Proms memories over the previous fifty years, memories very similar to those of thousands of others, musicians and amateurs alike.

"My musical education really began with the Proms. When I came to the Royal College of Music in 1923, I was pretty well ignorant about the concert repertoire. That summer I learned of the existence of the Promenade Concerts, and I think I went to almost all of them. I shall certainly always remember standing in the arena and hearing, for the first time, all the Beethoven symphonies, performed in sequence on Friday nights, as well as great gorgeous chunks of Wagner.

"I recall Samuel Dushkin playing, and Henry Wood conducting, Stravinsky's violin concerto which in 1933 was new to this country. I was so fascinated by the concerto that I obtained a score and parts from Schott's and tried it out on my South London orchestra of unemployed musicians. Very bizarre it was."

*   *   *

I got to the Albert Hall nice and early, about two hours before the Last Night was due to begin, but already the queues were right round the Hall and down the next street. It looked more like a street festival than a queue for an orchestral concert. There were Union Jack emblems everywhere, on hats, T-shirts, dresses, and street traders going up and down the queues selling flags, at 20p and 50p. Many of the young people were in fancy dress, with straw boaters, bow ties, blazers, frock coats and tails, or dressed like clowns with painted faces.

At the front entrances stood the ticket touts, offering good seats, very reasonable, so they said, just like at Wembley, which was where the orchestra had played a few unofficial 'Prom' concerts that year. They had been on strike about the B.B.C.'s plan to cut various orchestras, and the first twenty concerts of the official Proms were cancelled, until a settlement was reached. The hard-core Prommers had backed the orchestra all the way.

Some of the people in the queue had been sleeping outside the Albert Hall for up to ten days. All the tickets for the last night, for seats and standing, had been pre-sold by ballot, so the people sleeping out already *had* tickets. They just wanted to make sure they got at the front, beside the rail.

I talked to one young man aged eighteen, Mark Rogers, from Redhill in Surrey, who works in an insurance firm. He said he had had a sleeping bag on the pavement throughout the last ten days. "There were already five or six sleeping out when I joined. By the last night there was about a hundred people sleeping. It gets a bit noisy, till the traffic stops, but we usually sleep under an arch. We had a very friendly policeman this year, which helped."

On the Last Night they always decorate Little Albert, one of the statues at the back of the Hall, garlanding him with 'No Parking' notices, 'For Sale' signs and flashing road lights. "We never take road signs from holes in the road, but even so, some police get upset and come round the queue making enquiries."

You can leave the queue for a few hours every day, by arrangement with the other Prommers. Mark went to museums and several times managed to get tickets for the orchestras' morning rehearsals. On the last morning he went home to have a bath and change. Time, apparently, doesn't hang heavily when you sleep in the queue for ten days. There is so much to do.

The Albert Hall, viewed from the rear, with Prommers filling in time by putting on a show for each other.

"We always have the Prom Olympics, which was very good this year. You have to see who can drink a milk shake in the fastest time, who can dress and undress inside a sleeping bag in the best times, an obstacle race round the Albert Hall and then drink as much water as you can from a plastic cup in five minutes. The winner drank five pints. Only two people were sick.

"The other big event is always the Groperetta. It's a sort of concert-cum-operetta. This year it was called *The Strike Break*, a sort of skit on Tippett's *The Ice Break*. We formed a small orchestra of about thirty Prommers in the queue, called the Prince Albert Flying Orchestra Society. Pafos for short. We spent an awful lot of time rehearsing. We printed and sold programmes and hired a public address system.

"This is my third season as a Prommer. It's hard to explain how you join. Things don't appear to be organised, but then you discover little cliques up and down the queue, working away all the time. You just keep coming each year, getting a season ticket for all the fifty or sixty concerts. If everyone else likes you, you fit in. I've always enjoyed classical music. What I really want to be in life is a classical percussionist. The thing that made me come three years ago was watching it on telly and being fascinated by the chanting. I didn't know how it was done."

And how is it done?

"Ah, well, you'll have to wait and see. It's mainly spontaneous. We prepare banners, but leave the witty remarks till they happen.

"I'm also interested in other things, you know. I happen to hold the world record for the longest daisy chain. I organised that when I was at school.

Our daisy chain was 3,565 feet long. We're in the *Guinness Book of Records*. Look us up."

I then talked to one of the young stewards on duty, Chris Christodoulou, aged twenty-three, an electronics technician. He said he was only an *honorary* steward for the Proms season, a great honour, and he had to be specially vetted. For the previous seven years he'd been a Prommer, standing on the floor of the Hall, in the so-called Arena. "It's been strange these last few weeks, watching it from the other side. I thought it might look silly, but it doesn't at all.

"I don't think they've been as noisy this year as in the past, not that anyone ever gets out of hand. There was one year when someone from the Gallery threw down a bus ticket roll, which was meant to unravel like a streamer, but it didn't and went straight through a cello. All the Prommers had a whip-round to pay for the damage.

"When you stand down in the Arena, every night for eight weeks, you get to know everyone very well. It becomes like a T.V. soap opera, like *Coronation Street* or *Crossroads* – there's a new drama every day. A boy and girl come together for a few weeks, then they fall out and stand on opposite sides of the Arena. People then try to get them back together, and in the end they do."

I finally tracked down a gentleman called Ken Johnson who has become an unofficial leader of the Prommers. He prepares a list each year of the hundred or so regular Prommers who keep in touch with one another all the year round and have reunions. He also organises the queue lists, with a Day List and a Night List, so that people can leave their place in the queue with safety for a few hours at a time.

He is looked upon as something of a fanatic, even an eccentric, who lives his life for the Proms. He's been coming every season since 1954. When he celebrated his 500th Prom, the other Prommers did a special card for him. At the 800th, they organised a buffet dinner at the pub frequented by many Prommers, the Harrington off Gloucester Road, and gave him a set of Bruckner Symphonies. "Tonight is my 891st Prom. I should celebrate my 1,000th in 1982."

He is aged forty-one and works as a porter at a departmental store in Kingston-on-Thames. "Two years ago, sir, I was one of those who put the wreath on Henry Wood at the end of the last night. Next day at work, a lady said, 'Did I see you on television last night?' 'Yes, madam,' I said. 'Very well done,' she said. I always have that sort of business, sir, after the Last Night. It gets embarrassing at work because people have seen me on television."

Ken had slept in the queue for the last ten days, but not on the pavement, like all the younger Prommers. He always moves his car nearby and sleeps in that. He still lives at home with his parents and always asks their permission to stay out overnight.

"I'd hoped to cut down the number of days sleeping this year, but so many people joined the queue early I had to come. I'm *always* at the rail, sir, so I have to be here first. I don't think I'll ever get married, or all that sort of business. A wife wouldn't put up with me and the Proms, sir."

One of his self-appointed tasks is to organise the queue collection. This year they had collected £541.92, which wasn't as much as the previous year when they got £800. They buy a white carnation for each member of the orchestra and choir, which comes to about 250 people, wrap them in silver foil, and present them before the concert. The carnation is in memory of Malcolm Sargent who always wore one. They also buy bouquets for the soloists and a box of chocolates for the conductor. The rest of the money, if any, gets to the Malcolm Sargent Cancer charity for children, and to Multiple Sclerosis.

Ken is very proud of the close connection the Prommers have built up with members of the orchestra. One even gave him a card on his anniversary. In turn, they support the orchestra in any way they can, such as during their strike. He's particularly proud that he's met, in the flesh, two of his heroes, Malcolm Sargent and Colin Davis.

I then went round to the Artists' entrance where the white carnations were being given out to every musician and singer, all looking very smart, as they arrived in their evening suits and dresses. "The thing about the Proms is that the audience is here purely to enjoy itself," said Colin Bradbury, principal clarinettist of the B.B.C. Symphony. "They're not here to pose or posture or to criticise. The hard-core Prommer is the best audience in the world. They are genuinely attentive. They never make a noise when they're not supposed to."

This was his twentieth year playing at the Proms. It's a hard time for the orchestra as they have so many concerts, usually around twenty in the eight weeks, plus rehearsing, with a lot of new and unusual music to learn. "It can be very stressful. Even tonight, the Last Night, is not easy. There's some hard slogging in the first half, with some heavy orchestration. The 'Young Person's Guide' means every member is on show, with the magnifying glass going round every part of the orchestra. In the second half, there are lots of solos, and they can be nerve-wracking. That's when I have my clarinet cadenza."

Inside the Hall, the Arena was already full. The Prommers at the front were singing and chanting, waving their flags and holding up notices. 'Save the Westminster Hospital', said one slogan. Even in the posh seats in the stalls, Union Jacks and banners were being unfurled. The Gallery, which also contains standing Prommers, seemed miles away, with four tiers of stalls between them and the floor. Their faces were just blurs, but their voices could be heard and their banners clearly seen. 'Hello, Ulverston', said one. 'Romps 80', said another, which was a nice variation on the most common poster, 'Proms 80'.

The chants being exchanged between the Prommers in the Arena and those up in the Gallery were all very school-boyish. You could see them getting into little huddles, then shouting one two three, and out would come the chant. "Arena to Gallery – Anyone for Tennis?" Back came the reply. "Gallery to Arena – Merry Christmas." When the Gallery shouted 'Shuttle', the reply was 'Cock', then they'd all laugh and cheer at their own wit. When a piano had to be moved on stage, the Arena shouted immediately 'Heave' and the Gallery shouted 'Ho'. (When two pianos are being moved, the Arena shouts 'Double Heave' and the Gallery shouts 'Double Ho'.)

Another regular trick is for the whole front row of the Arena to produce their keys from their pockets and start jangling them. Then at a signal they all shout, "We're glad to hear you're in the right key . . ."

Several of the shouts and chants were a bit hard to make out from where I sat in the stalls, presumably full of in-jokes and references to previous Proms. It was very like a football crowd, with old-established chants coming out at intervals, known by all the regulars, but then now and again a new chant would appear, almost spontaneously, responding to a new incident.

"Arena to Gallery, repeat after us, How Now Brown Cow." This was shouted with such great power that I took it to be a very old one.

"We are a little hoarse this year," replied the Gallery.

"Message from Arena – What?"

This led to more cheers and a hail of paper darts, balloons and streamers from the Gallery.

Many of the Arena people were holding teddy bears and other soft toys, some enormous, dressed in tails and Union Jack boaters. One young man at the front rail had a huge silver heart, tied to his hand by a six-foot length of string, which floated gently in the air like a kite.

Five minutes before 7.30, there was a sudden move forward down in the Arena. Every remaining inch of space was quickly filled as people tried to get as near the front as possible. Then there was a great cheer as the orchestra and choir started arriving to take up their places. Looking round the Hall, I could see that every seat was now taken. At football matches, even sell-outs, there are always a few empty seats as some people have not turned up, but the Albert Hall's complicated ticket system fills every space.

By the time the evening's conductor, Sir Charles Mackerras, had appeared, his rostrum was completely covered in streamers. The orchestra meanwhile were busy throwing back paper darts to the Prommers.

Ken Johnson, in a world of his own, helps to conduct the BBC Symphony Orchestra. Mr Johnson, an unofficial leader of the Prommers, has been to every Prom season since 1954. He works as a porter in a departmental store.

When the conductor finally motioned he was about to begin, there was absolute silence. The whole first half was listened to with great reverence, though two balloons somewhere in the hall did go bang, by accident. The 'Young Person's Guide to the Orchestra' was done in great style, with the percussion department obviously enjoying themselves.

During the interval, there were several blinding flashes as the special T.V. lights came on for the B.B.C. cameras and the Arena immediately burst into 'Happy Christmas, B.B.C.'. Then Henry Wood's bust was ceremonially garlanded with a green wreath by two proud Prommers wearing white 'Proms 80' T-shirts.

The second half contained eight works, all short, and each was greeted with roars of applause and tumultuous flag-waving, especially for the first item, Elgar's first Pomp and Circumstance March. This piece has been greeted rapturously by the Prommers every year since its premiere at the Proms in 1901. "The people simply rose and yelled," wrote Henry Wood in his autobiography. He recorded that, before the concert could continue, it had to be given a double encore.

It's strange to think that a brand-new work, unknown to an audience, should be so immediately accepted. The main tune, 'Land of Hope and Glory', is now as famous as the National Anthem. It's been endlessly parodied, and the words adapted to suit all occasions, from college reunions to football terraces, yet its emotional power is still enormous. It can bring tears to the eyes of every exile.

Everyone knew it was coming of course, most of all the Prommers in the Arena, and they were bobbing up and down from the first note, rising and falling in time, row upon row of them, then slowly they changed to moving from side to side, still in time to the music. There was continuous flag-waving throughout, till the hall was a sea of red, white and blue. There were two encores, each followed by tremendous applause. On the final encore, the orchestra began deliberately slowly, just to catch out the regulars, which led to more roars and cheers.

Henry Wood's 'Fantasia on Sea Songs' also brought the house down. The hornpipe was completely drowned by the stamping of feet and cheering. Some of the front row tried unsuccessfully to jig and dance to the music, twirling arms, but they had too little space. At the back, several rather loud fog-horns suddenly joined in, but they were quickly shushed by the ones at the front. Whistles and little hooters are allowed, but they *must* be used at the appropriate and traditional times. All regular Prommers know that. The people at the back with fog-horns must have been new.

I worried that there might be fog-horns during the clarinet cadenza, but Colin Bradbury managed that beautifully, and in silence. Everyone gently joined in, humming discreetly in the background, for 'Home Sweet Home' which was played on the oboe and harps.

'Rule, Britannia' had the whole Hall once again in pandemonium, with literally everyone this time, all 8,000 people, standing up and joining in each chorus, then sitting down again for each verse. We all cheered like mad at the end, desperately pushing for an encore, but didn't get one. And then it was 'Jerusalem', the final number.

After he'd received his enormous box of chocolates, pretending to drop them, as if they were tremendously heavy, Sir Charles Mackerras then gave a little speech. During the whole concert, he had obviously been enjoying himself enormously, grinning and throwing himself around, while the orchestra had looked much more solemn and worried, concentrating hard on their parts.

"Good on you, sport," said a loud voice, putting on an Australian accent, as Sir Charles started to speak. Australia is his native land. Everyone laughed loudly and went on to cheer all his jokes, though the old Prommers still prefer Sir Malcolm, a conductor with true charisma.

He introduced Miss Sidonie Goossens, a member of the famous musical family, principal harpist with the orchestra, who was celebrating fifty years

with the B.B.C. Symphony Orchestra. It was also her sixtieth year as a player in the Proms. She got some very loud cheers.

"It has been a privilege to accompany you in the communal singing," said Sir Charles, finishing his speech. "In the hornpipe, you were magnificent." More loud cheers.

The last music was 'Auld Lang Syne', not on the programme, but no great British celebration can end without it, and we all stood up and linked arms. Then the lights went down and we all filed out, picking our way through the debris of streamers and balloons.

It had been a magnificent evening. I wouldn't have missed it for anything. The Prommers make it, of course. After eight weeks of patient standing and careful listening – for they don't shout, wave flags or dress up for the normal Proms – it was obviously a great release, letting themselves go for the last night, with everyone en fête.

During the whole of the second half, I'd noticed that Ken Johnson, the porter-Prommer, had gone into a sort of trance, much to the interest of the T.V. cameras who immediately focussed on him. He was of course right on the front rail, as planned, very visible, making his ten nights in the queue well worthwhile.

He had taken a baton from his pocket and proceeded to conduct every item throughout the second half, his brows knitted, his face deep in concentration, lost in his own world.

"I always conduct on the last night," he said afterwards. "I love conducting, but I stop myself from doing it during the rest of the previous eight weeks. But you must know what it's like, sir. I get carried away in the heat of the night, all that sort of business."

I found Mark Rogers, the young man who'd also slept ten days in the queue. He regretted they'd not forced the conductor to give them an encore of 'Rule, Britannia'. But he'd enjoyed everything. He'll be coming again next year.

"The attraction is simple really. You get the largest variety of music from the best orchestras in the world in the best hall in the world with the best atmosphere in the world."

Sir Henry Wood himself probably summed it up best, some sixty years earlier. "When it comes to the singing of 'Rule, Britannia', we reach a climax that only Britons can reach and I realise I can be nowhere in the world but in my native England ..."

Overleaf: Sir Charles Mackerras conducts the BBC Symphony Orchestra and 8,000 Prommers.

Goodnight Britain, goodnight....